Endorsements

"Don's perception of Margie Tyler makes me smile. While ingesting the messages that Margie delivers in her somewhat dramatic fashion, he captures her quirky ways and intense love and commitment to the Holy Spirit. Throughout the book Don slants his stories so one chuckles while learning the expansive communications from Spirit. I was compelled to return again and again to Don's entertaining, humorous stories, finishing the book in record time."

~ Meera Ballonoff,
Co-Author of the *One With God:*
Awakening Through the Voice of the Holy Spirit
Book Series 1-6

"The Earth is entering into a powerful inspiring time. There is a wave of energy passing through our world that is changing the course of all life it touches. I believe Don's book is written to touch as many people with Light as possible, replacing Fear with Love. God has enabled Don, through this book, to initiate spiritual growth for those who have chosen this path and have yet to experience a breakthrough. The enduring factor of this book is that it leads the mind to greater realities than our current vision has allowed."

~ Ron Hirsch, Inspirational and Spiritual Teacher,
Bridge Of Light Olelo Community Access Program,
Broadcasting from 2011 to present

"Amazing book! It is so well written and engaging that I started and finished it in one day. Don is a great writer with the gift of making the reader part of his story. I feel like I know Margie now, and her voice will light the way for all of us looking to find our true Self, our enlightened Self."

~ Vilmarie Zuenguaz

Awakening the Divine Mind

Awakening the Divine Mind

How a Little Old Lady's
Radical Spirituality Transformed My Life

Don McEntire

Awakening the Divine Mind:
How a Little Old Lady's
Radical Spirituality Transformed My Life

All quotes from A Course in Miracles, copyright 1992, 1999, 2007 by the Foundation for Inner Peace, 448 Ignacio Blvd., #306, Novato, CA 94949, www.acim.org and info@acim.org, are used with permission.

This is a true story. Some names and other identifying details have been changed to protect individual privacy. The timing of some events has been compressed or rearranged to facilitate the telling of the story.

ISBN: 978-1-7356932-3-1
ISBN: 1-7356932-3-5
Library of Congress Control Number: 2020919745

Cover photos by Deelia Nelson Photography
Cover design by Bill Van Nimwegen

Sacred Life Publishers™
SacredLife.com
Printed in the United States of America

For Kim and Kaya McEntire.

I'm so blessed to have you be part of my story.

Contents

Foreword

This book was a total surprise to me. I had no idea when I joined Toastmasters at age seventy-four to prepare for an upcoming book signing event that I was going to meet a tall, dashing, articulate young man who would be writing a book about me as his spiritual mentor. On that auspicious night, when I greeted Don as a potential new member at the Kihei, Maui Toastmasters group, destiny was clearly at play. Don was obviously touched by my speech about my recently published Book *One With God: Awakening Through the Voice of the Holy Spirit,* and at the end of the meeting indicated he wanted to buy one. The evening left me with a strong inclination that the two of us had a deep connection. After I returned home, I asked the Holy Spirit about my connection with Don and was given this message: "Don will be one of My powerful emissaries."

In our next Toastmasters meeting, just before Don was to give a speech, I handed him a small handwritten note stating that the Holy Spirit had given me a message that he will be one of the Holy Spirit's "powerful emissaries". At the end of the meeting, I was compelled to invite him to my home for tea, so we could discuss our seemingly unlikely conjunction. Eagerly, I looked forward to our first meeting together and was amazed that he towered over me while I stood on tiptoes to give him a big welcome hug. The meeting was obviously divinely orchestrated and would be the first of many subsequent Friday afternoons at my condo where we would talk about *A Course In Miracles (ACIM).*

I soon realized that Don was endowed with a brilliant mind and able to understand deep spiritual concepts with ease and express them eloquently. I watched as he became increasingly confident in his relationship with the Holy Spirit and proficient in his forgiveness of ego challenges around his family and work.

One afternoon, barely having settled down in his regular large comfy chair, bursting with excitement, he blurted out that the Holy Spirit had told him to write a book about us. It would be "our book" about how he had come to know me. I knew immediately it was in the divine plan for us both, which I had intuited the night he came to Toastmasters. It would be a privilege and honor to support him in whatever way I could.

A week later, I got to read his first chapter . . . it left me in stitches! His caricature of my appearance, although a bit exaggerated, was spot on. Not only had he captured my movement and mannerisms, he also reflected back to me the power of my role to embody the Presence of the Holy Spirit and present His message to those ready to receive it. Reviewing more chapters, I saw that Don was indeed a gifted writer, and after hearing each of his ten speeches at Toastmasters, I also knew him as a gifted speaker. It was no accident that he had been given a divine mission for his role in disseminating a message of *Awakening the Divine Mind* for the world. That impression was fortified on several occasions through my inner visions of seeing him speaking before huge audiences teaching the tenets of *ACIM*.

I remain open to however the Holy Spirit would have me serve His Plan in my support of Don's writing, and the continuation of my taking dictation for the *One With God* books. Of course, I look forward to sharing more afternoon "teas" with Don, basking in our experiences of being lived and spoken by the Holy Spirit.

~ Marjorie Tyler

Chapter 1

Meeting Margie

"You can choose a ready Guide
in some celestial Voice.
If you choose not to decide,
you still have made a choice."
Rush – Lyrics from the song "Freewill"

Margie was seventy-four years old when I met her at a Maui Toastmasters meeting, of all places. I had dubbed June of 2016 as Blue June because it was the most miserable month of my entire life. Having just recently separated from my wife and our five-year-old daughter in May, I moved out of our comfortable ocean view home on the golf course within the Wailea Resort, and into a tiny and sad 500 square foot ohana in the lower rent district of North Kihei. In Hawaii, ohana is the word for family, or what mainlanders would call a mother-in-law apartment.

As soon as the separation occurred it quickly became quite obvious that I had made a huge mistake. Seduced by the shallow promise of personal freedom and independence, I had willingly agreed to the separation when Kim suggested it after first exhausting all other reasonable methods of course correction with me. I was too stubborn and hard-headed to change my ways, and she was tired of being hurt by my actions and targeted by my anger. Angry was the most accurate descriptive word for me during this time. Anger had been steeping in my middle-aged mind for as long as I could remember, but now it had reached a full and unpleasant bitterness that I could no longer manage nor tolerate. I was much better at suppressing it when I was younger, but as I aged and life further distanced me from my hopes and dreams, the angrier I became. Sabotaging the best romantic relationship I ever had only added to my steeping anger, and when it became too heavy to carry, I tried to get rid of it by projecting it onto others. Of course, that didn't alleviate it, it just demonstrated my obvious possession of it, which only made me angrier. I was a ticking time bomb of temper, just as my father had been. No wonder I was now ending my third marriage.

Recently, an ornery older lady left me a rude voicemail message because she didn't like being included in my real estate postcard mailing. Although everybody knows how annoying we realtors can be with our direct mail marketing, I was appalled by her vicious verbal attack for such a trivial reason. So appalled, in fact, that I called her right back. As soon as she answered the phone, I launched my own attack, demonstrating with magnified viciousness what can be accomplished by combining pent-up toxic anger with profuse profanity at an undignified volume. I probably managed a cuss word per second by speaking fast and not pausing for breath at all. I didn't let up because I wasn't about to give her a chance to respond, but I was also running out of breath. She eventually hung up after a full fifteen seconds of verbal abuse and I gasped for air. As I caught my breath, I realized I didn't feel any better, only angrier. I remember thinking, as my elevated heart rate recovered, "What the hell is wrong with you? You just cussed out an old lady because she didn't want to receive your postcard." I piled the fresh guilt from this shameful realization on top of my stale anger and went about business as usual.

Once the separation was official, I thought I would simply distract myself by staying later and working longer at the office since there never seemed to be enough time in the day to run the real estate brokerage that I had founded over a decade ago. However, that distraction strategy promptly proved highly ineffective, resulting in increased dissatisfaction and unhappiness until my daily sadness morphed into a full-scale depression of such intensity that it fueled an overtly acrimonious attitude towards everything. I was suffering miserably and sinking in a bevy of bitterness that invaded every thought and imbued every action with the sour consequences of my negative thinking. I needed a better distraction than my real estate business provided, and quickly, because I was in a very dark and dangerous place. I didn't want to be verbally attacking old ladies just to project my anger elsewhere.

The poet Rumi said, "the wound is the place the light enters," but although I had a gaping emotional wound causing intense personal suffering, there was no light entering anywhere. Rumi was wrong! I never seriously considered suicide, but I did briefly and frivolously contemplate it during my darkest moments. However, that seemed over-the-top selfish because I knew there were people in my life that loved me and would be incredibly hurt by that action. Even though suicide wasn't an option, my existential angst did often find me wishing a huge hole would open up in the earth and swallow me involuntarily as a method of rapid departure and dissociation from my world of suffering. But instead of escaping by sudden involuntary disappearance, I remained a very visible prisoner of suffering. In social settings or around others I would often disguise my true emotions to attempt an acceptable showing, but I knew that disguise was a lie. I suspected they knew it too, but it was all I could offer and even that required tremendous effort.

As the weight of my unfulfilling life stacked up like bricks on my chest, it not only caused tremendous discomfort, but also made it difficult to breathe. The largest and heaviest brick was the emotional weight of the family separation, but there were also bricks for being unhappy, unsuccessful, anxious, fearful, lonely, angry, stressed, sad, self-medicating, and stuck in a career that lacked purpose and left me drowning in a crisis of meaning. I felt singled out by a cruel and unrelenting fate. My world view began to mirror the darkness I held within my mind, projecting a gloom which extinguished all light, leaving me in a darkened world. I was miserable, alone, and unable to escape the negativity now ruminating loops of victimization through my mind. This may sound bleak, but it still doesn't even begin to describe the deep heaviness and psychological suffering that I couldn't shake despite my best efforts.

I knew I needed to do something extreme; so, I joined Toastmasters. Many people have heard of Toastmasters but very few have actually summoned the courage to give it a try. I had called about it once before, but never took advantage of their invitation to attend a meeting. For those who don't know, Toastmasters International is a non-profit educational organization that teaches public speaking and leadership skills through a worldwide network of speech clubs. The organization's membership exceeds 364,000 in more than 16,200 clubs in 145 countries. Impressive, but none of that really mattered much to me at the time.

Although joining Toastmasters may not tip the scales towards extreme in most people's opinion, I had harbored glossophobia, a fear of public speaking, for as long as I could remember. I was a shy and introverted kid growing up and didn't much care to speak to anybody, including my own family, but speaking to a large group absolutely terrified me. Once as a teenager attending a church service, I was spontaneously called to the pulpit by the bishop and asked to share my testimony with the entire congregation. As I walked to the front of the chapel where the microphone was, I literally thought I was going to pass out on my way up there. I'm not sure if my fear in that moment pushed me into a frenzy of physical symptoms that began my public speaking phobia, or whether it simply confirmed what was already there. But there it was, nonetheless, and I knew early on in my life that the simple act of speaking wasn't all that simple when it was directed towards a crowd.

I later learned I wasn't alone, since a fear of public speaking is near the top of every human's fears and phobias list, exceeded only by the dual fears of loneliness and death. That may sound like lofty phobia placement for something as simple as speaking, which we all do successfully every day without much thought. But for those of us that suffer from this particular phobia, there is nothing lonelier than public speaking, and death is probably preferred to speaking before a large crowd. Perhaps that sounds irrational, but fear always contradicts rationality.

Since I was in sales, I became quite confident when only speaking to one or a few people, but any more than that and it seemed like my tongue and brain suddenly ceased functioning properly. I'd get so nervous my stomach would flutter like a kaleidoscope of ambushed butterflies and I'd feel incredibly ill. I couldn't understand what caused this physical phenomenon because I was so comfortable speaking one-on-one without any fearful thoughts or concerns at all, but this degree of resistive response to public speaking was really annoying and I was tired of involuntarily accommodating it.

The second reason I joined Toastmasters was for the distraction value due to the aforementioned separation from my family. Since I now had a lot of free time in the evenings, it was an exceedingly difficult adjustment after being accustomed to spending my evenings with Kim and Kaya. I became so lonely and depressed that this down time became unbearable, and I was desperate to fill that time with something, anything, that would prove to be productive and distracting. Why not distract myself with an activity that could meliorate a lifelong nonconsensual tongue-crippling condition that was also one of humanity's greatest fears? It was uncomfortable for me to even think about, and that meant it was a perfect choice. I needed something to jolt my numb brain back to life again. I remember thinking if joining a public speaking club didn't do it, then nothing would. That was my reason why Toastmasters seemed like a good fit at this point in my life, at forty-nine years old.

Margie was a huge curiosity to me right from the start. While I knew with sequential specificity my own reasons for joining Toastmasters, I silently wondered what dramatic turn of life events must have transpired for this ancient fossil to feel likewise compelled to join. I admired her courage though because she was by far the oldest member of our club. I mused the various possibilities that might have contributed to an old lady's sudden motivation to become a better public speaker in the twilight of her life. Then I interrupted this musing by self-consciously looking around and asking myself if the millennials in attendance were wondering the same thing about me.

Margie had a thin, wiry body that reminded me of my sons as teenagers when they were running on the high school cross-country team. Her face was quite wrinkled, but handsome, and clearly visible thanks to short and totally gray hair. She had large ears, a common feature for older people, and her short hair may have contributed to this characteristic appearance since they were always completely exposed. She wore black rimmed glasses whenever she was reading, which made her face look even slimmer. When she walked, she was a bit unstable in her move-ments; sometimes slightly wobbling or leaning to one side before noticing and correcting this apparently involuntary action. When she spoke to you her voice sometimes cracked. Speaking to her and not knowing when it might crack again was distracting and a little unnerving.

After Margie greeted me upon entering the meeting on my first night, and hearing that I was a new member, she smiled and told me she was also a newer member. Then she locked eyes with me and looked right through me in a way that made me feel . . . naked. Not naked in the physical sense, but as if she saw something in me that nobody had ever looked at before, and that I wasn't even aware of myself until she brought it to my attention with her piercing gaze. My instinctive reaction was to look away. I didn't know what she had seen or was looking at, but in my current state of mind I reasoned that if it was inside me then it wasn't worth seeing anyway. It was only for a second or two, but there was definite non-verbal communication on a level that I hadn't ever experienced before, and that really isn't even possible to describe. Yes, she was very curious indeed.

Toastmasters membership required bi-monthly participation in hour long meetings where each member would take turns delivering and having evaluated a total of ten speeches in a formal meeting structure in order to complete the program and earn a coveted, frameable certificate as a Competent Communicator. You couldn't get hired from it, but I was already a self-employment slave, so my dual purpose was simply to have a reason to get out of my lonely ohana and perhaps boost my public speaking confidence.

The meeting was shortly brought to order in a large room at the Kalama Heights retirement home in Kihei. As I sat down towards the back of the room, I wondered if Margie lived there by chance. There was an exercise area across the hall and there were no walls to separate these two areas, just an open hallway that narrowed into an enclosed hallway further beyond these two adjacent open rooms. There were several fluorescent lights burned out on one side of the room, so half of the room was darker than the other. It was all a bit strange and I wasn't sure what to expect as I settled in for my first meeting. As a new member, I was introduced and then given my first speech assignment to be delivered at our next meeting in two weeks.

The first speech of the ten that are required is appropriately called an Ice Breaker. It is a short four-to-six minute speech about yourself that is basically your introduction to the club and a way for everyone to get to know a little about you and your personal background, hobbies, and interests right away. The idea being that talking about yourself will make the first speech easier than speaking about any other topic. I was all for the first speech being easier. I could use all the help I could get, because just the thought of standing in front of all these strangers and delivering a speech was already making my chest tight and my stomach churn.

In this first meeting I learned that Margie had joined the club a month earlier and tonight she was scheduled to deliver her Ice Breaker speech. What fortuitous timing, I thought. I get to hear an Ice Breaker speech in my first meeting before I have to deliver my own Ice Breaker speech in the next meeting. Margie's name was called, and she slowly and unsteadily walked to the podium as we clapped our encouragement. But she moved so slowly that we tired of clapping long before she reached the front of the room. I half-wondered if she was going to succumb to her own mortality en route. I was so intrigued by this slowly unfolding scene that I quickly forgot my own anxious concern over my upcoming Ice Breaker speech and found myself leaning forward with great anticipation to see what this peculiar old woman would have to say. My curiosity was already pretty amped about Margie after our initial introduction, but there was no way I could have ever predicted what would happen next.

Margie finally arrived at the podium and looked out at us. But she was so short the podium obstructed her vision. She shuffled to the side of the podium until she could see us all without any obstruction, though now quite off-centered, but certainly visible with her wispy frame fully exposed. She clasped her hands together and took a deep breath as we watched her lungs slowly inflate with air. At the end of the long breath she briefly closed her eyes as she exhaled, and then opened them with a twinkle and began to speak.

"Fellow Toastmasters, my name is Margie Tyler and I am a brand-new club member. I was born and raised in a suburb of Boston, the oldest of three children. My father was the kindest, most patient man I've ever known, and my mother was the impetus for my becoming a clinical social worker, an artist on Maui, and for the desire to find my Self.

"When I was in college, I became acquainted with the ideas of self-realization and vowed to know my Self. I had no idea what it meant to be self-realized or enlightened, but I was determined to find out. My inner voice was revealed through dreams, which I recorded nightly and carefully analyzed. My Jungian dream analyst told me she had never met anyone with more synchronistic experiences than I reported.

"In the 1970s, during a visit to Sri Lanka, I became aware of Sri Sathya Sai Baba, a holy man in India who, to me, displayed the miracles of Jesus so familiar from my childhood connection with New Testament stories. I told my close friends that if Jesus were alive, I would go anywhere to be with him. Baba became my substitute for Jesus. From the mid-eighties to the early nineties, I visited Baba's ashram in India several times, observed and experienced his miracles, and studied his teachings that were grounded in knowing the Self and accepting that there is only One God.

"In 1991, a psychic friend described in detail two individuals I would work with. It took two years before I would meet and recognize them. The first was my Sufi teacher; when I met him, I felt that my prayer to find the means to open my heart was being answered, as I believed that Sufism, the mystical branch of Islam, held the key. I became deeply engaged with his community in Minnesota and was the leader of its branch in Denver for eight years.

"On September 11, 2001, Tom, my husband of thirty-five years, and I were planning to leave for our first trip to Hawaii. When the Twin Towers fell that morning, I instinctively knew that two pillars of my own life would crumble, but I had no idea which two. We didn't take the trip that day, but two months later we flew to Oahu where I visited a practitioner of a technique for uncovering layers of beliefs that prevent knowing the authentic Self. I received confirmation from my psychic friend that this practitioner and my Sufi teacher were the ones she had seen in her reading two years earlier. She worked with me during our days on Oahu, and I came to realize that I had become too dependent on my Sufi teacher and needed to leave him and his community, so I could pursue my soul's journey without an external teacher. The first Tower had fallen.

"The islands called for a return in March of 2003. Since my husband was unexpectedly unable to join me, I came alone. I stayed with the practitioner we visited on Oahu who had now become a friend. She had recently moved to Maui and now lived in Kihei. During the second day of that visit, an incoming wave broke my toe, so I ended up spending a lot of time sitting on a bench near the beach that day. While I was there, a man on a bicycle appeared at my park bench and we spoke briefly of his heart's call to move to Maui and his wife's refusal to move. Ultimately, he divorced her and moved alone. In that moment I was almost overwhelmed by the all-encompassing knowing that I, too, must do the same. I had no need or desire to leave my marriage, or my clinical social work practice in Denver, but I knew it was a Divine calling I had to follow. Tom was not willing to move with me to Maui, but he understood my complete dedication to my spiritual journey, after having witnessed it for the past thirty-seven years. He helped me make the move in every way he could, and soon, everything I needed to establish a new life on Maui materialized. The second Tower had also fallen.

"On Maui, when not immersed in my new art career with the Lahaina Art Society, I began delving into *A Course in Miracles* which I had studied in the 1980s. I became committed to come to know the Voice of the Holy Spirit, as described in the text and workbook lessons. I was determined to wake up from the dream of form and to know the Holy Spirit as the One Self that we share with every other human being on earth. I faithfully read it daily. I stayed on track and slowly witnessed I was becoming kinder, more forgiving, and more patient with myself and in my relationships with my family and friends.

"After eight years of working with the Course as the primary focus of my life, one night I was awakened at three a.m. and saw the word 'WRITE' on the screen of my mind. At the same time, I heard the word 'write' spoken in a voiceless voice within my mind. How would you react if you were woken up at this hour of the night and saw the word 'WRITE' in capital letters on the screen of your mind, knowing you are fully awake and not hallucinating nor dreaming? Have any of you ever heard of such a story? If so, did it make you question the sanity or integrity of the person telling the story?

"To confirm that I understood the command correctly, I asked for a dream that would show me the book and went back to sleep. In an ensuing dream, I was standing on a new sidewalk. Endless arches were seen over the adjoining street. A young boy came to me, covered both our shoulders with his blanket, and we walked together in peace. Then his father came toward us and offered me a light-blue book with a rotunda on the cover, which to me symbolized the unity of mankind. I wanted to protect it, so I slipped the book into a soft cloth bag. When I awoke from the dream, I sobbed in the realization that the command to write was truly from the Holy Spirit. I had been shown the book.

"From that day on, I took His dictation of about 1,000 words per day. The messages have continued without stopping for the past four years. I have now scribed ten books and the first two have been published.

"My experience of hearing the Voice of the Holy Spirit demonstrated that awakening to the Voice is indeed possible and immanent. The Holy Spirit clearly answered every request, and it became my practice to ask Him to comment on every question of my life. I would sit with Him, pencil and pad in hand or at the computer, stating my concerns and requesting His interpretation and guidance. I continued to ask until He brought me to the point of clarity and peace.

"The Holy Spirit answers every question, specifically addressing our personal needs on any topic we raise. His answers are always kind and loving. His Presence is constant. Through daily messages from Him, my trust in the Holy Spirit continues to deepen. My experience has continued to be a means for others to open up to hearing His Voice. We are assured that everyone has access to His Presence always, and we never have to make any decision alone. Now my days flow with unprecedented ease. I can observe the ego's thought system impersonally and know it is based in false fear and has no intrinsic power. I look back on the journey of this lifetime with new eyes, awakened to His vision. To live surrendered to the Holy Spirit as my trusted Friend, constant Companion and Guide, has given my life a peace and contentment that was unknown to me before."

When she finished, she passed the meeting back to the evening's Toastmaster and slowly made her way back to her seat. It took a few moments for everyone to process the surprisingly surreal speech we just heard. We thought we were in Toastmasters, but Margie changed the venue to some strange version of church. Since this was my first meeting, I looked around to see the group's response to her speech, since I was obviously expecting something entirely different.

I knew about religious philosophy, having grown up in Utah as a Mormon and later becoming a voluntary church missionary for two years. During that time, I read books, attended various denominational church services, and regularly engaged in comparative religious conversations with many people of diverse beliefs, but I'd never met anybody like Margie before. I scanned the room to observe the interpretation others formed from this intriguing but highly unusual speech about God, an Indian holy man whose name I'll never be able to pronounce or remember, a psychic premonition, Islamic Sufism, a divine divorce command, and having the Voice of the Holy Spirit awaken her at three a.m. . . . and what the hell is a Jungian dream analyst? Is that even a real thing or did she just make it up? I was happy to see I wasn't alone in my surprised reaction to her speech, which put my mind temporarily at ease. I was beginning to wonder what I had gotten myself into. If I wanted to be preached to, I could simply stop hiding whenever Jehovah's Witnesses came to the door. Maybe I should skip Toastmasters on the nights Margie would be speaking, to avoid being subjected to this type of nonsense in the future. As Margie slowly shuffled back to her seat several of us were already looking around the room at each other in congruous communication with various, "What the hell?" expressions.

Margie was oblivious to us and finally arrived back at her chair and sat down. The room's facial variety was interesting. A young lady near the front had a look of pity, as if, "that poor, delusional old lady has obviously gone crazy." Another expressed a look of wonder or bewilderment. I saw an utterly confused man, who clearly had no idea what she was talking about. It was harder to read a well-dressed man sitting in the darker portion of the room, but he seemed annoyed hearing such blather from a crazy old coot. But a couple of ladies sitting front and center were both smiling and very pleased with the content of her speech. Everybody heard the exact same speech, but there was a wide variety of different reactions to it. Whether the registered look was pity, wonder, bewilderment, confusion, annoyance, disappointment, or satisfaction, every face I saw also showed a subtle underlying hint of common intrigue. How could you not be?

There was no question it was a different type of speech, and I didn't know her well enough to figure out if it was all some fantastic delusion or just a strange combination of senility and imagination that only Margie was privy to. But one thing was sure; to her, it was obviously very real. She had no hesitation at all in telling us such personal and unbelievable things. Why would God have you divorce your husband after thirty-seven years? Even if that ever did happen to me, there was no chance I would ever make that information public in a Toastmasters speech and subject myself to the same judgment we were now heaping onto her.

However, regardless of the content of her speech, there was one undeniable thing that stood out to me in a rather unforgettable way, and that was the extreme confidence with which she said it. It was a bizarre story that didn't seem likely to be true, but the poise, self-confidence, and sheer fearlessness of her delivery was very real indeed. In fact, it was exactly the kind of public speaking confidence I was desirous of developing and was one of my purposes in Toastmasters to begin with. I may never speak about the same things she did, but I sure hoped I would someday be able to speak with her same fearlessness and confidence.

Then I noticed something else. Regardless of the obvious mental resistance I had to what I just heard; I noticed a subtle sense of peace for the first time since my separation from my family. It was as if a small light flickered in the darkest corner of my shadowed mind as a reminder of the temporary nature of that darkness. I had lived in such an unsettled and unhappy state this past month that I forgot what peace actually felt like. There was a lot of strangeness to process from her speech to be sure, but right now I was content to just be still and bathe in the peaceful afterglow of her intriguing speech.

But the peace didn't last long. Eventually a voice in my own head kicked peace aside and scoffed, "A voice in her head? Isn't that schizophrenia? Or is it called psychosis? At the very least it is an auditory hallucination." But my own countering thoughts were, "If she is crazy, then how is it that she wrote down what the Voice said and now has two published books from those writings? How could auditory hallucinations have been popular enough to publish a second book?" The reply from the first voice was, "Apparently mental health and sanity is not a prerequisite to be a published author. Probably only other crazy people are buying her books."

The irony of now having opposing voices within my own head was not something I had picked up on yet. Although I had always uniformly classified these opposing head voices under the single label of "personal thoughts", there was nothing uniform about them. They constantly contradicted each other with oppositional perspectives. Even with these two completely different thought systems existing within my mind, I still held the personal belief that separate and distinct inner voices must surely be a diagnosable mental disorder and dismissed my own vacilla-tion between such oppositional thoughts as mere intellection. This seemed easier than attempting to evaluate why each thought system was internally consistent and yet diametrically opposed to the other. Even though fundamental differences between them made partial allegiance to either impossible, I still made the futile attempt at reconciling the irreconcilable by constant vacillation. Had I exerted any serious effort towards self-examination I would have revealed only one of these thought systems could ever be right or true, a simple deduction which would have proven the other to be insane. I may have been walking a fine line to justify this impossible reconciliation, but I knew I wasn't as crazy as Margie was, and that was all I really needed to tell myself right now.

I wondered if the books themselves would provide answers to some of the questions that were now popping through my head like popcorn overflowing from a hot kettle. I felt a need to speak with her. It is not every day that you get to hear an intriguing speech like this from a published author in a small group setting and then have the opportunity to satisfy your immense curiosity by immediately asking direct personal questions. I had to find out more about these books and what this Voice was saying to her. I never once suspected the life-changing rabbit hole this initial curiosity had me crawling down into.

Once the meeting was adjourned the evaluation paperwork, the timing clock and the speaker warning lights had to be put away. I approached Margie somewhat tentatively as she was gathering up loose evaluation forms on the various tables and asked, "So you have published two of these books about the Voice that speaks to you?"

She looked up from gathering the papers left on a table and nodded, "Yes, two so far. I have written ten in total but only the first two have been published. The others are still being edited prior to printing."

"What is the name of the books?"

"*One With God: Awakening Through the Voice of the Holy Spirit.*"

When she said that book title the first thought that passed through my head was how I truly wished that were only possible. But if my life had taught me anything about God it was that He was incredibly distant. You'd have to know my own religious background to really understand why that book title both intrigued and annoyed me. I grew up in a highly religious Mormon foster family, so I had a basic belief in God, and although I no longer practiced Mormonism, I still considered myself a Christian. But I felt so far away from anything Divine that I eventually became indifferent and apathetic. I grew up thinking I belonged to God's only true church and everybody else was deluded. I thought this mindset was a Mormon thing, but I later learned this divisive "I'm right, you're wrong" mentality is pretty much the same in all religions, and among all people, religious or not.

Although Christianity is obviously conflicted and does promote teachings that oppose each other, could God's correction be to establish a religion that likewise conflicts and opposes all of the others? If so, God was trying to fix the problem by engaging in the same thinking that caused the problem, and I couldn't imagine God's mind thinking that way. It just didn't seem Godly. Rather, it seemed more like something a human would do. Were we really made in the image of God, or do we make God in our image by humanizing Him so that He will fit within our limited human perspective and understanding? Because why would a perfectly loving and all-powerful God display fallible human characteristics such as the divisive judgment that is required to burn or destroy both the willingly and ignorantly disobedient? This version of God was difficult to understand and defied a Being of perfect love to me. Religion seemed to be less about God and more about money, control, and manipulation through fear than anything else, and the end result was always massive amounts of burdensome guilt, with selective salvation often obtained through other means.

If God did exist, then wouldn't He be perfect? Wouldn't His creations be imbued with His same eternal perfection? And yet our entire physical universe is hurtling towards entropy without offering any evidence of His eternal perfection within a world He supposedly created. Instead everything we experience in this flawed world is impermanent and imperfect, which shouldn't even be possible if it was authored by eternal perfection. Something must have gone amiss because the system was rigged, and I concluded religion was part of the problem in that we were all being set up to fail only so we could then be punished for our inevitable failure. The Bible says that God is perfect love, but that doesn't feel like perfect love, and neither does the Bible's version of a God that conquers territories, kills enemies, and punishes sinners for not living according to certain laws. Once again, these are very frightening human-like characteristics. Nowadays God is apparently even demanding divorces of long-time marriages too. Thanks, but no thanks. This world God supposedly created was far too corrupt and insane for my willing attribution of its creation to a perfectly loving and all-powerful Being.

However, I wasn't an atheist and still believed in a higher power. Because just as the religion story didn't add up to me, neither did the highly unlikely possibility that the human race somehow won an improbable biological lottery of the perfectly fine-tuned and highly ordered conditions required to support sentient life on this planet. So, I was stuck somewhere between my disbelief in organized religion and an underlying belief in a divine creation. Hence my apathy and indifference. I definitely didn't want to go to hell, if there was such a place, but I just couldn't continue to endure all of the guilt and shame that religion fostered. Nor could I deny my own inner knowing of something else beyond my present sensory awareness, so the chasm between me and God only grew wider with every sinful thought and act committed. The result being a downward spiral of wrongdoing, with much of my life turning sour and becoming distasteful.

This wrongdoing was always followed by personal judgment, which assigned guilt that demanded punishment. This unpunished guilt caused me to fear God and further distance myself from Him out of fear of an inevitable, impending punishment, which only contributed to more fear and guilt. It was a vicious cycle that I could not correct nor justify, so I just subscribed to a belief in inadequacy, assuming I was a huge disappointment to a God who would eventually punish me for such. The Bible statement, "Vengeance is mine; I will repay, saith the Lord" caused me to fear whatever retribution God had in mind, rather than motivating me to love God or feel worthy of His love. If God permitted and encouraged Jesus to suffer because he was good, and could persecute His Own Son on behalf of salvation, then what would He do to me? The fearful answer to that question pushed me away from His love and into the arms of fear, where I reluctantly embraced the accumulated guilt from my sinful ways. Only a cruel theology would require God's blood sacrifice to achieve salvation and be redeemed from wrongdoing, and guilt easily saturates the mind indoctrinated by such religious dogma.

Although the book title obviously struck a spiritual nerve, I was still curious, so I asked another question.

"Each book has the same name?"

"Yes, books 1 and 2. The rest of them will also."

She clearly didn't have the books with her and wasn't offering me a free copy by virtue of my Toastmasters membership, but that would be an easy title to remember and look up on Amazon later.

Trying to make polite conversation and be complimentary, I followed with, "I have to say, I really enjoyed your speech. It was such an intriguing story and you delivered it with such clarity and confidence."

"Thank you. But don't give me too much credit, it wasn't me doing the speaking."

The confused and bewildered look on my face probably conveyed my true opinion of her sanity. I heard the speech. I saw who was speaking. There was nobody else up there. What is wrong with this lady?

Unruffled by my facial expression, she killed the uncomfortable silence by adding, "I do not speak. I am spoken. I do not live. I am lived."

Well . . . now that clears everything up. Alrighty then, you wizened whack job! I was just trying to be nice but now I was getting awkwardly pulled into a bizarre conversation with a loony old lady and needed to politely end it. I slowly nodded, while suspiciously watching her and waiting to see if she was somehow messing with me and would crack a grin or laugh at my puzzled expression. She looked back at me with all the seriousness and sincerity that you can possibly imagine. She was sticking with her response to my speech compliment, and this topic was clearly no joke to her. I looked into her eyes and she looked into mine, but then I looked away before she had a chance to make me feel naked again.

It was probably just because she was crazy but looking into Margie's eyes was like looking into another world. She was clearly not in this place in the same way that we are. She seemed removed, elevated, as if she was looking down on this world from an entirely different perspective. It was almost as if what she was seeing simply wasn't real to her. I've met some very strange people in my life, some actually hearing voices and muttering to themselves and making the very same claims as Margie. The only difference I couldn't quite put my finger on, nor let go of, was that look of absolute peace she projected at all times. Whether she was speaking to you one-on-one or to a room full of people, she never looked any different and was always supremely confident. She was absolutely fearless, and it showed. Since I was not that way at all when it came to public speaking, I was hoping I could learn her technique and that psychosis wasn't a prerequisite.

I left and went home to my tiny and sad dwelling, completely convinced that Margie was as off-center as her speech delivery had been. Yet I also remained intensely curious, even to the point of thinking about her and the strange voice in her head all night. Regardless of anything else I did; I couldn't get her out of my mind. When my needling curiosity eventually consumed me, I went onto Amazon and made an online purchase of *One With God: Books 1 and 2*. Even after the purchase, I kept thinking about the peaceful lunacy and obvious speaking confidence of a wrinkly old lady and the mysterious Voice that provided her with such valuable guidance.

I was definitely struggling and felt like my life was careening out of control into loneliness and despair, so guidance sounded nice. In hindsight, knowing what I do now, I could see that I was being perfectly positioned and prepared for an epiphany. There was no way my Teacher was going to miss this unique opportunity to make a lifelong contribution to my spiritual progress, but right now I was only mulling over the idea of sticking my head down the rabbit hole to see where it went. Being presented with an invitation to Crazy Town didn't mean I had to risk everything and go. What if I got lost inside?

And yet another part of me wondered . . . would that be so bad? It wasn't like I was happy with my life and how it was unfolding. Sure, Margie seemed crazy, but if I could somehow maintain that same level of personal peace and speak that confidently to a large group, would a brief peek or short visit to satisfy my Crazy Town curiosity be so bad? I slowly drifted asleep to thoughts of receiving valuable guidance and fearlessly speaking with Ciceronian eloquence, essentially with one foot firmly planted in "reality" and the other hovering in the air, positioned to probe the possibilities of a bold step into the unknown.

Chapter 2

The Light Enters

"Luminous beings are we. Not this crude matter."
Master Yoda, *Star Wars: The Empire Strikes Back*

Over the next couple of weeks, I spent a lot of time thinking about, writing and preparing my Ice Breaker speech. It wasn't easy, and I eventually concluded it was definitely not any easier for me to speak about *myself*. Maybe that was true for most people, but not me. I didn't want these strangers to know the failure and shame that was embedded into my personal history. What happened to my life? Where did I go so wrong? I had many big ideas and high ideals back in my twenties. I was going to shake up the world! Instead, the world kicked me in the crotch and when I fell to my knees it violently shook me up. And that is where I was now, on my knees, shaken, reeling in pain, and gasping for air.

Even if anyone did want to hear my story, too bad because I wasn't courageous enough to display the vulnerability to share it with them. I couldn't imagine telling strangers in a public speech how I've been married three times but was unable to make any of those relationships work. Or that I filed bankruptcy for a second time in my life just a few years ago and still hadn't recovered financially. I definitely couldn't tell them I was evicted from my last rental home after having had my cell phone and cable TV disconnected for non-payment during the Great Recession. Would anybody care that my kids and step kids were either distant from me or wanted nothing to do with me at all? Maybe some people could relate to these failures, but I seriously doubted any of them could compare their life challenges to mine. Saying anything personal would only relay the massive depression and self-loathing that followed my recent separation from Kim and Kaya last month.

I still missed my family so much that the pain of separation was sometimes intolerable. I was so incredibly unhappy at times that if I could have crawled out of my own skin, and into anyone else's, I would have. In my own mind, the self-pity reached such dark depths that I couldn't imagine anyone being unhappier, having worse problems, or needing more improvement than my current situation did. Life had victimized me by denying every wish, hope, and dream I ever had. All of it had gone horribly wrong, and nothing in my life was the way I wanted it to be or how it was supposed to be.

No, I couldn't share any of that. I decided to do the next best thing and write a speech that squarely placed the blame on my dysfunctional family. Not my religious foster family, but my actual family that made the foster family necessary in the first place. And I'd make it funny so that no one would see how sad, unhappy, and depressed I really was. I would mask my personal pain with humor, and self-deprecating humor was easy to find in my life and family history.

In a nutshell, I am the youngest of seven children. My mother's first husband went down in a freak airplane crash and left her widowed with a newborn and a toddler. She then met and married my father and had five more children, with me being the caboose baby. When I was four years old, and with older siblings aged six, eight, twelve, thirteen, nineteen, and twenty, my mother and grandmother were hit head-on by a drunk driver and killed instantly. My sisters, who were eight and thirteen, were in the back seat of that vehicle and both were hospitalized; one sister had stitches in her head to close up gashes from the collision, and the other was in intensive care with such severe vocal cord damage she was unable to speak. I remember when we went to the hospital to see her, she had to write down her questions or responses to communicate. Since I didn't know how to read or write yet I had to have an older family member either read her question or her response to me. At four years old, and with my mother and grandmother both dead from the same accident she was suffering from, these were obviously awkward visitations.

My father had a bit of a breakdown after the accident and was temporarily unable to take care of us, so he shipped the five of us still at home to live with our oldest half-brother, his wife and their three-year-old child. They became unexpected teenage parents who got married at sixteen and had a son, my nephew, that was about my same age. Even now they were only twenty years old at the time we arrived, saddling them with six children ranging from ages three to thirteen. I'm sure it wasn't easy for them since we were such an unruly bunch. My brother's approach to the situation was to be a firm disciplinarian. I don't remember very much at that age, except that I was always afraid of his belt "disciplining" us. That only lasted for about a year and then my dad came and got us and moved us to a gambling town in Nevada, where he had secured a job in a casino. Although my dad had a short temper, it seemed more directed at my older siblings than me. This caused my constant fear of disciplinary punishment to subside for the most part. My dad worked all of the time and even when he wasn't working, he mostly kept to himself. We never really had any parental guidance, so I learned to fend for myself from the age of five.

When I was eight years old, I was at school one day when I heard fire trucks and sirens rushing by the school. After school got out, I noticed the fire trucks were up near our house. I left school thinking I would check out the burning house on my way home, only to find out when I arrived that it was our house that was burning. I stood there in shock, watching everything that my family owned go up in smoke and then crumble into ashes. We stayed in a tiny apartment until the insurance money was paid out from the fire and then my dad moved us all across the country from Nevada to the Florida Keys. Much later I found out the fire happened specifically for the insurance money, in order to afford the move to Florida. In my eight-year-old naivete, that never would have occurred to me as an option, especially since our entire family was so traumatized by the loss of everything with no clothes, toys, or any other personal possessions.

We were only in Florida for a little more than a year before we moved again, and again, and again. Florida, Utah, Idaho, Nevada, back to Utah. My oldest half-brother that we all briefly lived with after my mother's accident never liked my dad much and joked that we moved every time the rent came due. I didn't know anything about the family finances at that age, but we definitely moved a lot. It seemed like every time I made friends and got settled into a new school we moved again. I had never repeated a school year at the same school.

When I was eleven years old my nineteen-year-old brother was killed in a single car accident when he struck a boulder while hot-rodding in the desert by the Bonneville Salt Flats. My dad didn't deal well with the death of my mother, and now he wasn't dealing well with the death of my brother either. As distant and detached from us as he already was, he became even more so. Insurance money from the accident meant we got to settle in Sandy, Utah for a few years. I actually attended the same middle school for two years in a row for the first time in my life, and then started high school with those same friends and classmates. My brother and I loved sports, but with all of the moving we never got to play on any sports teams before. Now we both played on the high school sports teams. My brother was two years older than me and played baseball, basketball, and ran track for Jordan High School, and I also played basketball and ran track and cross country. I eventually gave up track and cross country and became a one sport athlete, with all of my time and attention devoted to basketball only.

We were happy, until I was fourteen and a freshman in high school and my brother was sixteen and a junior in high school and my dad suddenly wanted to move us again. At that time, it was January and we were in the middle of basketball season. My brother was a starter on the varsity basketball team that was ranked number one in the entire state. He flatly refused to move again. My dad moved anyway, so his three remaining children ended up living with foster families in that same neighborhood so that we could continue attending the same school, which we did.

My foster family was strict Mormons, which turned out to be very good for me at the time because I needed the structure, never having had much of it growing up. My brother wasn't nearly as fortunate. My sister was eighteen at the time of my dad's move, and she met a guy and agreed to marry him within three weeks of their meeting each other, probably just so she wouldn't have to move again either. They had two children but are no longer together, an inevitable marital casualty of their hasty wedding.

Within a year of moving in with my foster family, the father contracted lymphatic cancer and died. I was a teenager too young to drive, but in my life I had already experienced separation by death from my grandmother, mother, older brother, and now my foster father, who was an absolutely wonderful man. I braced for more change, assuming I would now have to leave this family and school that I loved and go live with my dad in another dirty casino town in Nevada. But my foster mother put that fear to rest by expressing this didn't change anything as far as she was concerned, and I was welcome to continue living with them as long as I wanted to. It was a dream come true, a real and normal family, and it was the best part of my entire childhood.

After experiencing all that I already had in my young life, I knew a good thing when I had it, and this was it. They were a close-knit family with four other children besides me. There were two boys and two girls, and one of the boys was my same age and also my best friend. We enjoyed living together and eventually ended up as the starting guards on the basketball team during our junior and senior years, even winning the state basketball championship in our final year, which has always been one of the biggest thrills of my life.

As I thought of a humorous theme for my Ice Breaker speech, I could now see the comedic entertainment value of my childhood stories of dysfunctional family life before finding normalcy as a foster child. Truth may be stranger than fiction, but that also makes it harder to believe. Many of these stories were so bizarre that when sharing them people always assumed I was telling a funny but fictional story. With time I even began to laugh a little myself, so I decided to make this one of those times and wrote a somewhat silly speech about the life survival skills I learned being the youngest of seven children, and one little trick in particular that I actually used to get even with my older brothers for always beating up on me so much. I named the speech, "The Safe Seat." As I was writing it, I decided the only way to make it work would be to bring humor and vocal energy to the comically creative survival techniques of a small child with four unusually cruel older brother bullies.

On the day I was to deliver my Ice Breaker speech, I was obviously very nervous. That entire day was a blur to me with all of the anxiety over my upcoming speech lingering in the back of my mind like a guillotine waiting to drop. When I finally finished work and arrived at my second Toastmasters meeting, everyone was scurrying about and setting up for the meeting to start on time. I immediately noticed there were even more people here for this meeting than the last one, which seemed unfair to me since the guillotine was about to drop and I was already nauseated and anxious.

I saw Margie setting pencils and evaluation forms on the tables as I grabbed a table near the front and said a nervous hello. She looked up at me and her eyes immediately widened as she excitedly said, "I have a message for you from the Holy Spirit!"

Oh God. This was so annoying. I had enough to worry about with my speech tonight and didn't want to get caught up in her craziness immediately upon entering the room. I didn't want to hear the message or deal with her at all right now, so I just mumbled, "Oh really," and took my seat. She moved to the next table and placed some pencils and papers and then went to another table where she opened a booklet and pulled out a small piece of paper and began to shuffle back toward me. I looked down at my speech notes in an attempt to avoid eye contact with her. She placed the piece of paper on the table in front of me and shuffled away. I didn't *want* to read it now, but I couldn't resist, so I looked down and saw it was written in small, shaky penmanship that required a closer look. I picked up the tiny piece of paper with one line written on it and brought it closer and eventually deciphered, *"Don will be one of My powerful emissaries."*

My brow wrinkled as I thought, "What is an emissary?" I really didn't know, so as Ann Elaine took the podium to commence the meeting, I grabbed my phone and pretended to silence it while I quickly went to Dictionary.com and typed "emissary" and hit search. My phone screen displayed "emissary: a representative sent on a mission or errand."

Weird. This was only my second time seeing Margie and already she was passing me notes from the Holy Spirit like we were kids in grade school. This wasn't normal. Who does that? Once again, her fearlessness was impressive, although misdirected in this case. I was no emissary. I had no message, no mission or errand to deliver and right now I had bigger things to worry about, like the nausea in my gut as the meeting got underway and I was about to be called upon to publicly speak in front of this large, intimidating group of total strangers.

But as nervous as I was, when my name was called, I stood and walked briskly to the podium, in an attempt to fake confidence, and because I didn't want to arrive at the podium as slowly as Margie did in our last meeting. At six foot four inches and 240 pounds I did not have Margie's problem of not being able to see over the podium. I set my speech notes down and got ready to begin. I liked being behind the podium; it felt safer somehow than being exposed like Margie had been for her speech. I think I wanted to hide a little bit and the podium gave me just enough cover to feel like I was doing that. I tried to get my butterflies flying in unison but it wasn't happening, so I nervously greeted everyone and began my Ice Breaker speech:

"Fellow Toastmasters, I grew up in what some people may call a dysfunctional family. Being the youngest of seven children, with four older brothers, is not something most people passing through this life will ever have to endure . . . nor could they. Because I got beat up . . . *a lot*! I got beat up so much I think most people just assumed my bruises were birthmarks."

I tried to pause for emphasis after a line that I thought they would laugh at when I wrote it, but it is hard to predict how people will actually respond to your written speech until you deliver it live, and different people will respond differently, just as I had seen them do with Margie. They politely smiled but there was no laughter, so my pause created an awkward silence as I nervously forged ahead, though I really just wanted to walk away and go sit down and put my head between my legs in shame for my weak attempt at humor.

"It's tough to be the youngest, smallest, and weakest person in a large family, but the upside is you tend to develop some amazing survival skills that most people will never learn. The attempted explanation of this has become known as the 'Youngest Child Syndrome.' Yes, we even have our own syndrome."

More polite smiles, but they seemed a little looser and less forced this time. I seized this small amount of momentum and continued.

"Psychologists will say this about the youngest siblings, or 'lastborns,' that they are not entitled at all, they are more apt to buy used cars and second-hand clothes, they will answer to almost any name, they tend to be good listeners, learn from the mistakes of others, stay under the radar, and lastly . . . they get away with murder!" This line brought laughter and muffled chuckles, probably from those older siblings in the group remembering how the youngest child always did get away with murder in their own household.

But more importantly, their laughter felt like I was being injected simultaneously with both confidence and adrenaline. I stood a little taller and spoke a little louder and said with more confidence: "This happens because lastborns often try to differentiate themselves by being rebellious. They can also be quite manipulative . . . although manipulative is such a negative word. I prefer to call it 'creatively controlling.'"

My newfound confidence caused me to make a mischievous smile when I said it and they laughed again, obviously warming up to my story and feeling engaged with it.

"To give you some insight into the life of a lastborn, I'll relate a couple of situations that illustrate my creative thinking and the survival skills I learned in order to defend myself *and* pay back my brothers for all of their gratuitous beatings.

"The first survival skill I learned was Observation. I observed that older brothers who use lastborns as their own

31

personal punching bags will also exclusively reserve that punching right for themselves. In other words, anybody but my brothers beating up on me was strictly forbidden.

"Once I realized that, I became the toughest kid not only in my own class, but also one class higher . . . *as long as I had my older brother around.* So, when I was in the fifth grade and Bob Massell, who was the toughest kid in the sixth grade, was stealing my French fries, *and my brother was there,* I punched Bob right in the nose as hard as I could . . . .

"Unfortunately, my brother didn't see it. With my brother looking the other way as Bob's nose started to bleed, the look on Bob's face changed from shock and surprise, to complete and utter rage. I knew I was in serious physical jeopardy, so I did the first thing I could think of and turned and started running away as fast as I could. Never having participated in a 'punch and run' before, I wasn't quite sure how far, and for how long, I was supposed to run. But after seeing the look on Bob's face I wasn't taking any chances, and I didn't look back until I got all the way home. I found out later that my brother *did* eventually see Bob chasing me down the street with murderous intention, in an obvious attempt to violate his exclusive punching right, and he stopped the chase. So now Bob knew **not** to steal a French fry from a lastborn . . . at least whenever I had a brother around.

"But besides striking at French fry stealing bullies, I also needed a way to strike back at my brothers. They were so much older and bigger than me that I had no chance of taking them on by myself. I had to somehow recruit the help of someone even older and bigger than they were. The only question was who?

"Then it came to me . . . my dad! Our father was six feet four inches tall and weighed 350 pounds. Not only that, but he was a widowed parent with seven unruly children, he had a very short temper, and he already relished the corporal punishment of my brothers. He was perfect! I thus learned a second survival skill: <u>How to Enlist the Aid of an Unsuspecting Ally</u>.

"I learned a third survival skill shortly thereafter when my brother and I were in the back seat while my dad was driving, and I accidentally discovered what I now call . . . the Safe Seat. By applying <u>Careful Analysis,</u> I learned that the one and only Safe Seat in the entire car is the seat directly behind the driver's seat. The Safe Seat requires some explanation.

"I know lots of parents will threaten their kids with pulling the car over to distribute discipline when they are misbehaving in the back seat, but my dad *never* pulled the car over. He had the amazing ability to corporally punish us in the back seat *while* he was still driving the car! Here is how he did it.

"Whenever he would lose his temper because of something we were doing in the back seat, he'd grab the top of the steering wheel with his left hand, and then he would rotate his enormous torso while bringing his right shoulder and arm up over the seat until his right elbow was resting on the top of the seat between us, while his left hand still held the top of the steering wheel."

I demonstrated this rotation of the right side of the body while keeping my hips and left hand facing forward and holding onto an imaginary steering wheel in front of me, as the club members smiled and giggled in unison at my odd contortion. This reaction further fueled my enthusiasm to energetically demonstrate what came next.

"From this position, everybody in the back seat was now staring down the barrel of a ham-sized fist . . . and then . . . the punishment would begin. He would alternate *striking* and *swiping* in a crossing motion . . . like a musical conductor orchestrating a punishment masterpiece opus, and he wouldn't stop until he was sure he had adequately punished *everyone* in the back seat, guilty or not."

I demonstrated the striking and swiping motion dramatically, as a musical conductor would at the energetic climax of a
musical masterpiece, which brought howls of laughter from them.
I had them hooked, and it felt amazing! This confidence booster
caused me to actually put down my speech notes for the first time
and just go with the flow of the story from memory while I had
them engaged. My confidence was soaring, which provided a
natural high.

"Even an innocent was collateral damage during this
punishment. I once complained that it wasn't fair to punish me
because I was not even involved in the back seat dispute my
brothers were having. I'll never forget my dad's angry red face
shouting back at me, 'I don't care about justice! When I'm driving
this car, I just want *quiet*!'

"After my careful analysis helped me realize the value of the
Safe Seat, since it was the only location in the car that was free of
this painful punishment, from that time forward I implemented a
fourth survival skill—which was to <u>Plan Ahead.</u> Whenever we
were going anywhere, I would literally run to the car . . . not to
ride shotgun . . . but to secure the Safe Seat.

"Once seated in the Safe Seat, I'd then lock my door so that
my brothers would then have to get into the car on the other side,
and thereby take an *unsafe* seat. And then, as only a lastborn
would do, I'd pick a fight with my brothers that were now sitting
exposed and unprotected in the unsafe seats!"

Club members howled their appreciation of my youthful
creativity and deviousness. This speech was going much better
than I expected but the yellow light just turned on which meant I
had only one minute to wrap it up.

"The application of my learned survival skills worked
perfectly! It was a beautiful thing to be sitting in the Safe Seat as
my ally, the musical conductor, began his punishment opus of
striking and swiping at my very deserving brothers as they

squealed and cowered . . . exactly as I had planned after carefully observing, analyzing, and orchestrating all of it to happen.

"To those that are not lastborns, this illustration may sound like a sad way to learn survival techniques, but those big brother bruises, and ultimately . . . the brotherly love we all shared in our large, dysfunctional family . . . helped shape the resilient and resourceful person I am today."

The club members all clapped and cheered when I finished. I know they do that for everyone, but this was only my second meeting and I could tell they really liked the speech. After the speech and the evaluations were finished, I received a lot of compliments from around the room, which felt amazing due to my distinguished history of difficulty with public speaking. But the absolute kicker was afterwards when our club president and Distinguished Toastmaster, Ann Elaine, approached me and asked, "Would you consider entering that speech in the humorous speech contest?

"The what?"

"The humorous speech contest."

"What's that?"

She enthusiastically explained that every year each Toastmaster club sends their best humorous speaker to a contest with the best humorous speakers from all of the other clubs on Maui. The winner of that Maui area competition then flies to Oahu to deliver a speech for the division and district competitions if they qualify by winning the event. That all sounded fine and wonderful, but even still brimming with confidence after delivering my first speech, that just didn't seem possible for me. I tried to politely decline but she persisted. I learned later how good she was at that. I suggested she send someone else, more experienced, that actually wanted to go.

She then told me, "That speech is one of the funniest speeches I have heard in this club, and I've heard *a lot* of speeches.

I don't think you know how good it really was. Your physical humor is impressive. The way you described and demonstrated the backseat beating your father delivered while still driving the car was hilarious. Besides, nobody in our club entered a humorous speech for this contest, so if you would do it again at the area competition, you would represent our club. If you won't, then our club will be the only club on Maui with no representation in the humorous speech contest." I could only pry myself away from her by saying I would take her suggestion "under consideration". Yeah, right. There was not a chance in hell that was ever going to happen.

As I was preparing to leave, Margie approached me and asked me what I thought of my message from the Holy Spirit. I was so happy from my successful first speech that I didn't mind tolerating some of her weirdness for a moment, so I thanked her for the message. She then said she would like to meet with me, outside of Toastmasters, to discuss the message that she received and delivered to me. What was going on tonight? First, I deliver one speech and then I am asked to enter a humorous speech contest, and now crazy Margie wants private time with me to discuss a meaningless message that was clearly not even meant for me. For her to even think it was only proved the loony label that I had already assigned to her was accurate. Although I did receive her *"One With God"* books recently in my Amazon order, I hadn't taken the time to look at them yet because I was spending so much time writing and practicing my Ice Breaker speech during my free time. I guess it couldn't hurt to have a tea party with her. After all, she was probably lonely like I was. I told her Fridays were my slowest workdays, so I could meet her then. She gave me her condo address and we settled on Friday afternoon at three-thirty, and then I bolted for my car before anybody asked me to do anything else.

My happy speaking moment quickly vanished two days later when I attended a counseling meeting with Kim. The counseling was not for us, with the intention of fixing our relationship and ending the separation. The counseling was for our daughter, to help us transition to singlehood in a way that would not negatively impact little Kaya during the transition. The finances of the separation were not good. My friends joked how it is "cheaper to keep her" because it costs more to live apart and pay two rents and other expenses, but I thought I could handle it. I miscalculated how difficult it would be to perform adequately in straight commission sales when my personal life was in such disarray. My messy internal world was now externally hemorrhaging, and business income was draining away, which only caused more stress and tension. Even though my ohana dwelling was as inexpensive as I could possibly consider living in, we were still struggling.

For this reason, Kim wanted to rent out a bedroom in our home to a nice, older BMW salesman that was looking for a month-to-month lease because he was new to Maui. But the idea of another man, even a kindly older gentleman, living in my home with my wife and my daughter didn't sit well with me, and the full extent of my lingering pain hijacked the counseling session, and soon Kim was in tears as my familiar anger resurfaced and the counselor tried to back me down. But I resisted, wanting to unleash a heavy dose of bitterness so they could share in my misery. We never even got through the session and had to dismiss early.

When I got back to my tiny dwelling, the air conditioning was broken, and the heat was sweltering inside. The thought of my inconsiderate wife enjoying our luxury ocean view home on the golf course with central A/C and renting my bedroom to another man seized my mind and hacked away any reasonable responses. I was done. I wanted to end any attachment to all of it.

Why not? I didn't want this pain anymore! Body builders often tout the phrase "no pain, no gain," but I was about to learn that this applies just as much to spiritual development as it does to muscular development. I know every marriage ending is an emotional roller-coaster, but this was my third time, and the suffering was more than I could handle. In this state of complete misery, the emotional pain intensified until it reached a mental anguish so heavy that it pushed me off the bed and onto the floor.

Even the tile was hot as my legs folded under me while my upper torso remained on the bed, sobbing, and praying for a way to cope with the torture of this hell. It felt like I was being turned inside out emotionally, while being twisted at the same time. Eckhart Tolle once said, "When the ego weeps for what it has lost, the spirit rejoices for what it has found." During this weeping and wrenching, I remembered Margie's speech and one part about spirit in particular, "The Holy Spirit answers every question, specifically addressing our personal needs . . . . His answers are always kind and loving. His Presence is constant. We are assured . . . that everyone has access to His Presence."

A Voice? A Holy Spirit? I wanted to believe it. I needed something to change the emotional beating I was giving myself since my separation from Kim and Kaya. I cried out and begged the Holy Spirit, or whatever was there, to please help me! I sank down further and further until I was laying limp on the hot tile floor. I must have crossed an unknown pain tolerance threshold because I was now paralyzed and completely still. I had nothing left, no thoughts, no feelings, and no energy or mobility. My surrender was complete. As I lay awkwardly on the floor in complete defeat, I didn't know if I would ever recover from this frigid woe and apathy. I was entirely and completely broken. It was the lowest place I'd ever been in my entire life. It was also the precise moment when the help I had just begged for showed up in dramatic fashion, as my spirit rejoiced and liberated itself from what was left of my false reality.

It felt like an emotional earthquake initially, as all of the painful pent-up thoughts and feelings I had been holding onto suddenly began shaking violently as the Richter scale rose. Long before reaching its powerful peak, I simply couldn't hold onto them any longer and was forced to sever all attachment to them. After they got shaken loose, scrambled, and ultimately severed, they all drained away like dishwater swirling down the sink drain. As all of these negative thoughts and concerns were draining away, their departure created space for something else to begin to surface. It was light! Light began filtering through me and filling the space where I had been holding all of the thoughts and concerns that had just been torturing me a moment ago. Now none of it mattered, and it no longer even seemed real.

After the draining had finished, I felt . . . empty. I was no longer a physical form. I was shown my true identity, and it was pure light and nothing else. Suddenly from this emptiness a large blank screen of pure whiteness showed in my mind, and it was all I could see. I heard a loving whisper gently say "look" and on the screen images appeared. It was a simplistic scene of just me, Kim, and Kaya. We were together, we filled the entire screen, and we were not doing anything special or exciting, just talking and smiling, but we were very close. The love we shared between us was stronger than anything we had ever shared before. It wasn't just something I saw play out on the screen, I felt it in my heart as it swelled and filled with immense love. As I watched this simple scene unfold on the giant white screen, my heart continued to swell until it felt like a balloon stretched to capacity that would burst if it expanded any further. I really believed this swelling love would eventually cause my heart to explode, because it couldn't possibly contain this much love in one confined physical place without a massive rupture. But fear seemed wildly inappropriate, so I didn't resist; I simply let it expand and if it ruptured my heart, then so be it. This was the most amazing feeling I had ever experienced, and I didn't ever want it to end.

I watched the screen and felt the love between us as tears rolled down my face until exhaustion set in and the screen slowly faded, and I entered the peaceful darkness of sleep, on a hard tile floor in the sweltering heat. I had no idea how long I slept, but when I came back to conscious awareness, nothing appeared the same to me. The tiny and sad ohana was now a perfectly happy place. There was no pain. There was no suffering. There was only the lingering effects of the love and closeness that existed between me and Kim and Kaya that had almost exploded my heart. They were not there physically, but our love for each other still was, and that was all that mattered. I was at peace. There was nowhere for my mind to go that could ever compare to what I now felt, so I simply suspended thought and focused only on the love I had experienced and seen on that giant white screen. That was real, but nothing else was. My perspective was forever altered in a single moment, and nothing would ever be looked at with the same vision ever again. Rumi was right! The wound *is* the place the light enters, although it seemed like the light was already within me but was obstructed somehow. I had almost instantaneously gone from the lowest and worst moment of my life to the highest and best moment in my life. I even began to wonder if I somehow entered an alternate reality or a different dimension of time.

I may never fully understand or be able to adequately express it, but one thing was certain, nothing outside of me had changed. Everything that seemed to cause my suffering was still there. I still lived in a small ohana with a broken A/C, I had the same amount of money, all of my business matters were the same, all of my relationships were the same, everything outside of my own perception and perspective was exactly as it had been earlier in the day, and yet now absolutely nothing was the same. I never would have imagined it possible for everything to now appear so different without a single external change. Could just my own perception and perspective really be the sole cause of such a metamorphosis?

There was a purity to this new mental place that shined right through my previous perspective and illuminated all the shadows in my mind with love and light. No darkness remained, nor could any darkness ever hope to survive the presence of so much love and light within. The suffering caused by separation from love somehow caused the reveal of an inseparable unitive reality with love. When I was engulfed in darkness, I asked for light and learned that I was light. The irony of already being the thing I was asking for intrigued me and made me wonder how I had ever missed something so obvious, and also what other paradoxes might be likewise concealed within this false reality.

There were three parts to this epiphany that changed my perspective forever. The first was an undeniable recognition of something that clearly transcended everything. It is infinitely spacious, and it surfaced within me in a way that could never be confined to words, and yet it was connected to and seemingly contained within this temporal and finite human body. Although after this experience I knew such containment was entirely impossible, there was no denying that this was the experience I seemed to be having. For the first time in my life, I saw and contrasted *a different reality* than the one I had always blindly accepted without question. I had discovered my first real evidence of transcendent eternal perfection within this world, and it was in the last place I'd have ever thought to look. I was obviously not what I appeared to be. None of us were. Whatever this something else was, it definitely did not belong here and had been very effectively hidden.

This led to some important questions, and my second takeaway from this epiphanic perspective shift. Why would something so grandly magnificent ever diminutively conceal itself within such a tiny false image, subordinating the truth of its reality in favor of a much more limiting illusion? This made no sense to me. Why allow a painful delusion to substitute for a perfect reality that displayed such immensely felicific value, with more light and love than could ever be contained within an insignificant form? The reason a transcendent power of immeasurable value was deceptively relegated to a small false identity was a real mystery to me, since this curious concealment only kept most people completely unaware of it, just as I had been. The only conclusion I could conceive of was, it must be due to some unintentional and involuntary ignorance.

The third realization, and this was a big one, was how my new vision clarified the duality of my opposing thought systems and how each operated. One was of a lower order and knew absolutely nothing. Its primary purpose was to obstruct truth by demanding my full attention be placed on an illusory reality. The other thought system made no demands, already knowing truth from error. It had its own voice, but it allowed my mind to make its own choice, even if that choice was for limitation and illusion over reality. It only responded to my willingness and invitation, rather than bullying or making demands. The clear awareness of these two mutually exclusive thought systems both operating simultaneously within my bicameral mind explained the ambivalence and confusion that had always plagued my life. How could a split mind *not* be confused? When pain and suffering eventually caused me to surrender the reactionary thought system I must have crossed the threshold between them somehow, which allowed the clear emergence and discovery of something I had always suppressed and obstructed by the thoughts I had chosen to adhere to instead.

By stepping outside of and beyond the previously perceived limits of my awareness, I could now see how I had formed beliefs according to the perception of the thought system I adhered to, which, up until now, had been false beliefs formed from a false perception because they were based upon a false identification. These distorted beliefs were identified with *because I believed them*, even though they were meaningless, insignificant, and inaccurate. This created an external experience that conformed to this manner of thinking. Thus, all of my pain and suffering was only due to false beliefs I had adopted from a false perception. But from this new perspective of Self I could see that there was no guilt, there was only a belief in guilt. There was no sin, there was only a belief in sin. I formed those false beliefs from my own false judgments, and now that I had a better basis for comparison, I could see how inaccurate I had been. Only an accurate perception can reveal the Infinite, formless nature of uncontainable perfect love that makes the human heart feel like exploding, and it does so despite a lifetime of having been deceptively ensconced behind all of the errant beliefs and judgments of false perception.

The contrast was incomparable. One thought system believed judgment was necessary and justified, and always reacted quickly to pronounce it. Such judgment only kept false perception firmly in place, thereby making what is false appear real. By attaching belief to thoughts created from false judgments, I could generate a strong emotional response and resistance to something that I created in the first place! I wasn't a victim of this experience, I was creating my own reality and everything painful was only happening because of my own erroneous perceptions, false beliefs, and improper self-identification.

But when I surrendered those false judgments, an awareness of pure spirit and the blissful ecstasy of love was my experience instead. Light and love is our only true reality, but false judgment separates us from it and causes us to define an illusion of self, rather than our reality of Self. Seeing this so clearly brought unencumbered mental peace and non-judgment was the only prerequisite. Everything in this world is neutral and causeless until we judge it, and then we become the cause of positive or negative attribution. Our own perception and beliefs give whatever we see and experience any meaning it has for us. There is no good or bad until we judge it that way, thereby creating an experience that then cooperates and coincides with our own perception and judgment. If we believe something is good, that perception makes it good for us. If we believe something is bad, we make it bad with that perception. If we are angry then we live in an angry world. If we are loving, then we live in a loving world. But it is the *exact same world*! The only variable is how we allow our individual thoughts and beliefs to color and create our experience according to the mental perspective with which we choose to see, evaluate and classify everything.

We only imprison ourselves on the unstable scales of judgment. But when we refuse to hold anybody prisoner to the guilt that our judgment inevitably assigns, then our efforts not to imprison others with guilt frees us of it also and acknowledges our own innocence. Then we see our experience here as nothing more than an external representation of our internal thought processes, a reflection of what we think we see, how we judge what we think we see, and the labels or beliefs we then apply to those judgments to provide them with meaning. If it weren't for judgment, there would be no differences to use to create the illusion of victimization. There would only be the reality of self-creation and nothing would be external to us because it is all-encompassed by one unitive reality. Or as Margie would say, we are One with God.

I wasn't sure what to do next. The only thing I was sure of was that I wanted to hold onto this feeling of personal peace. I looked over on the nightstand and saw Margie's book, *One With*

God: Awakening Through the Voice of the Holy Spirit. I smiled, remembering our bizarre two initial encounters, and knowing that our third was scheduled for tomorrow afternoon. I had no idea what to expect from that meeting, but I knew it would be an entirely different meeting after this experience. It seemed planned that way, as if forces beyond my awareness were preparing my path as I subconsciously responded to certain cues. I thought about Margie's cryptic message from the Holy Spirit, *"Don will be one of My powerful emissaries."* I still didn't know about that, but it was stated in future tense two days before this experience. Coincidence?

Then I remembered the way Margie looked at me in our first meeting that made me feel naked and forced me to look away, followed by her delivering a speech about her search for and subsequently finding the Holy Spirit. I wondered if this something else I now recognized within me was what Margie had seen that day, and spent her whole life searching for. Was it possible she could have seen this light and love that was apparently always within me, even though I had never been aware of it myself? Could it be seen even when it was obstructed by all of my judgmental and depressing thoughts? Could the Holy Spirit be what she was looking for, when I looked away and shut the windows to my soul because I didn't think anything this valuable, perfect and eternal could possibly be within me? At least now I could commence with dispelling that belief.

Holy crap! Did I just find the exact same thing that crazy Margie had discovered? Did this mean I was losing my mind too? Are we both crazy? Or are we the only ones who aren't crazy, who have experienced our true reality in such a way that those who haven't discovered it yet have to label us just so that they can justifiably maintain their own delusion? I had just recently assured myself that I wasn't as crazy as Margie was, but now I was on her side of the fence with a lot of questions . . . and I liked it better!

The oppositional and judgmental thinking eventually tried to return, but these thoughts were so much easier to identify and discern between now because I had another way to perceive them and strip them of any assumed power. They were powerless, insignificant thoughts unless I assigned them power. Yet I also noticed it was a very real challenge not to fall into the judgment trap and allow it to disturb my peace and cause suffering. Controlling my mind was not an easy thing to do, even with my understanding of the meaninglessness of arising thoughts. I needed to reclaim that power and not release it for improper application. But I, and everyone in the world, seemed hard-wired to respond according to the lower judgmental and reactionary thought system. It's the default thought system we always tend to revert to, like bad posture if we aren't giving it any conscious thought, as if we were programmed to be judgmental and reactionary. But with focused practice, I found I could train my thinking to make non-judgment and non-reaction habitual, and thereby maintain my peace of mind.

I committed to only operate from the peaceful thought system. I decided to think and perceive truthfully for the rest of my life. The decision was the easiest I've ever made. I just needed to figure out how. Margie popped into my head again, prompting me to consider that maybe her book held a clue to help me find and stay on this path. I took Margie's book from my nightstand and decided to see what the Voice of the Holy Spirit had to say after waking her at three a.m. I read the first sentence of the preface, *"Without help, it is almost impossible to accept the unreality of the world you see, let alone that you are its dreamer."* I lowered the book and audibly gasped. In an entire universe of possibilities, I wondered what the odds were that I would read this first sentence from the preface of *"One With God"* within moments of being divinely assisted in unveiling the unreality of this world in a very personal and powerful demonstration, which brought me the clarity to finally see that I am the creative dreamer of this experience that gives it all the meaning it will ever have. I am the dreamer of the dream, and not it's unfortunate victim as I had previously supposed.

It's hard to imagine reading anything more pertinent and applicable in that moment than the opening sentence in the preface of Margie's book. It spoke to me in a way that would change the course and direction of the rest of my life. Just hours ago, that same sentence wouldn't have meant anything to me, but reading it now seemed like I was being shown with exact precision the powerful extent of infinite intelligence that had briefly surfaced within me and that I now knew I was part of. The confirmation of this realization gave me goose bumps as I sat there in perfect peace, enveloped by infinite love. I was no longer lost and had no excuse to remain imprisoned, nor was it even possible for me now that I had found this eternal perfection within. I could never be separated from it, although I could choose to deny it as the only real and truthful part of me. My identification with inaccurate perception had pushed the awareness of what I truly am aside in favor of weakness, smallness and suffering, until truth surfaced and offered me the help necessary to accept the unreality of this world and my place as the dreamer in creating it. Now I found myself looking forward to Friday for a completely different reason than I've ever looked forward to a Friday in my entire life . . . to have tea with a little, old lady.

Chapter 3

A Memorable Tea Party

"The mind is its own place, and in itself can make
a heaven of hell, a hell of heaven."
John Milton, *Paradise Lost*

After experiencing such a monumental and life-changing moment I couldn't wait to share it with Kim, of course. But in my excitement, I completely forgot how poorly things had ended during our last counseling session. Or maybe I remembered but didn't think it was very significant next to my miraculous revelation regarding the truth of our identity. So, I called Kim to tell her about my experience, but she didn't answer the phone. I texted her, but she didn't respond to my text either. It wasn't like her to not respond to me for an entire evening like this. I knew she was still upset with me.

The following morning, I was still excited and feeling the afterglow of my experience, so I was awake much earlier than usual. I checked my phone again; still no response from Kim. I decided to email her. I knew she usually woke up and laid in bed with her phone for a few minutes before getting up and going to the gym, so I wanted this email to be the first thing she saw when she woke up. It took me longer to draft than I expected and was much longer than I intended. Even so, I was able to send it by six thirty-five a.m. and figured she would see it within the next thirty minutes upon waking.

In the email I apologized about my reaction to the sublease of my old room to a strange man and explained that I just felt like it would make my visits to Kaya awkward if somebody else was always in the house when I visited. I proposed an alternative solution and then pointed out how we had been moving in a good direction until the rental situation surfaced that set me off. I told her all about my recent spiritual experience and how it had changed my heart and perspective, then I asked her for another chance to prove that I was no longer that same angry person.

This time she did reply, with a two-word response. The first word rhymes with luck and the second is a popular insect repellent. I couldn't believe it! I had to talk to her in person. How could she just dismiss such an amazing message from God Himself? I decided to let her do her morning workout and then speak to her later in the day before I went to meet with Margie. Later that morning she stopped by the office and when she left, I walked her out to her car and tried to share more of my experience with her. But she was very cold and still angry with me. She said it was just a ploy on my part to get my way when she had already provided me with more than enough chances to make the kind of changes that could have saved our relationship. She wouldn't hear any of it, and my heart sank.

It was frustrating to share a life-changing experience with the one person I wanted to share it with, only to have it tossed right back into my face with a refusal to acknowledge it as authentic. My longing to share something extraordinary that would benefit us both was being rejected without any considera-tion whatsoever, and I was being labeled a disingenuous fraud. Under any other conditions her response would have been understandable, but this experience really did change me, and I knew I was no longer the same person. None of that mattered to her. I remember walking back into the office feeling heavy again, weighed down by the frustration of having such an amazing experience mean absolutely nothing to the only person I wanted to share it with.

As the previous emotional pain and suffering began to return again, I tried to shift back to my new perspective, but it was difficult. I knew it was my own reaction to her response that was causing the feelings of negativity to return, but I just felt like I got surprised by a sucker-punch, so it was difficult not to react negatively.

The afternoon dragged on until I finally left early and went home to grab a late lunch before meeting Margie at three-thirty. After eating I read more of *One With God* to have some idea what Margie's book was about in preparation for our meeting. In the past twenty-four hours I had managed to read the first sixty-five pages of her book. I thought by reading it I could glean an adequate question selection prior to our meeting, but there were some serious gaps in my overall understanding. It wasn't that Margie's book didn't make sense or contain a lot of valuable information, but it was only available to me in small chunks since I was not well-versed on the whole basis of understanding that the ideas originated from. It was clear from just those sixty-five pages that the written words were helpful, practical, and coming from a higher place, but my own shallow depth of understanding caused too many of those words to float above and beyond my comprehension with ambiguous retention.

I decided *not* to write down any questions to ask Margie because operating at that level of mental precision was how I *used to* be. Now I was more interested in getting out of my own way and removing such self-imposed mental obstructions and making a list of questions seemed more like erecting obstructions than removing them. Nothing that had happened to me thus far needed my planning to be achieved, so why start now?

I was just going to trust the process and not give any thought to our upcoming discussion. Even though I definitively decided this, part of my brain didn't get the memo and started working overtime to raise its loud oppositional voice prior to our meeting. The very thought system that had just been exposed as powerless a day ago now seemed fearfully frantic to act to ensure its own survival. It was also still attempting to diminish my earlier experience, just as Kim had done. Although I knew that could never be diminished, described or even adequately explained. Something like that can only be experienced, and the experience leaves you with tremendous awe directed towards the Source of it.

The immediate effect of my new mental practice of non-judgment freed my mind by unburdening me of the need to constantly classify and judge everything. Although I wasn't always able to catch my habitually judgmental thoughts as they surfaced, even small improvements resulted in a dramatic increase in mental freedom and personal peace. I wondered how something so simple could be so far removed from the mindset of the majority, and how it had likewise managed to avoid my own understanding for so long.

By disallowing judgment, I was allowing truth permission to surface freely, rather than suppressing it in favor of contra-dictory false beliefs or obstructing it behind inaccurate judgments that kept it hidden. I wasted so much time in judgment prior to recognizing my true identity and regretted not surrendering it sooner.

Only in hindsight could I now see how ignorantly I had dissociated from truth by holding firmly onto opinions or mental positions. It was rueful to now realize how much of a negative impact my "psychosclerosis" had on my motivation for learning truth. After all, why bother learning something I already knew? So, I attacked truth and defended error, because truth contra-dicted my beliefs while error justified my judgments. But now I was committed to remaining open to everything and attached to nothing. The only thing I knew for sure was that I didn't know anything. I was finally ready to be a proper student of truth. I never suspected it would be possible to gain so much by letting go. This new understanding struck me so profoundly that I decided to make it my next Toastmasters speech.

Another of my previous problems was that I never bothered to question the veracity of what I was learning. I often accepted what others told me without even a cursory verification of reason, because I assumed *their* learning must be accurate or they seemed to be well-intentioned. So, the "knowledge" I was often gaining was false, coming from conditioned mental responses and forming a tainted operating paradigm constructed entirely of inaccurate judgments and perceptions. I never let go of them or changed them because they were useful in justifying my egoic position of superficial "knowledge," while unconsciously rationalizing my obstruction of truth.

A perfect example of this was being raised in Mormonism, clutching beliefs and claiming certainty in a manner that perpetuated this struggle to uncover truth. It was my own religious beliefs that kept me from moving towards truth if it ever ran contrary to church doctrine. The irony was that these beliefs were held in the name of truth, although they often obstructed it. I have since learned that many people do the same and hold onto traditional beliefs due to fear and judgment rather than opening up to love and forgiveness because that would require a release of certainty surrounding these beliefs. But I had been shown the completely causeless and insignificant unreality of this world, and subsequently witnessed the dissolving importance of a thought system I had ignorantly employed my entire life. Now I needed to unlearn a lifetime of useless "knowledge" that was stored in my mind and obstructing truth. If you think teaching an old dog new tricks is challenging, try getting it to unlearn lifelong habits. Unlearning is much more difficult than learning. Information flowed easily into my mind, but once I allowed it to establish residency as a belief then the eviction required it to be pried out with a crowbar.

I didn't mind this difficult extraction because I was now awakened to the realization that all of my past learning was wrong, simply because it caused suffering and did not make me happy. On that basis alone, its value should have been questioned much sooner. After all, if the purpose of learning is change, and I was not satisfied with the changes my learning had delivered, then that dissatisfaction should be recognized as learning failure. If I wanted to change my failed learning outcome, then a change in curriculum was necessary. I was ready, and something told me Margie was about to reveal my new curriculum.

When it was time, I got into my car to go find Margie's condo. It was in South Kihei near my Wailea office, so I expected to reach it within five minutes, and I did. I parked my car in guest parking, walked into her building and approached the elevator. My oppositional mind was racing in an attempt to understand, classify and judge what I was doing here in an attempt to make me fearful. I found it laughable to think of being afraid of Margie and wondered why I had never noticed before how silly some of my everyday thoughts were. I refused to acknowledge those thoughts as I continued in mental silence, resolving not to think too much about anything and just let things play out. I got off the elevator and began looking for Margie's unit number as I walked down the open exterior hallway of her condominium complex. I found her unit and raised my knuckles to knock on the door and was surprised by the presence of butterflies in my stomach. How relentlessly resilient these thoughts were! I rarely got butterflies for one-on-one meetings anymore. Oh sure, if I was meeting a buyer to show a multimillion dollar property or being interviewed for a high-end listing they invariably surfaced and fluttered a little, but that was because a potential six-figure sales commission could be hanging on the outcome of that meeting. But why would they surface now when I'm only meeting with a harmless little, old lady?

I disregarded them once again and knocked loudly on her metal exterior screen door, already aware from previous real estate sales of her floor plan that a loud knock would be required if she was anywhere but the master bedroom which was by the front door, due to the long hallway that leads from the bedroom to the main living area and kitchen. I heard Margie's crackling voice say something from a distance when I knocked, meaning she heard me and was coming but was all the way at the back of the condo. I couldn't hear her very well through the door, so I just waited, and waited, until she eventually opened the door and greeted me with an enthusiastic hello and swung the screen door open wide and wrapped both of her arms around me.

I wasn't expecting a hug, but in Hawaii hugs and kisses are often granted upon greeting or after an initial introduction. It took some time to get used to, because I was taught to shake hands, with men or women, but Hawaiian culture saw the handshake as far too cold and formal. I'd made some progress in the fifteen years that I'd been on Maui, but sometimes the quick hug still surprised me, especially as tightly as Margie was holding me now because not one of my three wives had ever hugged me this tight. I didn't want to seem unresponsive, so I squeezed her back, and when I did, I felt the bony ribs of her back indent where my hands were. I wasn't sure whether I had miscalculated my own size and strength, or her slender frailty, but I decided to be cautious and lessened my squeeze until I felt her ribs expand back outward. I wasn't sure how brittle bones can become at her age, but I wasn't about to find out by hurting her with a rib-breaking hug.

She eventually surrendered her surprisingly strong squeeze but kept her tiny hands rested on each of my broad shoulders as she pushed me slightly away to looked up into my eyes and practically shouted "How *are* you?" with a strong emphasis on the "are."

"I'm fine, thanks. How are you?" I queried as I diverted my eyes to the ground to avoid the awkward intensity of her gaze.

"I'm wonderful! It is so good to have you here. Come in, come in."

I followed her down the hallway and noticed the hall was covered with original paintings, and as the hall opened up into her kitchen, dining and living area there were even more paintings on the walls. I commented on the artwork and she told me she had painted them herself. I remembered from her speech that she was an artist when she first moved to Maui. From what I could see, she appeared to be a pretty good one. I don't really know much about art, but I liked that her paintings evoked both peace and beauty. She asked me where I wanted to sit. One side of the room offered a sofa and the other an oversized chair. I chose the chair. On the coffee table in the center of the room she had laid out some refreshments that consisted of grapes, cheese and crackers. She asked if I wanted tea, but I just asked for some water instead, so she shuffled into the kitchen and eventually returned with a chilled bottled water.

No sooner had I sat down with the water in my hand when she sat down across from me on the sofa and settled into her seat before looking up at me with that piercing gaze and asked, "Why do you think your name showed up in my daily dictation from the Holy Spirit after only our first meeting, especially when you probably already thought I was nuts?"

I looked down at the floor again and smiled a sheepish grin as I thought about how to respond. She wasn't wasting any time with small talk and surprised me with this quick first question, obviously not as oblivious to her surroundings as I had thought. She knew exactly what I had been thinking after hearing her speech and accepting her handwritten message from the Holy

Spirit. I wasn't fooling anybody by my judgments, especially someone as spiritually sagacious as she was, who has direct daily contact with perfect intelligence.

Not really wanting to answer, I mumbled, "I don't know."

Unfazed, she continued staring at me, as if looking through me to somehow see the answer on the other side, and then she leaned back on the sofa and said, "Why don't you tell me a little bit about yourself."

That seemed like a fair question. After all, I learned much more about her during her Ice Breaker speech than she learned about me. My speech only glossed the surface as I spoke of my family briefly and mostly for humorous effect, while hers detailed a lifelong spiritual search with incredibly personal details. I shared all of my family backstory. It was a lot of personal information and none of it was positive. It felt heavy just relaying it. When I finished, Margie continued to look at me, as if she wanted to say something but wasn't sure how to say it. I didn't know what else to say so I just stayed silent.

Finally, she spoke, "That is quite a life story." Another long pause as she froze me with her gaze while appearing to find and organize her next words. When she finally spoke, she said, "There is no time, place, or state where God is absent, because only God exists. Everything that appears to exist outside of God is a metaphor, a symbol that points the way towards our only reality of perfect, infinite oneness with God. Have you ever considered what your life story is symbolic of, or what message it is pointing you towards?"

I shook my head, trying to process everything that she just said. She continued, "Let's look at your life experiences and see if we can link their symbolism to the real cause of all these various negative effects."

That seemed like a good idea, although it made me a little uncomfortable to be diving into an analysis of my personal life and marital failures. We sat in silence for a moment, and when it became too awkward I eventually gave up and said, "I don't know."

"What is the common theme that has been shared in all of these circumstances, events, and people?" she asked.

She sounded like she was slipping into her clinical social worker background, but this was an easy question to answer.

"That they were all taken away from me by disease, disaster, divorce, or death."

"Yes, making it difficult to imagine that this is what God created for you, since every one of these examples is a painful separation story. Do you have any idea what this is symbolic of?"

I had no idea. She must have thought I was a very poor student, but I just didn't know what she was getting at or implying. More silence as I pretended to think, though completely baffled. Sensing I had no answer but not wanting to let me off the hook, Margie asked another question, "Do you know how you got here?"

I knew after my epiphany yesterday that my stock answer to this question would be wrong, and because I was trying to unlearn anyway, I tried to take the safe route and answer her question with a comical question of my own. "My parents?" I regretted my unamusing attempt at humor as soon as I did. She knew I was trying to make my evasiveness funny, but she responded anyway.

"That is the answer the ego would suggest, in an attempt to persuade you to believe you are a body, made by other bodies, and bound by what the body orders you to feel. But we are constantly choosing between our own weakness and the strength of God. I'd like to invite you to choose again regarding how you think you got here, and remember that what you choose is what you think is real, and every choice you make establishes your own identity as you see it and believe it is."

I'd never been reprimanded so eloquently and politely for being facetious. I decided I better choose again and correct course.

"I believe I was created by God and He sent me here."

"A better choice, but still not completely accurate because although God did create you, He did not create this world and He has nothing at all to do with your being here now."

Now I was confused. I was trying to follow, but this statement seemed contradictory. If God created me, then how was it possible that God had not also created the world and had nothing to do with my appearance here? Nobody who believed in God had ever said such a thing to me before. As I'd already discovered, Margie was different than anybody I'd ever spoken to about God, and although I was trying to remain open, I realized the lifelong conceptual framework my religious beliefs had formed was obstructing my understanding.

After all, you didn't have to go very far into the Bible to find a contradiction to this statement. In the very first verse of the Bible, Genesis 1:1, it says, "In the beginning God created the heavens and the earth." Seems pretty clear to me, but now Margie was telling me something different. I could see my religious unlearning was going to be harder than I expected. Responding to the confusion that was now registering on my face Margie backed up and tried to explain, "The world you see is an illusion of a world. God didn't create it, because what He creates must be as eternal as Himself. But there's nothing in this world you see that will endure forever."

"Then who created the world?"

"What world?"

"This world!" We were beginning to sound like an Abbott and Costello skit.

"This world doesn't exist in God's reality, which is also your reality since you are One with God."

"Then how did this illusory world appear to get here?" I asked.

"That is an interesting story," she said and then took a pause so lengthy it made me wonder if she was going to tell it to me. I was starting to understand her pauses were not just to allow me time to process radical concepts, but also for her to listen to her own internal Voice to ensure that I received the very best explanation possible. She decided to start me with milk before meat, replying:

"I think it will make more sense to begin with what you are, and then we can circle back to this illusory world and how you appear to be here now. I already said your reality is not what it seems, because it is not just outside of time and space, but also outside of all limits and beyond all boundaries. In this reality, beyond everything you think you see, is a perfect oneness of spirit called Heaven. This oneness is so completely and infinitely inclusive that before your separation from it, there was no possibility of awareness of anything else.

"In this perfect oneness, Love is shared by extension, and the extension of this Love creates identical perfect, loving, indivisible, and unalterable Spirit that is exactly the same as the Spirit that created it by extending. This extension of Love from Source creates, shares, and expands the perfect Love that exists within this perfect oneness, and that expansion of Love created is called Christ, and Christ is the same as the Source—without any separation, distinction, or difference.

"The Love that extended and created Christ is the one and only Source of all creation. Jesus used the word Father as a metaphor for this Source, which metaphorically made the creation of His exact likeness His Son. It is important to remember that these are only metaphors and that God cannot be limited by gender, nor can Christ. In fact, millions today refer to our Source as a Divine Mother. As long as you recognize this Source as the

Author of your creation, with no name but Love, then it doesn't matter which term is used because no word is adequate. I use Christian terminology because *A Course in Miracles* does, but Spirit is impersonal and, in Its eyes, all persons are One. Remember that Christ's creation did not dilute God nor change the nature of God in any way, it only extended the whole. This perfectly united spirit of God encompasses everything, and there is not anything, anywhere that is not encompassed by it."

"If parents told that bedtime story, I don't think children would ever have nightmares," I quipped.

"Wait until I get to the idea of separation being introduced into Heaven. That part of the story has caused every nightmare there has ever been."

"It's too bad the story doesn't end here then," I added.

"You determine where this story appears to end with your own beliefs and power of choice, and the only reason the idea of separation can ever cause any nightmares at all is because of your belief in it and by exercising your power of choice to seemingly create it. The truth has never completely left you and the separation that you think you see now is really only a product of your own belief. This whole idea of separation is a false idea that only appears real within this backwards world. All of the separation you appear to see, and experience, is just an illusion superimposed upon your actual reality to create a false experience that then causes you to grossly misidentify with a false self-image that is infinitely smaller and weaker than the Self you really are."

As intense as that statement was, I could understand exactly what she meant because of my experience yesterday. But had she told me any of this before then, I would not have had a clue what she was talking about. Timing is everything.

She continued, "Look, the world seems to present you with a lot of different problems, so many that you feel overwhelmed by them. But isn't it possible that all of your problems have been solved and you have removed yourself from the solution?" I eyed her curiously as I slowly shook my head and then realized I meant to nod.

"That's because lots of problems is the ego's desperate attempt to distract you from recognizing that you only have one problem, and that problem only has one solution. One problem, one solution. But you'll never find the solution if you don't even know what the problem is. Because your one problem is the singular cause of multiple effects, and as long as you are focused on treating the effects and not the cause of the problem itself, then the effects will never go away. Their endless repetition will inevitably continue, leading to anger, dismay, frustration, and depression, which you know all too well. It is like when modern medicine treats the symptoms but not the cause of the illness. This is important for you to understand because it makes the necessary correction very simple, though not always easy." She slowed down and pronounced with emphasis every single word of her next sentence, "*The only problem you have and need to correct is your distorted perception of separation from God.*" She paused once again at the end to allow that statement to sink in before continuing.

"The problem of separation is really the only problem you have, and it has already been solved. You just don't recognize the solution because you have removed yourself from it. When your mind perceives separation as real, it becomes real for you. But it isn't, and the Holy Spirit will assist you with a perception correction when you're ready. Until then, your life will continue to re-enact the separation, the loss of power, and the ego's futile attempt at reparation. These repetitions are endless until they are voluntarily given up. Otherwise, they continue to show up in your separated life and are adhered to as your present reality, when they aren't. Correct the false perception that stems from the mistaken idea of separation from God, and you will never suffer from separation again, because it will no longer be perceived as your reality. The truth is within you, because this knowledge has been kept for you in the Mind of God, the Source of all life. You cannot ever leave the Father's Thoughts and will always be in them, among them, one with them, and therefore one with Him."

Although I liked the one problem, one solution idea, this seemed like an extreme oversimplification for my prodigious problems. Was it? Or was I the one that had overcomplicated everything? Until recently I had never considered the possibility that I had sure knowledge within me. Now she was telling me that it had always been there, outside of my awareness but available to me, linked directly to the Mind of God. I thought back to yesterday's experience and that beautiful moment of seeing beyond all thought, perception and judgment, when this sure knowledge of light, love, and truth that was usually buried beneath everything superficial surfaced and made itself known. Was that the Mind of God she was referring to? It sure seemed like the same thing. This thought caused a return to the same peace I felt yesterday, which I took as a confirmation of this truth, which then made me want to tell Margie about my experience. But it was extremely personal, and I hardly knew her. Besides, after Kim's reaction I figured I better wait.

Although that experience was life-changing in its effect on me, I noticed there was still a hitch to some of what Margie had said because it contradicted everything I had ever been taught about God, and how He had created my individual soul. I thought I was a uniquely special child of God, separated, and less than God but with a divine seed of tremendous unrealized potential. What Margie was sharing was radically different from what I was used to hearing, but that didn't necessarily mean it wasn't true, it only meant I may have more unlearning to do.

"So . . . how exactly did the separation from God seem to occur? It is one thing to say it didn't, but that is hard to believe when your entire experience is screaming something completely different."

"Somewhere within this perfect oneness, something happens that seems like a dream, and a small aspect of the Son's mind has a tiny, mad idea. This idea was really more of an innocent wondering of a 'What if?' scenario than anything else, as it considered, or dreamed, what it would be like to exert independence from the perfect oneness of God to go off and create and play on its own in a world ruled by the experience of individuality, departing from God's reality of oneness to entertain the idea of separation. Even Jesus referenced this idea of the Son's willing separation from the Father when he shared his parable of the prodigal son."

"I thought that was a parable about forgiveness."

"There was nothing for the father to forgive since he never condemned his son for leaving. The son was not kicked out of the house or banished in any way. He left innocently from his father's viewpoint, although he foolishly believed he could do better on his own and quickly squandered his inheritance for nothing of any value, because he had not understood its worthlessness at the time. He was then ashamed to return to his father, because he thought he had hurt him or made him angry. The only guilt in this story was the guilt that originated within the mind and thoughts of the prodigal son and did not come from his father who only saw him as innocent and loved him unconditionally. When the son later returned home feeling unworthy the father wouldn't acknowledge any of that because only his son's innocence existed in his mind, clearly demonstrating that what the son thought of himself and what the father knew to be true were incompatible ideas. The father welcomed him with joy, rushing out to meet him before the son even arrived at the father's house. The father hugged and kissed him, possessing only love and approval of his son, and proving that the son himself was his father's only treasure, and he wanted nothing else. Likewise, you are God's only treasure, and He wants nothing else but union with you. If you are the treasure of God, and what He values is valuable, then there cannot be any question as to your worth. How then can you not regard yourself as valuable unless you are making *yourself* unworthy, just as the prodigal son did?"

I slowly nodded my head, mentally connecting the parallel of our spiritual separation from God to this parable of the prodigal son. When Margie noticed the dawn of understanding spreading across my face, she winked at me and said, "Isn't that a great story?"

I nodded and smiled as she continued, "The Bible is rich with symbolism of this concept, and *A Course in Miracles* provides a very detailed explanation of the origins of separation, which it calls the 'detour into fear.' The Garden of Eden represents the pre-separation condition as a state of mind in which nothing was needed. Adam listening to the 'lies of the serpent' represents all the untruths told by the ego to sell the idea of separation. But the mind is free to believe what it will, and you do not have to continue to believe what's not true. The deep sleep that fell upon Adam caused a dream that seems to make this lie appear real, but you can awaken at any time and see for yourself that we are at home in God, dreaming we are in exile but perfectly capable of awakening and restoring our reality of oneness with God. Being cast out of the garden of Eden, Revelations referencing a war in heaven with angels being cast out of heaven, the parable of the prodigal son, these are all symbolic of this "detour into fear" that originated from the tiny, mad idea of separation. The dream has become a nightmare and the only way to escape it is to awaken from it. And when we do, our waking eyes will rest upon God and we will know it was all a dream, and our sins and errors never really occurred. It is silly to assume we have the ability to usurp the power of God or be separate from Him if that is not His will.

But within the dream that is how we seem to be, somehow departed from our perfect reality after having left truth in favor of delusion. The free mind of Christ, being creative like God, was capable of entertaining this tiny, mad idea and making it possible of both accomplishment and real effects. The Son obviously did not realize the magnitude of this thought of separation, which was so vast and incredible that from it a world of total unreality had to emerge, and with it seemed to cast you out of Heaven, shattering perfect oneness into fragmented and meaningless bits of disunited perceptions.

"That is why I told you that God did not create this world and has nothing to do with you being here now. The Son decided to leave and create a world to satisfy his shortsighted curiosity, and when that symbolic apple was bitten it initiated the Big Bang that created our illusory universe as an apparent answer to the Son's hypothetical 'What if?' question. The effect of this errant thought seemed to cause the manifestation of an experience where time and space appeared to suddenly spring out of eternal oneness and create a place where the deathless come to die, the all-encompassing can suffer loss, the timeless are made slaves of time, and the changeless change. But in reality, it is not possible for the peace of God to give way to chaos, hate, pain, and death. The dream is deceiving you if it ever appears that way."

"Wow, so the Big Bang that created our universe was nothing more than an errant thought by the extension of God, or Christ?"

"Never underestimate the power of the mind. The mind made the entire universe, each body and every form that appears to be in it, and there is only one mind that encompasses it all, although it appears to have been split into many. Each separated soul split off from this mind is a fragment of the Christ Self that has chosen the wrong teacher. There are only two ways of looking at the world, with two teachers that each point in a different direction. Your perception will reflect the teacher you have chosen, and you will follow in whichever direction your chosen teacher leads. The right mind represents the Holy Spirit Who points you home to God, and the wrong mind represents a belief in separation or individuality, known as the ego. It points to anything in this world that you believe is good and valuable and worth striving for, because it knows your pursuit of such will require you to remain in the world, separated from God in awareness, and subject to continued imprisonment. The ego distracts you into believing the illusion and its multiplicity of problems are real, when none of it matters because none of it is real. Once you understand this you can choose again, and your right-minded vision will show you that your reality is One with God. As soon as your mind has changed, and you have chosen to believe this is your reality then that is the reality you will see. You see what you seek because what you seek you will find.

"If you choose the ego as your teacher, it inevitably leads to pain and suffering. But this is always only a temporary choice because an imprisoned will produces a spiritual situation that ultimately becomes intolerable. Eventually, everyone begins to realize that there *must* be a better way, and this realization becomes a turning point that allows the Holy Spirit the little willingness He needs to release your mind from wrong-minded thinking. But you have to choose again and surrender the wrong mind to allow the Holy Spirit to put you in your right mind instead. It is this turning point where the Holy Spirit gently takes your hand and begins to lead you home, retracing every step taken and decision made that brought about your separation from God. You don't need to do anything except surrender and allow the Holy Spirit to restore your true reality of perfect oneness with Source."

She didn't know it, but she just described exactly what had already happened to me. I was tormented by pain and suffering from my identification with the ego's world of separation. But when the situation became intolerable, I couldn't take it anymore. I surrendered and let go, allowing the Holy Spirit to come rushing in to remind me of another option. I liked the imagery of the Holy Spirit gently guiding me home to God, but gentle isn't the word I would have used when I felt the emotional earthquake violently shake loose all of my negative emotions and then expand my heart until I thought it was going to explode from an over-dilation of Love. But at least my Teacher left no doubt as to Who held the real power and who didn't. Margie must have sensed she was probably giving me more information than I could handle so she finished with: "The Holy Spirit unites Christ to our reality of perfect oneness with Source. What God says is one will forever be one, regardless of what the ego gets you to believe temporarily.

"The instant the idea of separation entered the mind of Christ, God's Answer was immediately given as a correction for this tiny, mad idea. This is the pervasive message of the Holy Spirit's daily messages to me and why I was instructed to title His books as *One With God: Awakening Through the Voice of the Holy Spirit*. People need to know that the mind can elect what it chooses to serve, whether the ego's wrong-minded thinking or the Holy Spirit's right-minded thinking. The only limit placed on this choice is that you cannot serve two masters, another of Jesus' teachings. This just means that you must pick a side, and that choice determines whether your mind is operating under oppressive or authoritative control. Only by choosing the right Master can you correct the error of separation and unravel the ego's lie to verify that we really are One with God."

Could it really be as simple as just changing my mind, accepting God's Answer and letting His Teacher handle the details? If that was true, I was ready. But first I needed a break before my head exploded. This was mind-bending stuff, so my head was hurting from trying to comprehend it all. With my awakening experience, Kim's accusation of it not being genuine and Margie's radical spiritual explanations all happening within the last twenty-four hours, I'd say it was a safe bet that I was at a crucial turning point. But it was clear I had a long way to go before I would reach Margie's level of understanding, because much of this information was not fitting within my dearth of intellectual capacity.

Since Margie just described a sure process of eventual spiritual awakening that coincided perfectly with mine, before I knew it, I was sharing the details of my experience with her. I told her everything; the shortened counseling session, the break that caused true reality to briefly shine through all my false perceptions and illuminate my mind with the light of truth that was my real identity. I told her about Kim and Kaya showing up on the screen of my mind, and the exquisite bliss of having been shown our reality of being light and infinite Love that cannot be contained within any form, nor understood by anything but true perception. I finished with the unlikely coincidence of reading the first sentence of the preface of her book immediately afterwards. She didn't say a word but was absorbing everything I said with an intensity that made it hard to look directly at her. When I finished talking and looked back at her, she was crying.

I took that to mean she thought my awakening experience was authentic. She stated the obvious, that it could only have come from the Holy Spirit. She wiped her tears, genuinely moved by the gift that was bestowed upon me. Then she said, "Thank you for sharing that with me. Now I know why I was told to deliver that message to you."

Chapter 4

Gathering Mentors

"There are only two ways to live your life. One is as though nothing is a miracle. The other is as though everything is a miracle."
Albert Einstein

When I left Margie's condo, I was surprised to see that the sun had already set, leaving only a red and pink luminescence along the horizon. I loved living in South Maui, where year-round sunsets over the ocean, or their afterglow, can be seen simply by looking west. I never tired of them. Kim and I used to watch them together every night in the beginning, before I stopped making an effort to do so. I looked at my watch. 6:52. I had been at Margie's for over three hours. But after my awakening experience, being able to sit down with someone like Margie less than twenty-four hours later could not have been timed more perfectly. Not only did she understand exactly what had happened to me, and possibly even been instrumental in it happening, but she was willing to help me learn the lessons it delivered and explain the truth this experience had opened up within me. She said I could come back anytime. I'd heard the phrase, "When the student is ready the teacher will appear." But really? This all seemed way too coincidental, yet it also included an air of inevitability. I was definitely in unfamiliar territory, but I had no doubt I was right where I needed to be.

My trust in perfect alignment was undeniably buoyed after meeting with Margie. She inspired and fascinated me with her confident answers to all of my questions, and with such pin-pointed and specific information as I had never heard before. More importantly, what she had told me resonated with my own personal experience. She wasn't always easy to understand, but neither was calculus. New ideas that stretch the mind to greater capacities can be uplifting but may initially challenge us. It just comes with the territory, and I wouldn't have it any other way. I don't mind a challenge as long as there is a commensurate reward attached to its completion. Plus, I was extremely curious, and looked at my new spiritual surroundings as a kid might gaze upon Disneyland for the first time. I was vitalized and paying close attention, enchanted by something I had never witnessed or experienced before.

Margie was unique, I've listened to many who confidently proselytized their own delusion, but her peaceful manner and poignant message spoke to me in a way no other teacher or teaching ever had. Her words were received with perfect resonance. I suspected it was the Holy Spirit in her speaking to the same in me, declaring a unity of mind in an effort to restore what was never meant to be separated. I spent my entire life seeking and searching for a better way without finding anything until Margie told me in a Toastmasters speech that I already had within me exactly what I'd spent my entire life externally searching for.

As a result of Margie's inspiration, I called Ann Elaine that same night and told her I would deliver my "Safe Seat" speech in the Humorous Speech contest in September, to represent our Toastmasters club in the competition. Later that week as I was looking through Toastmaster Magazine, I saw an advertisement for speech coaching. I didn't know there were speech coaches, but I figured if I was now entering speech contests then it couldn't hurt, so I sent an email to inquire about the cost.

Not only that, but it became clear with regards to Kim what I should do. I decided to keep it simple, and I was just going to love her without any conditions or demands. It didn't matter what she thought of me and whether my love would ever be reciprocated. I would stop worrying about whether she loved me and just love her anyway. I figured if I did that then she would see I had truly changed, and if she didn't, then at least I'd be leading with love and living in alignment with my true identity and not some false version of myself. I'd let her be the judge of my authenticity and just focus on being authentic. My own spiritual perception correction had nothing to do with her anyway. I was pleased with the simplicity of this decision.

It was almost three weeks until the Humorous Speech competition. During that time, I did a lot of reading on spiritual topics and thought a lot about our three hour tea party, trying to get a grip on this strange new world I had stepped into. I thought Margie was crazy long before her deviation from virtually every religion in the world, all of which teach of a Source being the Creator of something which is not Itself, and then interacting with the separate creation. But it rang true deep within me that God created me like Himself and gave Himself to me as an eternal gift that would be insane to deny, and any description or definition of God also defined and described my true Identity. Once again, this required me to unlearn my previous understanding of God, and of myself, and replace it with His Own. This took me beyond all previous misconceptions of a separate or distant God and brought Him closer by believing myself to be more divine. Margie mentioned removing obstructions to hear the Voice of the Holy Spirit and that is what I planned to do. If she had found and heard the Voice within her, then I should be able to find It too.

Interacting with others while seeing them as the One Self, or the One Son, had an immediate positive effect on my outlook towards them. I saw them as equals, an extension of spiritual oneness that included myself, with more similarities than differences. Seeing them this way unified us with each other, and with God too. It reminded me of another of Jesus' teachings about oneness of spirit when he said, "In as much as you have done it unto the least of these my brothers, you have done it unto me." A phrase like that was no longer just an admonition to be nice to others, it was a literal description of spiritual oneness. Another benefit of identifying with spirit was how much of the weight or heaviness of the world was lifted. Before my awakening I felt like I could hardly breathe, but now all insignificant thoughts, false judgments, and self-assigned meanings dissipated. I was sure it was the same world, but it was almost unrecognizable from the world I knew before.

Although the effect on my attitude and outlook towards others was immediate and positive, it also required the reversal of an entire lifetime of habitual judgment that had been used to construct my current thought system. This meant I often met with resistance from my previously established mindset, but there was no arguing the positive results I was obtaining. Although the change was internal, the results were externally visible in all of my interactions and relationships. I remember thinking even if Margie was crazy, this was still a better way to live because I was so much happier and more peaceful. But after spending several hours with Margie I knew she wasn't crazy, and I also didn't need any further confirmation about the truth of my own Identity. Jesus once said, "By their fruits ye shall know them." As my mind slowly moved the new information from an intellectual concept into an actual spiritual practice, my distorted perception was in constant correction and there was no denying the beneficial reality of these fruits. My downward spiral into hell had become an upward spiral into the infinite beyond.

With Kim and Kaya, I stopped seeing them as a means to some selfish end and started to see them as an extension of the One Self. As such, anything I could do to improve their life condition would only benefit mine. There was no negotiation or compromise necessary, whatever was best for them was best for me too. My old thought system was screaming to change back from this new perspective, but I had already evaluated and compared the two thought systems and there was no comparison. One brought pain and the other brought joy and peace. No exceptions or compromises can ever be made between the right mind and the wrong mind, between everything and nothing, between God and the ego. This is because belief in the ego or the wrong mind represents nothing and choosing it indicates a denial of Source, while the right mind represents everything real and unites us with the all-encompassing nature of Source. Any compromise at all with regards to this choice limits and reduces our wholeness. I was not interested in choosing error or nothingness. I was committed to the choice that brought happiness and peace, and now that I had found it there was no way I ever wanted to lose it again. This fruit was addictive, and I constantly craved it.

Of course, the beneficial results of this choice were immediately noticeable to both, if not somewhat suspiciously received by Kim at first. She seemed to really like the ease and comfort of interacting with me now. There was no anger, no judgment, no demands, only love and acceptance. She understandably maintained her dubious nature about the validity of this change, but I couldn't really blame her after seven years of manipulating her needs to suit my own. I held the mental image of love and unity that I saw on the white screen of my mind that day and knew reuniting with my family was eventually going to happen. Why else would I have been shown those family images? So, I relaxed into and trusted that knowledge, looking forward to someday ending the separation from my family, just as I would eventually end my separation from God.

Since I had already extensively practiced my "Safe Seat" speech and didn't need to deliver it until September in the Area

Humorous Speech contest, I started working on my next speech. I titled it "The Danger of Certainty." I chose this speech topic because all of my life I had held cherished beliefs about God and other things that I thought were valuable additions of knowledge, only to learn in the end that those beliefs were nothing but self-erected obstructions to truth, allowing it to hide behind my own certainty. I wanted to challenge these cherished beliefs and previously protected values, because truth does not need the protection of belief. Truth stands alone, beyond all beliefs governed by the ego. Truth is the spiritual center that is approachable from any angle and direction as long as thoughts and ideas can move freely and are not attached and anchored to a belief system that restricts them, thereby keeping truth hidden and unapproachable.

Consistent with the theme that when the student is ready the teacher will appear, as I was writing this speech additional mentors began to show up in my life, once again, as if on cue. The personal assistant of the speech coach I inquired about responded to my email and told me the coach was out of the country and would be in contact with me as soon as he returned. Two days later I received this email:

> Don,
> I'm back in the USA.
> I have some time to talk today about what you want to accomplish.
> Let me know if we can chat today.
> Afterwards, I'm on tour (out of the country) for 10 days.
> Ed Tate
> CSP – Certified Speaking Professional
> World Champion of Public Speaking

Of course, now I'm curious what a Certified Speaking Professional is and how you become a World Champion of Public Speaking. He had a website link at the bottom of his email signature with a hyperlink that said, "See Ed in action." So, I clicked it and watched a couple of the speeches posted on his website, including the speech that won him the title of Toastmasters International 2000 World Champion of Public Speaking. There was no question he was an excellent speaker, possibly the most dynamic I had ever seen. Not only that, but after winning the World Championship himself, apparently finishing ahead of 354,000 members from 141 countries, he subsequently coached the 2009 World Champion as well as the most recent 2016 World Champion. I didn't entertain any delusion about someday becoming a World Champion, but he clearly had the credentials to help me become a better speaker.

I also looked up Certified Speaking Professional (CSP). It is a designation from the National Speakers Association (NSA) and is the highest speaking designation in the United States, and only seventeen percent of NSA members hold it. The twenty page document I pulled up online detailed the qualifying require-ments, which seemed unattainable to me. You had to document at least 250 paid speaking presentations over a ten year span, with at least 50,000 dollars in speaking fees collected each year. Each qualifying speech had to be at least thirty minutes long and given to an audience of a certain size, etc. I couldn't imagine anybody that wasn't already a professionally paid public speaker giving two-to-three speeches per month to large crowds for thousands of dollars per speech . . . over a consistent ten year period.

Yes, he was definitely qualified, so I called him to discuss the possibility of hiring him as a coach. I told him I was new to Toastmasters but that I had just won my club competition in the Humorous Speech contest, leaving out the part about winning by default because nobody else participated. We chatted for a while and then he told me of his fee structure. It started at 4,500 dollars and went up from there. He explained everything that was included with his coaching. I politely listened, but after hearing 4,500 dollars I knew there was no way that I could ever afford it. I told him I'd consider it and then wished him well on his international speaking tour and said we could touch base when he returned.

That bought me a couple of weeks. Although I would love to have speech coaching, it wasn't cheap. The only way I could afford it was if I landed a large sales commission quickly, so I put that intention out into the universe. I decided I would hire him only if a huge cash infusion somehow made it possible. Otherwise, it simply could not be done. Hey, stranger things have happened . . . and they were about to start happening to me.

The same week I had my conversation with Ed Tate, I met Ocean Love. Ocean was an apparent rental lead that supposedly became a buyer lead. I say apparent and supposedly because I think, in reality, she was pretending to be those things just so the Holy Spirit could connect me to exactly what I needed, right when I needed it most. Ocean could not be labeled, being one of the most intriguing people I had ever met. She represented a divine dance of spirituality, creatively woven into the world of form to demonstrate, organize, and arrange whatever necessary to yield the most significant teaching value, provide the most spiritual comfort, and heal the most suffering from separation.

When I answered my cell phone that day from a blocked caller, Ocean was on the line and she said, "Hello, I'm a single older lady, in my fifties, financially stable so money is of no concern, and I see that you rent properties. I was wondering if I could talk to you about helping me find a suitable rental." I liked the part about money being of no concern, but I would turn fifty myself next month and didn't appreciate her thinking that was "older". We started talking and she told me how she had no A/C in the place where she lived now and that she doesn't need much because she lives alone and meditates a lot, but she has to be comfortable during her lengthy meditations or they are not as effective. Then she said something nobody seeking my services had ever said to me before; that it wasn't about the money, it was about the *mana*.

In Hawaiian culture, *mana* is spiritual energy of power and strength. It exists in places, objects, and persons. *Mana* has a supernatural origin and is a sacred, impersonal force. Having *mana* implies influence, authority, and efficacy, and its possessors are accorded respect. It is the Hawaiian belief that you gain *mana* by acting *pono* (right actions) and lose *mana* by violence or wrong actions. It is also the Hawaiian belief that *mana* is external as well as internal, meaning it is everywhere and you either align with it or against it. I'm not Hawaiian so I didn't know any of this at the time, but since money is of no concern and I get paid by commission, I must now pretend to be a *mana* expert.

I had never been asked to find a property by *mana* before. People tell me all kinds of different criteria they want: how many bedrooms, bathrooms, a certain view, a specific location, square footage, a swimming pool, a hot tub—but never *mana*. So now I've got to find mana. Since her name was Ocean, I assumed the ocean must have a lot of *mana* and being a small company without a lot of rental inventory, I told her about the only oceanfront condo rental we had at the time, at Menehune Shores. She asked a few questions and said she wanted to see it and meet me, so we set up a showing appointment. The appointment was with me, and although Kim and I were business partners, we never went on appointments together because that was inefficient (my feelings, not Kim's). But when I told Kim I had a showing at Menehune Shores with a lady that appears to have plenty of money, but the property has to have *mana*, of course Kim wanted to come along and meet her. Kim loves meeting new and interesting people, so renting and selling real estate on Maui has been a dream job for her.

Kim and I went together to show the beachfront rental to Ocean. When we arrived, we saw Ocean get out of a new, full-sized pickup truck. She had a stocky, masculine build and extremely short, pure white hair and piercing blue eyes. It was not a crew cut but not much longer than one. She was also wearing what appeared to be Air Jordan basketball shorts and a T-shirt. This wasn't exactly what I was expecting after our phone conversation. She looked like she was headed to the playground for a pickup basketball game, and would kick back and have a beer afterwards, Maui style. She ignored my raised eyebrows and greeted me warmly and introduced herself with a firm handshake, not a hug. We all chit chatted as we walked to the elevator and I noticed she was wearing a knee sleeve and appeared to be limping slightly. She saw that I noticed and explained how she tore ligaments in her knee long ago and now under certain weather conditions it acted up and bothered her. She then said that is the bad news, but the good news is she can predict the weather better than most meteorologists. I laughed. She was very pleasant and had a warm smile and happy eyes. We couldn't pinpoint exactly why but being around Ocean made Kim and I both feel good.

As soon as we went into the condo it didn't take Ocean very long to give it a thumbs down for *mana*. I asked her why and she told me there were too many people in the high-rise building, there was another high-rise building visible within the ocean view, and it was close enough to the road to see and hear cars on busy South Kihei Road. Then she emphasized once again what she was looking for and I learned that by *mana* she meant quiet with serene energy. High-rises and busy roads ruined the *mana*.

All this time we talked I realized I still didn't know what she did for income, so I asked. She told us she performed spiritual healing work. I joked that I didn't know it paid so well. She laughed and said she has built quite a reputation for her work and now she works with a lot of celebrities, and they pay her thousands of dollars an hour. She said she doesn't charge them, but she accepts donations if they offer them. Intriguing. I looked at Kim and could tell she was also fascinated. Then we started chatting about her celebrity clients and she mentioned her spiritual work with Oprah and Tony Robbins. I furtively wondered what wealthy celebrities like that thought of her Air Jordan basketball shorts. She told us a few more stories and we asked a few more questions and before we knew it an hour had passed.

The more she talked, the more I could tell she was connected to a power that most of us never fully realize or will ever hope to access. When Ocean referenced God, she always said the Universe. It didn't matter what she called it; you got the strong impression that she was *very well* acquainted. As we stood in the parking lot and prepared to say goodbye, we kept chatting, and then Ocean turned to me and said, "You've obviously had a spiritual transformation and alignment recently." I nodded knowingly to Ocean as I turned to look at Kim. She looked like she just got shocked by a cattle prod. I didn't say anything, and I couldn't tell if Kim thought I put Ocean up to saying this or what. I just stood there stunned, until Kim spoke and asked her why she said that. Ocean replied that this is what she does, she picks up spiritual vibrations and mine had just recently been tuned. I couldn't believe it, but I loved it because this was now coming directly to Kim from a spiritual worker, and apparently a very good one if celebrities are paying her handsomely to show up in her Air Jordan's to spiritually align them.

As Kim and I drove back to the office we were both shaking our heads about Ocean. She was so engaging and fun to speak with and then to throw out that last comment like she did was a bit spooky. It made me feel like nothing is private. I had only told

Kim and Margie about my experience, but now I meet someone who doesn't have to be told and can apparently just sense it by my spiritual vibration. I told Kim how cool it was that Ocean could just pick up on something like that because that really did just happen to me and I reminded her that I told her about it, without mentioning her two-word retort when I did. Kim now knew my experience was genuine. It was the first time she acknowledged it, not that it mattered to me because I had already decided to just love her regardless, but from that day on our mending relationship hastened its improvement.

I decided to seize the momentum from this experience with Ocean and told Kim about some Couples Communication classes in Kahului that our insurance covered, and she agreed to attend with me. She had tried to get me to go to couples counseling before the separation, but of course I refused because I already knew how that was going to go. I wasn't going to be able to justify my bad behavior to a third person, especially one trained to quickly identify all of my signs of misconduct. I wasn't willing to stop doing what I was, so I simply refused to go, which demonstrated that I didn't care much about Kim or our relationship. But now that I'd been through the refiner's fire, I was thrilled to have the opportunity to attend a Couples Communication class and really work on our relationship. I don't think Kim would have ever agreed to do it if it weren't for Ocean's confirmation to her. Ocean made me believable again.

I returned to Margie's condo again the following Friday afternoon, and as soon as I arrived, I asked Margie if she knew or had ever heard of Ocean Love. She tilted her head to the side and looked up to the ceiling out of the corner of her higher eye as she contemplated whether that name was familiar to her at all, and then she shook her head. I told her what happened with Ocean. She replied, "That can happen because we all share one mind, and once you remove the ego's obstructions to oneness you are able to access this mind fully, without being subject to the ego's self-imposed separation limitations. This allows unity with other minds, because we are already connected. Being One with God means that we have no more nor less than everything He has, and only the ego's phony belief system can ever make us feel deprived of this wholeness. The Holy Spirit tells me things all the time that I never could have known on my own, such as that you are one of His powerful emissaries." I still wasn't sure about that, but I knew better than to doubt or question it if Margie said it. She then explained that all spiritual masters such as Buddha and Jesus had accessed the one mind and learned from it.

"Didn't you say you grew up as a Christian?" she asked.

"Yes, although many didn't see it that way."

"Why not?"

"Because Mormonism is a religion that is somewhat outside of mainstream Christianity, so other Christians didn't always want to acknowledge our beliefs as being Christian."

"Never underestimate the ego's ability to divide and separate, especially within religion. Although religion is supposed to lead us back to God, it often obstructs the path to God through easy identification with the ego's plan of separation instead. God-fearing is a common phrase tossed about among religious practitioners, but those two words are oxymoronic and should never be placed together."

"Why is that?" I questioned, curious because I knew exactly what she was referring to and often did hear that phrase used with a positive connotation to piety, like a badge of honor to their belief system.

"Because God doesn't want you to fear Him. God wants you to acknowledge that fear doesn't exist, except within the ego's thought system. You are as God created you, and what you are cannot be threatened. So, fear is an illusion. Its presence will always obstruct the peace of God within you. Fear indicates you have forgotten your true Identity and identified with illusion instead of the peace and perfect love that God created. Anytime you feel fear the ego has deceived you into separation from Source. Escape from fear requires acceptance of the Atonement, which is the undoing of our belief in separation and remembering our perfect oneness of spirit, and that can only happen by withdrawing belief in the ego's idea of separation.

"Perfect Love casts out fear, and if God is perfect Love, then so are you. But you can't serve two masters, so you need to choose between being Love or being fearful, between total freedom or total bondage. You can't combine both because your choice of one automatically negates the other. Fear perpetuates the unconscious guilt caused by choosing separation from our Father, just as with the prodigal son. But we are not separated and distant from God, so separation and fear are synonymous miscreations that must be undone. The fundamental cause of all conflict in this world is always between God's creation and the Son's miscreation. All fear is implicit in the second, and all love in the first. Therefore, the entire human conflict is simply one between love and fear."

It was refreshing to see how easily she was able to distinguish between the two thought systems and then isolate the ego and strip it of any power. It was quite logical when she explained it to me even though I had missed the correlation myself. Because Margie had undone her ego and identified so strongly with the Voice of the Holy Spirit, she enjoyed the true perception that comes from the Holy Spirit's constant guidance, and she carried that perception with her everywhere she went, like a lantern slicing through the darkness of misperception. She once told me that misperceptions produce fear and true perceptions foster love. Now I understood why she was so fearless. God's unobstructed love flowed through her because *she truly perceived* no separation between her and God, and therefore her real Identity could never be threatened, and this removed all cause for fear. Her awareness of perfect oneness with God was effortlessly expressed in every-thing she said and did, and it was a pleasure to witness, even though it did get confused with craziness by those who were not yet awakened, just as I had initially done.

This expression of love and oneness was not an act, but the most genuine thing you've ever seen or felt. Something as simple as Margie giving me a hug became a confirmation of God's love. It was unmistakable and undeniable. We talked a lot when we were together, because I had so many questions and wanted to accelerate my spiritual progress and understanding, knowing this was a rare opportunity for me to learn from such a truth-realized being. But my visits would have been just as meaningful if we would have simply sat in silence, as long as I could feel that peace emanating from her which seemed to drain my own anxiety. I felt like I was patronizing a peace spa with every visit.

"Anyway, since you grew up Christian, as I did, it may be helpful to realize Jesus knew this world was an illusion. He figured it out and tried to tell us, but his message got confused. He pointed out our eternal reality by saying he was One with God and identified so strongly with spirit that when he died, he was awarded Godhood by his followers. Jesus even says of himself in *A Course in Miracles*: 'There is nothing about me that you cannot attain. I have nothing that does not come from God. The difference between us now is that I have nothing else.' His reference to nothing else is a reference to the illusion of separation that the ego has us believing is real. Remove that belief and you will attain the same oneness with the Father that Jesus claimed. He knew that any perception which included separation from God was false and therefore must be an illusion."

"I never really thought about Jesus as an equal, because Christianity has always elevated Jesus as unique and special, having a relationship with God that we didn't."

"Yes, but you can't find light by analyzing the darkness within you, or by seeking a distant light to remove it while emphasizing the distance. This obviously only perpetuates belief in separation. It is true that Jesus is God's only Son, but so are you. Jesus said he and the Father were one, but so are you. There is only one Son and you are it. To see Jesus as any different than yourself bolsters belief in uniqueness and individuality, which is the thought system of the ego. His uniqueness is not in his birthright because you have the same birthright, it is in the sense that he was probably the first to fully identify with our true reality of perfect spiritual oneness and then communicate and demonstrate it as well as he did, even though his message was largely misunderstood. Nowadays there are over 20,000 different Christian churches that each have their own interpretation of Christianity, none of which truly understand his message. If you are serious about wanting to understand what Jesus was trying to teach, then read *A Course in Miracles*. There he explains and teaches in tremendous detail. It really gives you a chance to get inside the mind of God and correct your misperceptions."

"What does it say his message was, and why was it so largely misunderstood?"

"His message is that you are a non-spatial entity having a spatial experience, but that experience is a false one because you are not a body, and therefore death is not applicable to what you are. These were actual lessons Jesus taught and then demonstrated with his own resurrection in an attempt to awaken us to the truth of our reality and the falsity of the dream. He recognized the dream for what it is and knew that only a sleeping mind could ever dream up separation from our Source. Jesus proved this world is not as it appears, and that we don't belong here. We belong at home with God, one with all there is and ever will be, and not as a small, limited human existence trapped within a false experience. He told us to stop making illusions real by believing we are something we could never be and end our suffering by joining him in perfect and complete oneness with God, instead of sleeping and dreaming an illusion of individuality. And he is still saying that to us even now. That's essentially what *A Course in Miracles* is, his dictated teachings for a perception correction so that we can reestablish our true Identity."

"So . . . the dictated teachings of *A Course in Miracles* are from Jesus and not from the Holy Spirit that speaks to you?"

"Pure spirit cannot be divided except within illusions, so in reality there is no difference between the Father, the Son, and the Holy Spirit. It is all the same spirit; it is just that Jesus is specific to you and the Holy Spirit is abstract. God cannot be divided except through a distorted perception that makes Him seem divisible."

"You've mentioned *A Course in Miracles* a lot, in your speeches as well as our discussions. I guess I should buy it and read it."

"I guarantee you won't be disappointed if you do." And with that she got up from the couch and walked over to her desk and picked up a tattered old copy of *A Course in Miracles* and brought it towards me to get a closer look. She carried the book with great reverence to where I sat and then opened it to show me her highlights and notes in the margin. The pages looked like they had been turned a thousand times. She gently laid the book across my lap and then slowly stepped back while maintaining a fixed gaze with me. I would have looked down at the book, but she was backing up with her eyes locked on me and after several small steps I thought she was going to fall backwards over the coffee table that was between my chair and the couch.

I hadn't seen anybody move so slowly and deliberately with such a fixed gaze since my brother hilariously did so in an embarrassing moment as children. Once we were home alone watching his favorite baseball team on TV when he got the sudden urge to run to the bathroom. While he was in the bathroom his favorite player hit a homerun and I announced it to him from the living room, which caused him to come barreling out of the bathroom with his pants around his ankles, shuffle-running to the TV like a prisoner in ankle chains making a jailbreak, to watch the instant replay of the homerun hit. I laughed as he stood behind the couch with his pants down watching the instant replay.

As fate would have it, with him in this unsightly position, I see the landlord coming up the sidewalk to the house. I should have warned him, I really should have, but after all he put me through as the youngest child, I guess I was looking for a little payback. So instead of warning him, I took a stealthy step back into the kitchen where I could see the front door and living room but remain undetected. I felt a unique combination of anticipation and excitement as the hilarity of this scene began to unfold before me.

The landlord reached the porch and knocked on the screen door, to which Danny snapped out of his homerun trance and turned to lock eyes with him just a few feet away. He didn't move, he simply stood aghast as his mind tried to register what was really happening. I watched as the shock of being caught with his pants down reflected on his face and his eyebrows shot up and his jaw dropped nearly to where his pants were.

He clearly didn't know what to do, so he simply did nothing. He just stood very still, as if not moving would somehow keep him from being seen. The landlord asked him if our father was home. Danny didn't answer him nor attempt to move, he just continued to stare: I'm sure the landlord could hear the uncontrolled laughter coming from my concealed location. Finally, Danny slowly—as if in slow motion—did the prisoner shuffle all the way back to the bathroom. In his acute brain shock he never bothered to pull up his pants nor took his eyes off the landlord during his entire time of transit, swiveling his neck to maintain constant eye contact with the landlord the entire time he moved in slow motion back to the bathroom, much as Margie was doing with me right now.

Margie must have sensed the coffee table behind her because she stopped stepping back just in time and didn't comically crash down on it like Chris Farley on Saturday Night Live. With that crisis averted I looked down at the book she had so demonstratively placed in my lap and asked her, "How did Jesus dictate all of this? And to whom?"

Margie replied that it was dictated to Helen Schucman, an atheist educator and psychologist that was a Professor of Medical Psychology at Colombia University in New York. Helen was struggling through a difficult and strained relationship with the head of her department when he told her he was tired of the angry and aggressive feelings her attitude reflected and told her, "There must be another way." She agreed and vowed to help him find it.

That willingness to cooperate in finding a better way opened up a new chapter in her life as she started to have symbolic dreams and descriptions of strange images coming to her. She was surprised when a voice spoke clearly in her mind and said, "This is a course in miracles. Please take notes." That was her introduction to the Voice, which made no sound, but seemed to be giving her a rapid inner dictation that she took down in shorthand. Although it made her uncomfortable, she never stopped recording it and never claimed to be the author of the material. She reported it to her colleague who was head of her department, Bill Thetford, who agreed to help her by typing her shorthand dictation while she read it back to him. The whole process took them seven years as they recorded some 1,500 typewritten pages.

"That sounds like it pretty closely resembles your experience and how your books are being written," I said.

"Yes, it is. My experience was similar and so will yours be once you start to consistently hear the Voice for God. The Voice is your voice also, and He promises to respond to your willingness to consider a different thought system, one that undoes the ego, ends suffering, and instills peace. The Voice is quite literally already within you, but it has probably been drowned out by adherence to an opposing thought system that coincides with your belief in separation and the ego. Helen and Bill wanted to find a better way, and they did, and *A Course in Miracles* is that way. The Course teaches you about these two different thought systems, one for the ego and one for the Holy Spirit, and you learn by comparing and contrasting them."

"It sounds like you have read it several times."

"I have because it is life-changing in so many ways. Just turn to page one and read the Introduction and tell me if this isn't a book that you *must* read."

I flipped back to page one at the very beginning and read out loud:

"This is a course in miracles. It is a required course. Only the time you take it is voluntary. Free will does not mean that you can establish the curriculum. It means only that you can elect what you want to take at a given time. The course does not aim at teaching the meaning of love, for that is beyond what can be taught. It does aim, however, at removing the blocks to the awareness of love's presence, which is your natural inheritance. The opposite of love is fear, but what is all-encompassing can have no opposite.

"This course can therefore be summed up very simply in this way:

>Nothing real can be threatened.
>Nothing unreal exists.
>Herein lies the peace of God."

"It sounds theological. That is a strange thing for an atheist to write."

"That's because Helen wasn't the author. She only wrote down the message the Voice delivered to her, and since she was an atheist and worked in a prestigious and highly academic setting she often disagreed with the content of her dictation and resisted the process, even though the Voice which spoke through her clearly identified himself as Jesus. Helen maintained her paradoxical position of consciously clinging to her avowed atheism even though she could not deny what and who was involved with the scribing. Despite this ambivalence she was unequivocal about not being the source of the writing. Even after all of the dictation was finished and *A Course in Miracles* was published, she said about it, 'I know it's true. I just don't believe it.' Even though she knew the truth of the Course's teachings, she didn't implement them in her life."

"That's interesting. I can't wait to start reading it," I told her. "I'll order it today."

"There are lots of spiritual paths one could take, and they all lead to God eventually, but if you want to accelerate your progress and save time it would be difficult to imagine having a better or more qualified teacher than Jesus. By the way, as a lifelong Christian just be prepared that you may find this version of Jesus a bit different from how he is perceived within Christianity, since his message is pure and has not been corrupted by the annals of religious history or the interpretive misunderstanding of those recording it. Perhaps that's why it came through an avowed atheist like Helen, to keep religious interpretation from clouding his message."

I thought to myself, "Why stop the spiritual surprises now?" I went home and immediately ordered my own personal copy of *A Course in Miracles*. After I did, I felt a strange anticipation. I wasn't sure if it was because of my purchase of the book or the miraculous manifestation of three mentors that transpired within a week of my spiritual awakening experience. I knew the appearance of Margie, Ocean, and Ed Tate meant I was on the brink of something significant. Perhaps this was the turning point Margie had mentioned in our first meeting, where renunciation of guardianship of my thought system would allow the Holy Spirit to correct my misperceptions and gently lead me back to God. It was an easy decision to renounce control and stop doing things my way, since I obviously never had any control anyway, and my way clearly wasn't working. My attempt to avoid God had been futile. God is inevitable.

Chapter 5

A Different World Emerges

"In order to ascertain the truth, one must doubt
all traditions, scriptures, teachings, and all the
content of one's mind and senses."
Buddha

Two days after meeting Ocean and with speech coach Ed Tate
having fled the country after assaulting me with his astronomical
coaching fees, a cash buyer who owned a lot of property on Maui
(but never bought any of them through me) called to ask if I could
show him some luxury condos. As I silently performed my happy
dance with him still on the phone, I told him absolutely. I showed
him two Kai Malu condos and he bought the more expensive one
for 1.196 million dollars and closed it in three weeks. I didn't
know if Ocean had anything to do with that, but I was beyond
questioning these things anymore.

Since putting the speech coaching out into the Universe, as
Ocean would say, when Ed followed up with me two weeks later,
I was only a week away from a 35,000 dollar sales commission,
my largest of the year. Obviously, I took this quick cash sale as a
sign that the Universe wanted me to hire him, so I did. And I have
to say, Ed was fantastic! The first thing he did was ask me for my
speech copy on "The Danger of Certainty." Then he went over it
with me in great detail and showed me how to shift or alter key
words for the most vocal impact. I was indubitably being coached

by a highly skilled speaking professional. He really improved my speech content and layout.

Then he had me video conference my speech to him while he watched every detail of my delivery. Afterwards we discussed it, and he pointed out where I struggled or where something didn't come off quite right. Then I would deliver it again, and again a few days later, and even again if possible. Ed demonstrated the art of public speaking and taught me things I never would have known had I not hired him.

With Ed's fingerprints all over my revised speech I walked into Toastmasters that night feeling prepared and confident. No longer the glossophobic guy, I was actually looking forward to giving a speech, with no butterflies or concerns whatsoever. I couldn't wait for my name to be called. When it was, I smiled and excitedly stood and walked to the podium. I loved the beginning that Ed and I came up with. I waited until the entire room was silent and then I shouted the first four words of my speech loudly:

"'They're peeing on you!' my wife shouted as the back of my head and neck were doused with warm liquid. Without looking up, I began to sprint down the narrow, suspended hanging bridge we were standing on and away from the territorial Howler monkeys in the trees above us." I stepped from behind the podium as I mimicked fearfully running away from pissing monkeys while looking back over my shoulder at the imaginary critters in trees above and behind me. When I looked out at my audience after this opening, I saw a lot of white in their eyes. I loved it. Ed taught me stories are sticky, meaning remembered, and the first thing you have to do in a speech is break any preoccupation and grab their attention. Mission accomplished.

"This sudden sprint by a large man . . . on a highly unstable hanging bridge in Costa Rica . . . caused some serious consternation for the Japanese tourists ahead of me, as they grabbed the side ropes and crouched to regain their balance on the violently bouncing bridge as I came barreling towards them ... screaming like a banshee and covered in monkey urine."

I demonstrated their crouching, holding and bouncing while raising my voice and vocal energy as I finished these lines. The combination of my wide-eyed physical humor and the way Ed helped me perfect the delivery of these exact words brought more smiles and laughter, and complete, total engagement with my speech in thirty seconds, as planned.

"Seeing their obvious fear and distress, and knowing I was now far enough away from the Howler monkeys to not be subjected to any further acts of territorial aggression by way of a golden shower, I stopped running and looked back for my family.

"I was surprised to see both my wife *and* my daughter doubled over, laughing uncontrollably! Then my wife held up the *empty* water bottle to show me what had been poured on my head and neck when she shouted what she did." They were laughing uncontrollably by the time I said "neck", and nobody heard me say the final six words. Ed later said if I deliver this speech again to leave those six words off. He called it "stepping on laughs" when you are speaking while the audience is laughing, and you should never step on laughs. Instead, you want to milk laughs with longer pauses that include comically expressive faces. It had never occurred to me when practicing and timing my speeches to budget punchline pauses so that I wouldn't "step on laughs." He dissected every speech with me like this, both before and after delivering it to a live audience.

"Madame Toastmaster, fellow Toastmasters and guests, have you ever been *absolutely certain* of something that simply wasn't true? President Ronald Reagan once commented, 'The trouble with some people is not that they're ignorant; it's just that they know so much that isn't so.'

"Indeed, everyone seems interested in getting their questions answered, but nobody wants to have their answers questioned.

"But it is important to question your answers because the knowledge you think is serving you may actually be harming you instead. For example, how many of you were taught to eat all of the food on your plate because there were starving children in other countries? Perhaps that thinking needs to be reconsidered within the context of our current global obesity crisis." I had another example here, but Ed suggested this one and it is better and more applicable.

"Knowledge is definitely desirable, as long as it is accurate and not being used as a tool of deception. Socrates is considered to be one of the wisest men to ever live and yet his Socratic paradox states, 'I know that I know nothing.' When the wisest displays wisdom by claiming ignorance, that indicates there is simply too much we don't know to attach our beliefs to anything with any real degree of certainty." I knew this from recent personal experience.

"We may think we are locking knowledge *in* with our certainty, but in reality, we could be locking it *out*. Because we destroy our motivation for future learning if we think we already know something, and we thereby close ourselves off to any new information that might contradict our currently held belief. We need to allow truth the freedom to be what it is, rather than distorting it to fit within our predetermined beliefs.

"Dr. Wayne Dyer said, 'Be open to everything and attached to nothing.' Our attachment to certainty can be a real problem because all certainty is held at the possible expense of openness, flexibility, unity, truth, motivation for learning, and ultimately, intellectual freedom and personal peace." A few eyebrows raised.

"The reason for this is because certainty encourages rigid rules enforced by divisive actions. Clashing belief systems spawn strife and discord as both sides display an unwillingness to yield their positions, regardless of truth or accuracy of information. We only need to look at religion and politics to see how clearly this is demonstrated. Money is not the root of all evil, conflict is. But the love of money often causes conflict, and so does certainty.

"Certainty also makes you small, by limiting your perspective and shortening your range of psychological space, imprisoning you with rigid attachment to knowledge that may not even be accurate, but which you still won't let go of. My small company struggled for years because _I was certain_ that hiring an employee would be expensive and unnecessary. But eventually I asked myself, 'What if I'm wrong?' What if you're wrong? What a great question to liberate yourself from the confines of intellectual imprisonment caused by certainty.

"Jesus said if you seek you will find, and this is because seeking is usually done with an open mind and a detachment from certainty. According to Rumi, even your seeking may not be necessary because he said, 'What you seek is seeking you.' If this is true, then perhaps you can stop seeking and simply allow what you're seeking to find you, by removing the obstructions that are obscuring you from it; obstructions like certainty." I didn't want to come right out and say that everything we are all looking for is already inside of us, but that is what I meant. Time to lighten up and wrap up by restating my main message.

"Knowledge often cannot find you when you're hiding behind certainty but if you are willing to remove this obstruction then it will bring truth into clear view. This world is not really what it seems to be. The monkeys are not really peeing on you. Life is full of many interesting paradoxes: giving is receiving, letting go yields control, and freedom requires surrender.

"Your liberation and personal peace depend upon surrendering certainty because certainty is a defense held by the ego. Truth needs no defense, and offers none, so when you surrender certainty you also surrender the ego that is defending it, which removes the obstruction, brings spiritual liberation and restores personal peace. But true surrender cannot happen as long as you are certain. It will only happen when you are 'open to everything and attached to nothing.' Madame Toastmaster . . . ."

I stayed at the pulpit until the Toastmaster arrived as everyone applauded. I realized this speech may not be that meaningful for many of them, but it meant a lot to me. I was finding my public speaking voice and using that voice to deliver speeches with humor and sincerity that demonstrated my commitment to opening my mind to the truths that were changing my life.

Since we had no rental inventory to satisfy Ocean's housing needs, and with money being of no concern, she expressed an interest in purchasing something. But like Margie, Ocean danced to the beat of a different drummer. She had a very specific procedure to determine which properties she would visit. First, she gave me some loose criteria for the acreage and general location, and I would email her a comprehensive list of potential properties. She would then meditate on each property sent, and let me know which, if any, the Universe wanted her to see. When I did schedule a showing for her, I was to instruct the listing agent in advance that she did not want to be spoken to at all during the showing, because she needed to maintain a meditative state the entire time she was on the property.

She always drove her truck and met me at the property at the designated time, instead of driving with me, which was my customary procedure when working with a buyer. We would briefly greet each other upon arrival, and then I would go into the property alone to prepare the listing agent for her peculiar showing procedure by explaining that she would be walking the four corners of the property by herself first, to gauge the *mana* before coming into the house. When she did eventually come into the house, I instructed them not to say anything to her and just let her walk meditatively through each room. Needless to say, this made for some interesting showings. Some listing agents were able to keep quiet and some weren't, and sometimes Ocean was the one to break her meditation and ask a pertinent question.

Although this method of *mana* property search was totally unlike any I had ever done, I had already been meeting with Margie, so I was accustomed to the eccentricities of the spiritually enlightened. It really is a different mindset that emphasizes total trust in an unseen reality. So, the next time somebody seems excessively weird or even a little crazy, listen and look a little closer, they may just be spiritually enlightened and taking their cues in accordance with a different reality.

Both before and after these showings to Ocean, we would chat and every time she managed to share something different about her life and spiritual journey that helped me understand and advance my own. She often joked with me that no donation was required. A lot of times she shared examples like the one we experienced on our first meeting, where she gets information from the Universe that wasn't told to her through traditional forms of communication. I always looked forward to these showings, but they often took a long time. Sometimes Kim would come with me and get to share in the Ocean experience. Both of us felt something unique about her and enjoyed being around her whenever we could. I didn't know if she would ever actually buy anything, but I didn't really care, because the spiritual education she was providing was far more valuable to me than a sales commission.

After several rounds of showings following this procedure, I showed her a house that was listed for 4.995 million dollars. It was on a large several acre parcel that was oceanfront, and the land abutted a steep cliff with the ocean far below. There was a wide gulch separating any neighbors to the south side, with a waterfall view from the subject property to the other side of the gulch where the waterfall flowed. There was also a detached yoga studio that was built partially suspended over the cliff with unbelievably expansive ocean views and where one could see and hear the waves roll in and crash against the rocks and cliff wall below. It was spectacular and I commented to the listing agent that I had never seen such a breathtaking view. It was unfortunate the main house wasn't built there instead, because it sat further back on the property with not nearly as dramatic of a view.

Ocean broke her meditation twice on this showing. The first time when she looked out at the waterfall on the other side of the gulch that ran adjacent to this property. She asked the listing agent how popular that waterfall is and how easy it is to hike up to. He said that it frequently has visitors hiking up to it, just about every day, but it is so far away that there is no noise or any adverse visual impact. We could barely see ant-sized people admiring it at the base. Ocean then announced to us that the people at the waterfall now were high on drugs and that type of behavior so close to this property could cloud the clarity of her meditation. The listing agent looked at Ocean the same way I looked at Margie the day she handed me the note from the Holy Spirit. He didn't quite know what to say, and I'm sure he hasn't ever had a buyer make a statement like that before or since. I was surprised too, but I also understood it because of Margie's comment about how Ocean did this by tapping into the one mind that created this universe. Apparently, Ocean didn't want to unify with your mind if it was on drugs because then she also shared your intoxication, which clouded the clarity of her own connection to the Universe.

The second time she broke her meditation was when she walked into the main house after viewing the yoga studio. She came right up to me with wide eyes and said the *mana* was so prodigious in the yoga studio that it almost knocked her down. As the waves came rolling in and crashed into the cliff wall, they pushed the *mana* all the way up the cliff and into the yoga studio, infusing that whole area with the most powerful *mana* she had ever felt in a property. This obviously excited her, which excited me too because we were standing in an expensive listing. Excitement is exactly what you hope for when showing a client property in this price range.

When we finished the showing she asked me to find out if the seller would rent her just the yoga studio. She said she would pay *any rental price* they desired. I tried to pin her down on how high she would be willing to pay so that I could try to negotiate within her desired payment range, but she just reiterated to me that she would pay *any price*. I had a conversation with the listing agent, even throwing out a rental amount of 50,000 dollars per month, but ultimately the sellers wanted to sell and not rent. It was not about the money for them because they were already extremely wealthy, they just wanted out of the property for other reasons.

Another time after Ocean had walked a property and the listing agent said something about being Hawaiian, Ocean responded, "I've lived many lives as a Hawaiian. But this is my last lifetime and I needed to take a non-Hawaiian body this time to finish my work on earth." Never having believed in reincarnation myself, I found this comment to be a little shocking. Had anybody else said it I would have immediately dismissed it. But if anybody knew about these things, I figured it would be Ocean and Margie. I had never asked either of them about reincarnation and this statement was made so matter-of-factly that it surprised me and made me curious. Knowing that Kim didn't believe in reincarnation either, I told her about it and asked her opinion. She replied to just remain open and see if any other signs show up.

At the next Toastmasters meeting, I wasn't speaking but Margie was. After her introduction and being told the title of her speech was "Given a Gift of Power" Margie walked to the front and seemed a little more animated than usual.

"Fellow Toastmasters, if you were to be given a gift of power, what would you want it to be? Think for a moment. This speech was to be a speech about power, the power of persuasion, and I was driving myself nuts thinking about how I was going to start this speech."

Her voice cracked on the word "power" and she was doing a lot of hand gesturing as she spoke, which I had not seen her do before. She continued, "I do have an inner Voice that speaks to me and gives me dreams. This morning I woke up with the most magnificent dream. I had been given a gift of power. Guess what that gift was?" She held up her bony index finger when saying "gift of power" and then waved it side-to-side like Dikembe Mutombo did on the basketball court after blocking an opponent's shot, as she asked the question.

"I was leaving an auditorium where I had given a speech, and I was holding this enormous rifle. The rifle was this long, it was bigger than me." She fully extended her short, skinny arms to indicate the rifle length and it still didn't look like it would be a very long, but we all knew what she was trying to convey. "It was brand new and absolutely weightless. In that moment of awakening, I knew this was the gift of the Holy Spirit Who gave me the dream. I was being told 'This is the world's symbol of power.' The world believes that weapons are their power." Her face was incredulous.

"I had no feeling about this thing that was in my hands. I just walked out with it. I made no judgment about it at all. It wasn't anything that was fearful or dangerous." Her face is now carefree. She is clearly becoming a better speaker, and showing more energy and emoting better, just as Ed was coaching me to do. "It had no meaning whatsoever, but it was a symbol of power. The meaning then, which I asked the Holy Spirit for, Who I knew had given me this dream, is that every single thing in this world is a symbol, and its meaning only comes from who we ask what it means." She told me in our first meeting that everything but God is a metaphor, and I liked the addition about the meaning of the symbol depending upon who is doing the interpreting, the ego, or the Holy Spirit.

"I ask everything of the Holy Spirit Who lives in me. So, I asked, 'What is your meaning of that gun?' And He said, 'That's just a symbol. Everything is a symbol, and you and everybody you'll be speaking to tonight has My gift of power in them. They carry My gift of power everywhere.' The power that is real is the internal power, and it's the power and the love of God that we are," she says as she moves to the other side of the podium, still being very expressive with her hands.

"I've been to churches where the preacher looked like he had a lot of power and he was telling everybody in the church, 'Sinners come on down and be saved.' As a child I was terrified of this red-faced preacher. And as a child, I was so overwhelmed with guilt from my birth onward that I could never have gone down to be saved. I was totally unworthy, as I say, from childhood all through my life, until I finally came to read a book that has really helped me understand the source of my guilt, which is *A Course in Miracles*. As a result of reading the book I actually learned for myself what it talks about, and that is about having the Voice of the Holy Spirit within us. I came to know that inner Voice. It actually spoke to me one night and told me to write the books that I've written and are now published. So, I know that power is in me, and I know that it's the same power and the same Voice that is in each and every one of you."

She says this so confidently and sincerely that we get a true sense of the power that is in her, and the still silence brings a palpable peace to the room that is pleasant to sit within.

"Two weeks ago, I was driving, and I was listening to this beautiful music by a woman who was singing about her connection with Jesus. Suddenly I had an image of the crucifixion pass in front of my eyes. I saw Jesus on the cross, he was drooped over. His image was so real. I had to go, of course, to the Holy Spirit within me and ask, 'What is it that I saw? Was that just a vision or was that something that was true?' And I was told that I was present at the crucifixion in another lifetime."

I guess that answered my question about reincarnation. Typical fearless Margie, she just tells it like it is and never holds back.

As Margie pauses, I look towards Ann Elaine, the speech timer sitting in front of me, to see which light is on and how much time Margie has left to speak. I can see the timer stopwatch is well beyond six minutes, but no light is on. She is supposed to get a green light at five minutes and a yellow light at six and a half minutes, but we are at six thirty-three on the stopwatch and there is still no green or yellow light.

Sitting close enough to see what was happening, I almost leaned forward to tap Ann Elaine on the shoulder and remind her she was supposed to be timing and there were no lights when there should already be two. But when I saw how enthralled she was in Margie's speech, and looked around the room to see the impact it was having on others as well, I stopped myself and we all just accepted the speaking gift that is Margie. As we basked in Margie's powerful peace and presence, it was evident that it really didn't matter what your religion or spiritual background was, Margie simply sliced through all of that by speaking eternal truths. Peace is a universal language that we all crave communication with, and Margie was satisfying that craving and adeptly demonstrating theology doesn't matter. It is all metaphoric and pointing to the same thing.

Margie looked to the timer but saw no lights and seemed bewildered by that timing mystery but continued with aplomb about her lifetime with Jesus, "I have actually known that, but this was a clear picturing of having been there at that time. And even then, in that lifetime, I was guilty. I was feeling that I was not worthy of his love and was actually relieved at his death that I was not going to have to deal with my anger and guilt for not being free to love the way that I wanted to love."

The aplomb was gone. Margie was struggling to maintain control of her emotions now, and just then Ann Elaine looked down and saw the clock timer at past seven minutes and flinched as if she had just been stuck by a pin. Margie looked at her just as she turned the warning light from off to red, skipping green and yellow altogether and letting her know she was already over her allotted speech time without being offered any warning lights. Margie knew Ann Elaine had messed up, but I wasn't sure if she knew why. Margie's speeches were effective, and not only on me since our Distinguished Toastmaster just botched a simple timing job because she had been so engrossed in her speech.

She finished with a flourish as her misty eyes released the tears that she had been struggling to hold back, "And the Holy Spirit within me told me 'There is nothing to fear. You are a being of love.' Everyone has that Christ Self within them. We are all one. We all have that same inner Voice that we can learn to know. So, know the power of God is within you. You are one with Him, and you carry His power everywhere you go."

As Margie walked back to her seat Ann Elaine leaned over to Rita sitting next to her and whispered in awe, "She is such a great speaker!" I smiled in agreement, and then smiled again as I imagined what Margie's response would be to this compliment if Ann Elaine ventured it forth after the meeting. Maybe I'd delay my typical quick departure and stick around to eavesdrop on Margie's responses to the various compliments she was about to receive after this moving speech. Perhaps I'd get to hear Ann Elaine's reaction to Margie's "I don't speak, I'm spoken" response. How quickly things change. A couple of months ago I was annoyed and frustrated by Margie's speech and mannerisms, and now they were my favorite part of Toastmasters meetings. What I initially thought was crazy was now proving to be spiritual truths emanating from an enlightened being.

Rumi, the thirteenth century Persian poet, said, "I want to sing like the birds sing, not worrying about who hears or what they think." I modified this Rumi phrase by altering just three words, "I want to speak like Margie speaks, not worrying about who hears or what they think." I needed to become a more fearless speaker.

I was really enjoying the Couples Communication class I was attending with Kim. It was nice to have that time with her, showing that we each cared enough about our fractured relation-ship to implement healing strategies. The other benefit to this weekly class was that since we both needed to be there, we had to get a babysitter for Kaya. I convinced Kim that since we already had a babysitter and were already out, we should go to dinner, a play, a movie, or anything else fun that we wanted to do together. We were still separated, but now we were enjoying a weekly date night after our Couples Communication class, often discussing my most recent meeting with Margie or Ocean's latest teaching or story. Ocean was still bringing us closer, even months after beginning to heal our relationship by unexpectedly confirming the authenticity of my spiritual awakening to Kim.

During one class the instructor spoke about communicating appreciation to your partner and suggested we each write five positive sticky note messages expressing this appreciation and posting them in places your partner will see them. I thought it was a good idea so when I was with Kaya at the house and Kim wasn't there, I performed this exercise. But you can't do something like this around a six-year-old that just learned to write without creating a desire for active participation. So, little Kaya did it too, completely stealing my thunder because her notes were so much better and cuter than mine. They were six-year-old sweet and usually had misspelled words, which only added to their charm.

The surprising thing was that she didn't just write them for her mother, as I was doing, but she started writing them for me too, and she still does today. I am always thrilled to find one of her sweet notes of appreciation. Sometimes she leaves me a note by the coffeemaker in the morning, pinned to the counter with a mug she made me in Quebec that has a red heart glazed onto it with her handwritten words "I Love You Daddy" inside the heart. I have found these notes on my dresser, bathroom mirror, pillow, and even on my copy of *A Course in Miracles* (*ACIM*). I still have these notes, now permanently attached, to my writing notebook and on the cover of *ACIM*. The notebook says "Best Dad Ever" with a smiley face, and on the cover of *ACIM* there are two notes, one of them has a picture of a mermaid in sunglasses with the words "I love you so much" written to the side of the picture. But since she drew the mermaid first, the "h" at the end didn't fit and now lies horizontally on top of "muc." The other note has no drawings and simply says "Hi Dady I Love You."

With a weekly date night and the positive vibe that we were enjoying as a family again it was easy to confidently predict the final outcome, unlike the first time my Puerto Rican mother-in-law rode an escalator back in the 80s. We were in Las Vegas and I didn't know she had never ridden on one before. We had just parked and now we needed to take a long escalator that connected the parking structure to the front desk, so several people were bringing their luggage down the escalator. After some initial hesitation by my "suegra" that was followed by jocular teasing, we showed her how to step safely onto the escalator. She eventually did so and down we went.

As we moved down the long escalator everything seemed fine until up ahead someone's luggage didn't get lifted over the lip of the escalator at the bottom and fell over. As the luggage owner scrambled to recover the fallen luggage, the next lady on the escalator reached the bottom and tried to step over the fallen luggage but her legs were too short, and the luggage was too large. So, she went down, leaving a lady and a luggage sprawled out at the bottom of the escalator, blocking the exit for everyone else coming down. Seeing that we were next to arrive at the bottom my wife and I naturally started stepping back up the escalator to give them time to clear the area before we got dumped on top of this sprawling pile of escalator obstruction. Her mother didn't understand what we were doing. My wife said something to her in Spanish, but she just looked up at us with a confused look and didn't dare take a step on the descending escalator. After a few ignorantly nonchalant seconds she arrived at the bottom and was deposited on top of the growing pile of humans and luggage as her own suitcase fell on top of her upon landing. This caused a hurried hotel attendant to rush over and shut down the escalator, help take the luggage off them, and pick them up from the ground as my embarrassing wife cachinnated hysterically.

That was the first and last time my mother-in-law ever rode an escalator. Some things are harder to predict than others, but Kim, Kaya, and I eventually reuniting as a family seemed fairly easy to accurately predict at this point.

After delivering my speech on "The Danger of Certainty" in late August, I received and immediately started reading *A Course in Miracles*. I wasn't sure what to expect after such a lofty recommendation from Margie and how she presented it to me. Margie was the most spiritual person I knew, along with Ocean, and she literally promised me this book was life changing. I was apprehensive because in the past whenever I got a super strong recommendation for a book or a movie, I built up my expectations so high that I was often disappointed later. But *ACIM* did not disappoint, and as exalted as Margie's recommendation was, and as ambitious as my own expectations already were, the book easily exceeded both. It really is life changing.

The length of the Course may be intimidating for some, and if so, then just read the first fifteen pages. I guarantee that is all that's needed to find something valuable enough to justify whatever expense or effort was invested to acquire it. It didn't take me long and very early in my initial reading I felt my life beginning to pivot in a different direction, as if everything that had ever happened to me was just a lead-in to this perfectly framed moment of discovery, as *ACIM* registered its intriguing and unquestionable impact upon me. Although I didn't really know what this meant or what I was pivoting into yet, I could somehow sense that my life was never going to be the same because of this book.

It is not puffery when I say that reading *ACIM* has resulted in the most spiritually beneficial impact of anything I've ever done in my life. That may not be everyone's personal experience, but that is what it did for me. I personally believe it is one of the most powerful spiritual documents the world has ever seen, and I felt privileged to be extracting such life changing truth from it. I couldn't believe it had not already taken the world by storm. Although it has sold over three million copies without the benefit of paid advertising since it was first published in 1976, Harry Potter arrived twenty years later and has already sold over 120 million.

I'm not sure an attempted explanation would do this remarkable book justice, but I'll try. There were three initial concepts that jumped out and deeply impacted me right from the start. First of all, the channeled voice as presented in *ACIM* is familiar, like a faint recollection of something long forgotten that returned and reminded me of a pleasurable memory I never wanted to forget. It was my first time reading it, yet it felt instantly recognizable. I was drawn to the spiritual tone of the voice immediately in an entirely unexpected way. I admit a possible bias here because this voice clearly identified itself as Jesus with several unmistakable first-person references. Having been a Christian all my life, this obviously heightened my interest. The more I read, the more I felt as if I had just unwrapped one of Willy Wonka's invaluable golden tickets, except instead of a lifetime supply of chocolate I had won a lifetime supply of spiritual instruction from a master teacher, uncorrupted by millennia of mistranslation or misinterpretation. It doesn't even matter if you don't identify with Jesus, because any symbol of unconditional egoless love will work. But Jesus worked just fine for me because I always liked his wisdom and teaching style.

The familiarity and recognition of the voice was exciting enough, but the real excitement derived from the voice's sheer depth of wisdom that jumped off each page as it expanded and uplifted my heart. Reading *ACIM* provided the sensation of deep diving into an ocean of spiritual wisdom because the message transcended words and concepts and directly penetrated my heart like an injection of the purest light and love. Regardless of whose voice it was, it resonated within me as someone undoubtedly connected to truth that can express it eloquently. The level of spiritual understanding that flowed from each page completely contradicted the world's thinking, yet made so much logical sense, much like speaking to Ocean or Margie did. I was filled with humility and gratitude for the good fortune of having discovered such an unbelievably powerful resource of profound wisdom.

The final reason the Course grabbed me as it did and lubricated my mind for an easy acceptance of its ideas, was the purely spiritual pull of perfect love. It was obvious the words were coming from a place of unconditional love, which is often spoken of but rarely communicated so clearly. Regardless of the amount of love we currently have in our lives, we will always crave more because God is limitless love and we are not meant to be limited or separated from His love. Since love binds, the more love we have the more unity we enjoy, and unity heals and restores our Divine Mind, causing us to think like God. The more we can unite and heal the hidden hates and secret sins that the ego keeps us distracted with, the closer we move towards our spiritual reality of perfect oneness with He Who is perfect Love. There is an unmistakable and overwhelmingly powerful extension of divine love attached to and imbedded in every word, concept, and idea of the Course. So even if the ideas are unbelievable, or are too difficult to accept or apply, or if the Course teacher being Jesus is off-putting, there is still tremendous value in dissecting the mind of a teacher who obviously knows unconditional love and can teach it so powerfully.

Having been a lifelong Christian, I had always been amazed by Jesus' capacity for love and forgiveness as depicted within the New Testament, but I never imagined I would have the opportunity to climb inside his mind in such an intimate manner. Is there any way to accurately estimate the value and magnitude of such detailed teachings of love and forgiveness? To me it is priceless, and surpasses anything I've ever seen, felt, or experienced before. Reading *ACIM* commenced an intensely blissful and miraculous healing deep within me. It is one thing for someone to tell you that God loves you, and quite another to experience it directly for yourself through the Voice for God. Jesus obviously knew and experienced this ineffable love firsthand and was able to convey it in a manner that touched the deepest core of my being, which added heaps of credibility to the message and contributed to my immediate acceptance of it.

Although Margie was right about this being a different Jesus than the perception Christianity holds, I didn't see it as a bad thing because I knew this Jesus was the real deal. I had never felt this much emotion or clarity in his message before and I truly enjoyed getting to know the mind and thoughts of this ascended spiritual master. From the very beginning of my reading journey I had no problem unlearning what I thought I knew about him and reveling in his first-person account instead. Once again, it was important for my spiritual growth to remain open to new information even if it contradicted any current belief.

I already knew Margie had introduced me to what some may consider radical spirituality, but it is still worth mentioning that some of the ideas within the Course will be hard to believe, and others may seem quite startling (even for Christians). This does not matter. We are merely asked to apply the ideas, not judge them. We do not need to welcome them, believe them, or accept them, and we may even actively resist them, as Helen did. None of these things matter because it is the use of the ideas that gives them meaning and shows us their truth. Their efficacy is in their application, which can be achieved regardless of our judgment, belief, or even our acceptance.

I never anticipated this dramatic of an impact from *ACIM* . I was soon craving the message and cherished my reading time, devouring it for hours at a time whenever I could. I'd let the words take up residency in my mind, always increasing, advancing, and elevating my spiritual perspective, while constantly accessing higher portions of the Divine Mind. It was like stacking priceless gems within my mind as ammunition against the ego's thought system. I could then draw from them throughout the day and spend them like currency to transform my thinking and change my mind, infusing meaning into a life experience that had been sorely lacking it. Situations arose daily that challenged my new perspective and invariably one of these gems always tumbled down through my thoughts to correct a perception that was veering off course.

Eventually my learning established a mindset that spoke to me from this higher perspective; constantly countering the ego's thought system, and awakening my own inner Voice that pulled from my voracious reading of *ACIM* and edified me from a place I never knew existed, transforming my thinking and greatly improving the quality of my life. This happened repeatedly until my right-minded thinking strengthened enough to begin nudging the ego thought system right off the mind's stage. There was a new master in my mind, and this master was all about love and peace, not suffering. My subtle change in thought caused some not-so-subtle results to immediately begin manifesting into my life. My entire perspective shifted from one dominated by the loud voice of ego to a quiet inner voice of perfect clarity that was no longer repressed or bullied by ego.

This new voice joyously stepped right onto center stage, overwhelmingly happy to be free from whatever dungeon of mental imprisonment the ego had banished it to. I'd never felt better, happier or more peaceful in my entire life. My fifty years of seeking was over. I discovered how easy it is to be happy when I identified with my true Self and freed my mind from being a shackled slave of deception to a false and illusory reality.

When Margie introduced the Course to me, she told me you can't serve two masters and will have to choose one. But she said it was an easy choice because it was one between total freedom or total bondage. When I restored communication with Source all anger left me and was replaced first with joy, and then with peace. This is what we all crave, but so fleetingly find. This union with Source is our primary purpose in this earthly experience, to uncover a buried piece of the Christ mind within the ego and bring it to the surface to shine light and love into a darkened and loveless world. I was personally witnessing in my own life the inspirational, perception-expanding miracle referenced in the title. *ACIM* may not be the only method to make this all-important shift in perception, but it has certainly proven to be an effective method for me.

I never would have imagined the grip this book took on my mind, quenching my constant thirst for truth. I had been seeking God through a liar's voice when I was already an inseparable extension of God, with His Voice within me and willing me to align my thinking with His. This recognition of the spiritual oneness of the Christ Mind opened my spiritual eyes and forced me to take a good, hard look at what I used to think was important and caused apathy for the illusory lie as I began embracing reality instead. Of course, this created some uncomfortable but necessary adjustments to my daily life. But I maintained vigilance of my newfound spiritual position, while constantly attempting to incrementally move beyond it. How often can all of the above be said about the impact of reading a single book?

It was so refreshing to engage a spiritual practice that recognized and harmonized with the truth we share in God's mind. I felt like I was really beginning to think as God thinks and see as God sees. Beliefs are not always true, but they are always true to the believer. We choose what we believe, and it's not necessary to make those limitations real by believing in them. The truth is easy to choose if we fairly evaluate the results that will be derived from our choice. How hard is it really to choose between total freedom and total bondage? Does it make sense to hold onto the belief that there is a reason to continue the pursuit of what has always failed to deliver any joy and happiness? It's been said that the definition of insanity is doing the same thing over and over again but expecting different results. My choice for separation was a lie the ego sold me in order to ensure its own survival, a survival that guarantees God remains distant and separate.

When I was twelve years old, I was getting a ride from a friend whose father was a realtor and he had Dennis Waitley's "The Psychology of Winning" playing in the car. I made a positive comment to him about it after he dropped me off and within a few days he had violated the copyright and duplicated it for me on cassette tapes (yes cassettes, and I remember 8-track tapes too). I would listen to it in my bedroom at night to be inspired and motivated, and I've been listening to personal development programs ever since. I decided to order *ACIM* on CD to listen in my car, so I could hear the message as well as read it. I also bought the audio book on my iPhone so I could listen at the office, and especially when I lay in bed at night before sleeping. Perhaps I'm a better auditory learner because the audio seemed to make the message come alive even more deeply for me, especially when I combined meditating and listening. I'd lay still and get a master's course in spirituality. The experience felt as if I sat at the feet of Jesus himself and was personally instructed. It was an unbelievably beautiful experience.

The next time I met with Margie, we discussed my speech on certainty, and she told me I was becoming a better speaker. I confided that I hired a speech coach. She was intrigued but probably thought it was unnecessary. She agreed that the certainty of beliefs was a huge setback to most spiritual seekers in that they are often so attached to and obstructed by false beliefs that they could never let go of them to find truth. She told me, "Beliefs are just perceptual judgments we accept as true when they usually aren't. Everybody is looking to find truth and add it to their belief system, but truth is already within them, and it is their beliefs that are often obstructing it. What we really should be doing is removing beliefs that cause cognitive dissonance with truth. You were very effective at pointing out how we can, and do, hold onto false beliefs that obstruct our arrival at truth. Perception always involves uncertainty and interpretation, but knowledge doesn't because it transcends perception."

"What do you mean?" I asked.

"Do you believe your true identity is spirit or do you know it?"

"Well, now I know it."

"And do you believe the Holy Spirit within you speaks to you, or do you know He does?"

"I know He does because it happens all the time."

"Would the truth of this knowledge ever change even if you allowed your perception to form and hold a different belief?"

"No. The truth would remain true and the perception would be wrong."

"Then your perception has been transcended by knowledge, and you found that knowledge within you, not from any external source. It only happened when you demonstrated a willingness to allow your perception to be transcended by what is, rather than be formed by what you believe. If you hadn't suffered enough dissatisfaction adhering to the ego's unpleasant thought system to surrender it and open yourself up to truth, then your perception could still be believing what obstructs truth instead of knowing the truth already within you."

With regards to *ACIM* , I told her all about the effect it was having on me, how much I was enjoying it, and how it somehow opened a door to my own inner Voice. Margie quickly admonished me to "Write it all down!" So, I did. Soon every page of my planner was filled with profound spiritual writings. Kim noticed this and when I explained what was happening, she purchased me a writing notebook in September for my fiftieth birthday. The more I wrote, the more the Voice spoke to me. Sometimes I would finish writing a long passage and then read it as if for the first time, even though it was entirely in my handwriting, and I often had to look up certain words in the dictionary that I wrote but didn't know the meaning of, even though they were always perfectly used within the context of the message. I showed some of the writing to Kim and we just shook our heads because we both knew it was not my writing, just like the Course wasn't Helen's writing and the *One With God* books aren't Margie's writing. I was hearing the same voice they were. I now had three spiritual mentors (Margie, Ocean, Divine Mind) and they were triple accelerating my spiritual progress.

Chapter 6

Glitches in the Matrix

"The Matrix is the world that has been pulled
over your eyes to blind you from the truth.
No one can tell you what it is.
You have to see it for yourself."
Morpheus, *The Matrix*

After taking Margie's advice to record everything that the Voice told me, I quickly filled up my writing notebook. I remember thinking it odd when Margie said she sat down with her notebook and asked the Holy Spirit questions, and now I couldn't stop doing it myself. It was like mining for gold from the mother lode of Divine Mind. Even years later I still read these messages and am struck by the profound spiritual wisdom that was unknowingly inside of me, and accessible to my mind all along.

Between my discussions with Ocean, my meetings with Margie and the inner Voice I was hearing as a result of reading *A Course in Miracles*, mystical or multisensory experiences soon began flowing to me in abundance. Whatever spiritual door I had cracked open was now gathering momentum and swinging wide open. I had already been shown the unreality of this world in an unforgettable way, but additional confirmation never hurts. Was all of this really happening just because of a simple shift in perception regarding the blatant unreality of our world? Could I assist others in their awakening by pointing them to this same inner Voice as Margie had done for me? I will share examples of the changes that were becoming my new normal, and if they seem unbelievable that is understandable because had they not happened to me then I probably wouldn't believe them either.

One day Ocean called me and said she needed to see a property in a very specific area, but she wasn't sure which one. She asked me for a list, as usual, but she had never been this location specific before. I sent the list to her to meditate over and she called me back the following day with a request to see only one property. She said she wasn't sure why she had to see it; she just knew she needed to. I set it up and prepared the listing agent, and we agreed to meet at the property at the designated time for what would turn out to be one of the strangest showings of my life.

The property was a home that was built to straddle two ridges that joined at the end of a small gulch, but the house's location made the access by car limited. As we walked together with the listing agent down the winding path that led through the trees to the house, Ocean slowed her pace until the other agent and I both stopped walking to see what was wrong. Ocean then came to a complete stop, told us this was going to get a little weird, and then stomped the ground a couple of times with her right foot as she raised her hands to the heavens and started singing a chant in the Hawaiian language. She was right about the weird, but the weirdest thing was not so much the stomping or the Hawaiian chant as much as it was the beautiful, angelic voice she was singing with. I had never heard a voice like that before. It was an otherworldly sound that made my soul flutter and feel incredibly loved. I later told Kim that if I could record that sound, I'd play it on loop all of the time.

To my auditory delight, she did this a couple of more times before arriving at the house. Once we arrived at the house, she explained that the house had been built in such a way that it was blocking or cutting off the land's natural flow of spiritual energy (*mana*) and she was going to try to clear it. At least now we knew what she was doing. She opened all of the doors and windows to the house and stood in the middle of it and began to stomp her right foot and chant in Hawaiian again. I looked over to the listing agent and her eyes were as large as golf balls when Ocean started moving her hands and arms in an upward motion as she chanted, and then that angelic voice lifted my spirit again, this time quite literally. As she chanted, I felt a fluttering pull from my solar plexus and then I had the sensation of the pull elevating me. The fluttering continued as I slowly rose up above my body somehow. I was still in the house, but my entire visual perspective shifted as I hovered several feet above and behind my body and could see myself on the ground below. My first thought was "I'm flying!" That thought was followed by a query, "How can I be floating above my body and also be on the ground at the same time?" I didn't know if the land's spiritual energy was being cleared, but something was definitely happening to mine.

When Ocean finished, she was physically spent, but I felt completely energized. She needed to hold my arm going back up the path to where we parked. As we walked, she told us that every spiritual message is about love, because that is what we truly are. She also said signs from the Universe are everywhere if we will just look for them and pay attention. This reminded me of Margie saying everything but God is a metaphor, and that there is no time, place, or state where God is absent. Ocean then pointed out a couple of these signs for us. I told her I didn't know she could sing like that and asked how she learned to. She replied that she can't sing, or at least she never had any formal training or lessons. I was shocked. I also said I didn't know she spoke Hawaiian. She said she doesn't speak Hawaiian, nor does she know any Hawaiian chants. This was difficult to believe because I just watched and listened to her chant in Hawaiian. She said this happened once before and there was a Hawaiian man present

121

who told her afterwards that she had chanted something about the spirit of the eagle coming down and some other very specific Hawaiian language references, none of which she understood the meaning of or knew that she had chanted. I didn't understand what she chanted either, but I'll never forget that angelic voice that she chanted with, nor the out-of-body spiritual elevation sensation it produced.

After hearing both Ocean and Margie mention reincarnation, I was curious so I read a book called "Journey of Souls" by Dr. Michael Newton, a hypnotherapist that applied age regression therapy in his practice and surprisingly discovered that he could regress his clients beyond their present lifetime. This was disconcerting since he did not believe in an afterlife or reincarnation. But the scientist in him was fascinated. He did more regressions and achieved the same result. He continued this research until he had an entire book full of very specific case studies he had recorded of many different souls and their experience in the soul's spiritual life between earthly lives. I thought it was an interesting read and an intriguing idea, so I looked to see if there were any of these hypnotherapists on Maui. There was only one and she was forty-five minutes from my house. I called her, we had a chat, and I made an appointment. Before we started, she said the full past life regression often takes several hours, so maybe we should just do a shorter session this first time and then we can block more time for later, if desired. I agreed and we started the hypnotherapy.

Although she put me into a deep state of relaxation and hypnosis, I was alert and aware of everything that I said to her the entire time. Imagine my surprise when I suddenly started accessing information I never thought I knew. She asked questions I didn't think I could answer, and then surprisingly I did. I told her I had been channeling spiritual messages. She asked me what I called them, and I said they are "inspired writings". I told her I felt the presence of others. She asked who they were, and I didn't know all of them, but one was named Jess. She asked me what I felt from them and I noticed a gentle breeze of their love surround me and go through me, and I said "love." When I said the word "love" her dog, who had been sleeping on the floor by her feet, got up and jumped onto the couch with me and laid his head and upper body across my chest and made a deep, moaning sigh. I guess he could feel the love emanating from my heart chakra and wanted to immerse himself in it. I knew what the dog did, but I didn't want to move or disturb my session, so I let him stay there. Then came the big surprise, she asked if there was anybody helping me with the inspired writings and Margie appeared in my mind. When she did, I realized that we didn't just meet, but that I knew her from before we were born. I could see that we had made an agreement, or a soul contract, to do something together before we ever came to earth. I initially expected it had something to do with her helping me find the Voice of the Holy Spirit within me. But now I suspect my telling of this story about Margie's influence on my spiritual awakening may have been the pact we made together.

When we finished the session, the hypnotherapist apologized and commented that she had never seen her dog do that before. She then told me animals are adept at sensing energetic messages and mirroring them back with brilliantly appropriate responses, and she knew this because she was also an equine-assisted psychotherapist that practiced the treatment of equine-assisted psychotherapy (EAP). She even gave me some examples of recent EAP sessions that showcased her EAP assistance with astounding results. I'd never heard of such a thing before, and it seemed a bit bizarre to me, but so was her dog moaning and laying across my chest at the precise moment I said "love." When she asked who Margie was and why her name had come up during the session, I shared some of my awakening experiences with Margie and Ocean. She got very excited upon hearing Ocean's name and described her and asked if this was the same person. I said it was. She asked if she could get Ocean's phone number from me because she had lost contact with her and Ocean was a horse whisperer. At this point, nothing anybody said about Ocean would surprise me. She explained that in her practice of EAP she was referred to Ocean because they had a sick horse that was dying, and they couldn't figure out why. When she got Ocean involved to spend some time with the horse alone, Ocean told them exactly what the problem was, apparently from the horse's perspective. They treated the horse accordingly and the problem immediately went away. After hearing that story, I couldn't resist and told her one of my own, about how Ocean had called out my recent spiritual alignment to my doubting wife, and also about her stomping and Hawaiian chanting in an angelic voice and how it created an out-of-body experience for me.

I was curious about the presence of others that I felt during the hypnosis and who Jess was. Later, I was reading Lorna Byrne's worldwide bestselling book *Angels in my Hair* and in it she mentions we all have a guardian angel or angels, and we can confirm that quite easily by simply asking them for a sign. She said they are good with electricity and one easy sign you can ask your guardian angel to give you is to make a light flicker. I read a lot at night after the girls went to bed and in my four years at this location, I'd never had my reading lamp flicker before. So, I put the book down and asked Jess for this sign and as soon as I did my reading light flickered! It startled me when it actually happened, and then it made me feel briefly eerie until I felt a gentle swirl of love and peace encompass me and wash over and through me so that I wouldn't be fearful. There was no question a loving entity, or guardian angel, was always near me. Apparently, mine is named Jess.

One Sunday, we went with some friends to a beachfront swimming pool at Wailea Ekahi where they own a condo. I was quietly reading my book in a chaise lounge under an umbrella while our kids played in the pool. When I looked up, I saw all of the people in or around the pool had what appeared to be a tube or cylinder of light extending from the top of each head up into the sky. I watched these cylindrical light extensions for several minutes, rising from the crown of their heads and shooting a light beam into the sky like a high-powered flashlight, but very steady because the beam was always directly above them like an unmoving extension that kept them connected to whatever light was at the other end of their beam. After several minutes of this observation, the light beams stopped. This temporary shift in light vision was an awkward mystery that raised questions I couldn't answer, so I didn't tell anybody about it.

Shortly thereafter the answer appeared in my reading and further confirmed the perfectly coordinated spiritual education I was receiving. I realized I had briefly been shown true vision when I read in *ACIM* , "As the ego would limit your perception of your brothers to the body, so would the Holy Spirit release your vision and let you see the Great Rays shining from them, so unlimited that they reach to God." Although I don't know if I would have called them "Great Rays," they were definitely rays of light that extended beyond my usually limited perception of bodies, and higher and farther than even this expanded range of vision could see. Envisioning these light rays reaching all the way to God created a unique visual of 7.7 billion light projections all emanating from and connected to the same singular Source of Light that was somehow projecting this Light into a dark and shadowed world.

Later, I also read a saying by Jesus in the non-canonical Gospel of Thomas discovered near Nag Hammadi, Egypt, in December 1945, "His disciples said to him, 'When will the kingdom come?' 'It will not come by waiting for it. It will not be a matter of saying 'here it is' or 'there it is.' Rather, the kingdom of the Father is spread out upon the earth, and men do not see it." But sometimes they do. Because I witnessed that we are the Father's kingdom, spread out upon the earth.

The hypnotherapist asked me if I meditated and I told her I didn't because I didn't know how. She said I should look into it and told me how beneficial it is. Margie had told me to ask the Holy Spirit about everything, so I decided to ask the Holy Spirit about meditation. That dialogue went something like this:

"Are you there?"

"I'm always here."

"Then why don't I always hear Your Voice?"

"Because you're listening to another voice. Without silencing the mind, the voice you hear is that of the ego."

"How do I silence the mind?"

"Through meditation."

"I've never really meditated so I don't know how."

"Meditation is collaboration with God to extract truth from the Divine Mind. Truth is inseparable from you and is always accessible to those with a still mind."

"So how does it work? What do I do?"

"There are two parts. First, you find a comfortable position and then close your eyes and still your body. Do not move at all. Soon the stillness of the body removes it from your awareness and reveals only your thoughts. Now still even those. Do not allow any mental meanderings. Control the mind and focus on stillness, not on continued manic thinking.

"It may take time but by focusing your awareness only on breathing you will see how you can keep the mind still and push manic thoughts from the mind. A still mind with no thought will unite you with the Divine Mind, causing a state of joy, peace, and contentment, for this is your natural state when self-will surrenders to Self-realization.

"That peaceful state of mind is a sign you are successfully leaving the distractions of the world behind and remembering God. Slow your breathing with deeper breaths. Focusing on breathing helps you dissociate from the ego's thoughts by placing your awareness on their observation instead of the thoughts themselves. Thoughts come and go like clouds in the sky, but the observing awareness remains constant. Once the mind is clear and still you will hear Me, and My instruction. I will tell you all you need to know. My thoughts appear on the same platform but are derived from a different Source. There will be a clear distinction between My thoughts and the thoughts of judgment and fear that are proposed by the ego."

I was then pulled into slow breathing as if on autopilot, and I felt the peaceful relaxation increase in my chest near my heart with each slow exhale. I went with it and felt my soul sinking into a groove, so I wiggled deeper into the groove and when I did so I felt peace and love wrap around me like a soft, comfortable blanket and then everything started to expand. It was strange how expansive I felt by going within myself. I soon realized that my finite physical form should have limited such expansion . . . but it didn't. The expansion continued well beyond my body's limitations. I wasn't aware of my physical body anywhere, but I knew this expansive state could not be possible within it. I was no longer a physical form. I knew my body had not moved, and yet somehow, I was clearly in a different place.

As I expanded, I felt like I was being bathed in exquisite peace, and the expansiveness extended beyond all anxiety, and any restrictions of form were removed. I felt loved, supported, and connected to something much larger than the limited, insignificant body I had left behind. This peaceful expansiveness was beyond anything I had ever felt before. I felt I was blissfully floating in space, but also that I *was* all of space. Could this wonderful state really have been within me all of this time?

When the questioning nature of this thought surfaced then the Voice spoke and told me, "The Kingdom of Heaven is within you because the Kingdom of Heaven *is* you. The ego creates and causes separation from the reality of this expansive state of Being, but that separation is an illusion. It is a temporary obstruction of reality, due to your belief in and choice for such separation, but that belief can be corrected by choosing again. There is nothing you can interpose between yourself and your reality that affects truth at all. The truth of your reality envelops you completely and cannot ever be lost, although you can temporarily deny and obstruct it."

In addition to this lightness and expansiveness, it felt like there was a finger point of light pressure right between my eyes. I knew that had to mean something, so I asked the Voice about it.

The level of joviality in the Voice surprised me when it replied, "That means you are doing it right," making me feel like I was receiving a good-natured ribbing.

I replied in the same manner of jest, "You are very jovial. I expected You to be more serious."

"Joy and happiness are the essence of My nature and, like love, they cannot be contained and must be extended. You are only able to contain them yourself because you have forgotten who you are. If you hadn't, then you would *always* be happy because joy is woven into the very fabric of your Being. Only the ego can inhibit joy, and depression is a sign of withdrawal from God and allegiance to the ego. But you cannot forsake God because you were created as part of God, as a divine expression of His Holy Thought. As His creation, you are whole and wholly connected to Him and always will be. What is there not to be happy about?"

An experienced meditator could probably elaborate on or critique the simplicity of this meditation instruction, and that is fine. I asked and this is what I was told. Maybe this is something that will work for you and maybe it isn't, but it definitely worked for me. It is a very simple technique; close your eyes, still your body, still your mind, and focus on your breathing. This simple meditation instruction worked so well for me that I had some highly interesting meditation experiences after learning and practicing it.

I was curious so I looked it up later and learned that the pressure point of light between my eyes was my sixth chakra, also known as the third eye. I still don't know what that means, and I guess it isn't important for me to know, since joviality ensued when I asked about it. I'm sure that's the right call because I've never forgotten the experience although I forgot everything I researched and read about chakras. Although years later I remembered this chakra again upon reading The Bhagavad Gita for the first time when chapter 8, verse 10 said that through "the power of meditation, with your mind completely stilled and your concentration fixed in *the center of spiritual awareness between the eyebrows,* you will realize the supreme Lord." I also learned later that the entire experience was one of astral projection, which I had heard of but never experienced before. Once again, the term for it and my description of it isn't nearly as important as the experience itself.

After that experience, meditation became an important part of my spiritual practice. When my foster mother and her seventy-six-year-old husband visited me on Maui for the first time (she remarried after being widowed when I was living with her as a teenager) I told them I frequently have spiritual experiences during my meditations. To which her husband commented, "I need to get some of your drugs." I laughed and told him that although I had read about the mind-expanding mystical or spiritual effects of psychedelics, I had never actually tried them. However, I was obviously intrigued by the abundant research regarding their ability to get some individuals temporarily transcending identification with their bodies and experiencing ego-free states.

As appealing as the temporary dissolution of ego sounded, I was more interested in an abiding dissolution that didn't require the ingestion of a schedule one substance to achieve. Psychedelics may be a rather effective shortcut to these same benefits of meditation and can often cause an enduring shift of perception by initially uncovering access to an alternative reality most people never become aware of. But I was already aware of that alternative reality and I didn't care to risk any potential side effects such as "bad trips" in an attempt to rediscover it. Psychedelics would probably be more beneficial for those who *haven't* discovered our unseen reality yet, or ever perceived of anything beyond their five senses.

More than anything, I liked asking the Divine Mind questions and getting truthful answers. Being a lifelong Christian I just had to clarify the long-held Christian belief that salvation only comes through Jesus. So, I asked Him with great curiosity.

"Is salvation only obtained through belief in Jesus?"

"That depends upon your definition of salvation. What does salvation mean to you?"

"You know, being saved."

"Saved from what?"

"From sin and death."

"Then the salvation you speak of is nothing more than being saved from the effects of a harmless dream. Can God's Son lose himself in dreams when God wills Heaven to be his? You need no help to enter Heaven because you have never left. God's will cannot fail, and neither sin nor death exist within the reality of the holy Son of God. It is only your belief in their existence which forms the walls of imprisonment that you seek salvation from. You do not need a mediator to eradicate sin and death, since they do not exist. You only need to stop believing that they do. Helpers are given to you in many forms. Jesus offered you a demonstration that it is impossible to kill God's Son; nor can his life in any way be changed by sin, evil, malice, fear or death. These are illusions that cannot affect the wholly innocent Son of God. Salvation and freedom do not require a key held by anyone else. Salvation is easy *because* it asks nothing you cannot give right now, simply by purging your belief in sin and death. Since salvation comes from God it is your birthright as His creation, and will always be yours. It is as sure as God, since God Himself placed it within you, joining your mind with His and unable to be broken. There is no chance that Heaven will not be yours because nothing can prevent what God wills be accomplished, though it can be temporarily denied. You will know your salvation and freedom when you stop denying it. The prison door is not closed, nor are your chains locked, but you cannot know liberation while believing in separation."

The Holy Spirit taught me that Jesus was a man who *only* saw the face of Christ in everyone because he remembered spirit and its knowledge of God, so he became fully identified with Christ and One with God. Jesus himself was constantly pointing to God, acknowledging his total dependence on God and it was that dependence which aligned him with his true and authentic power of complete union with God, and not a phony external power derived from the ego that the world perceives as real. He is a Savior in that he saw the false without accepting it as true and we needed his form so that we could see God within us to save ourselves from our own illusions. His misquoted and often misunderstood message was for us to know we are One with God, not just that he is. In the first chapter of *ACIM* he tells us "awe is not an appropriate reaction to me because of our inherent equality." If together we comprise God's only Son, then how can we not be equal?

When Ocean discussed love the day she restored the flow of spiritual energy to that property, lifting my soul into the air and above my body, I asked the Holy Spirit about that too.

"It seems like everything is about love."

"Love *is* everything, because God is everything and God is love, and so are you when your perception is not distorted by idols and illusions. Love encompasses all and has no opposite. There is no time or place that is void of love. When it seems love is not present, fear has obstructed the obvious, and fear is a false creation of the ego. Only love is true. You feel love when you feel Me, and you initiate My presence with thoughts of love. Since love is what we are, and God is, we can join minds simply by holding loving thoughts. Look on all things with love and I'll always be present. Abide in love and abide in Me. I will never judge you, and since all are one, I'll never judge another. If any judgment is present, then so is the ego, which reinforces itself through judgment and cannot survive without it. Judge not, for judgment is derived from fear and demonstrates deference to the ego."

Judgment was a constant struggle for me, as it is for many people. Then one day I read the following in *ACIM*, "A dream of judgment came into the mind that God created perfect as Himself. And in that dream was Heaven changed to hell, and God made enemy unto His Son. How can God's Son awaken from the dream? It is a dream of judgment. So, must he judge not, and he will waken." The words "judge not and awaken" stuck with me and I would repeat them whenever I was tempted to judge something that my ego decided needed judging. I really wanted to be a fearless speaker like Margie and not worry about what people said or thought. I could tell I was making progress, but it was difficult because I remained concerned about the judgments of others towards me, attesting to my ongoing belief in separation rather than the oneness of spirit that my shifting perspective was trying to adjust to, and that the Voice was trying to teach me at every opportunity. I didn't care as much as I used to, but I was still holding identification with that separated self.

I was also spending more time in the house with Kim and Kaya, even though I still had my rented ohana. Once, after having had the flu for a few days, I was staying at the house so that I wouldn't have to be both sick and alone. After a brief bout of fearful hesitation, I decided maybe it was time to try holding down some solid food. I went to the pantry to see if anything looked appealing to my still queasy stomach, and as I stood there the Voice spoke to me very clearly in a louder voice than usual, startling me by saying, *"You don't have to live in fear! You're not a body."* I actually turned and looked behind me when I heard it, but of course nobody was there. After confirming I was alone, my perspective then shifted just as it had during Ocean's Hawaiian chant. I could now see myself and hear my body's thoughts from an elevated external perspective.

I felt incredibly calm and peaceful. As I had been sick, I contemplated how comforting the concept of not being a body was. The Voice spoke again, saying, *"That is why I'm called the Comforter."* I left the pantry to go sit down on the couch. When I did this, the Voice spoke again, clarifying His initial statement, *"One is the cause, and the other is the effect. The body causes the effect of fear. But you are not the body; you are love, so you have nothing to fear. Love encompasses all without exception, and cancels fear when it is not obstructed or denied."*

After a pause, to allow that statement sufficient time to slowly sink in, the Voice continued, *"You can always tell whether you are identifying with your true Self or your false self by whether you are feeling love, or whether you are feeling fear."*

As I continued to incredulously observe my body sitting at home on my couch the Voice continued to speak and teach, *"This is not your home. You are living within an illusion.*" Then, simultaneously upon saying the word "illusion," the mirror in the room rippled, as if it were a pool of water and a pebble had just been tossed into it.

After the rippling mirror was restored to a clear reflection, I asked, "How am I living within an illusion?"

The response was swift *and* emphatic, "*Because you believe you're separate but you're not; you believe you're a body but you're not; and you believe you're temporal but you're not.*"

These words spawned a temporary remembrance of my real home in my mind. Just remembering it made me yearn for it and feel closer to it, and also so much further from this world, which now seemed foreign and insignificant by comparison.

The home I remembered is a place of unity, equality, oneness, all-encompassing love, and transcendent peace. This remembrance of home confirmed the illusion for me. Any place where we can feel fear, and see distinction, division, separation, and individuality *must be* an illusory dream, because it is *not* our real home.

I immediately wrote down the entire but somewhat bizarre experience in my notebook, in speech form and without making any changes or rewrites in only a few minutes. This was extremely quick considering that I usually spent between four and six hours writing a speech before I practiced it on video conference with Ed. My gratitude for such a profound experience caused me to thank the Divine Mind for the clear communication, immediately hearing this response:

> "*What is undeniable should never be doubted, and what is irreversible cannot be changed. This is My message, and it is not about contests or competitions, but about truth, no matter how uncomfortable it may be sometimes to speak it in front of a room full of people, or even an entire*

ballroom of people. Speak the truths I share and free your mind from perceptual imprisonment. This freedom is your undeniable and irreversible reality."

I had never spoken to a ballroom of people before, so I didn't understand that reference. But after always having felt vaguely estranged on earth, being told specifically that this place is not my home was quite comforting. The entire experience from start to finish was so surreal that I woke up the next morning wondering if it really happened. Then I smiled when I saw my unopened granola bar snack on the end table by the couch.

Once again, my spiritual curriculum calibrated experientially with impressive timing from my daily reading in *ACIM* as I read shortly thereafter about the restoration of the Kingdom to God's Son, "Heaven waits for his return, for it was created as the dwelling place of God's Son. You are not at home anywhere else, or in any other condition. Do not deny yourself the joy that was created for you for the misery you have made for yourself. God has given you the means for undoing what you have made. Listen, and you will learn how to remember what you are." Perfectly timed teachings such as this getting quickly and "coincidentally" confirmed were now becoming commonplace. I was not obtuse in the recognition, once again, of the extremely personal customization the Divine Mind was demonstrating in the delivery of my curriculum.

I told Margie about the experience and said I would be giving a speech about it, which seemed to please her. Then I wondered what a speaking professional like Ed would make of a speech with this content. Would he think of me what I had thought of Margie initially? When we had our coaching appointment, I delivered my speech to him exactly as it was written for his evaluation and commentary. When I finished Ed was silent, which was unusual for him. I knew he wasn't feeling it, or at least that version of it. He expressed his concern that seven minutes is not enough time to adequately develop and speak about such an experience, which I agreed with. He then said it would be better as a longer keynote speech but based upon what I had been told by the Voice to speak the often-uncomfortable truths He shared, I tried to remain firm regarding my speech content.

Ed told me, "It is your speech and you can deliver it this way if you want, but a seven minute speech is not sufficient time to cover a Voice that startles your awareness with spiritual wisdom, provides an out-of-body experience, uses a potentially polarizing Biblical term, and miraculously causes a mirror to ripple. Without more speaking time to adequately develop and explain all of this story content then you will only alienate your audience."

He had a valid point, and I was paying a lot of money for his coaching advice. So, with his input and advice, I made some revisions but tried to maintain the same general message while making it more universally applicable and having less of an alienating effect. We needed less story and more message. There had to be a better balance. When we finished, I think it was a better speech, but I had to lose some of my story content so the rippling mirror and my memory of home with personal commentary was removed.

Still, it was a different speech than anything I had ever tried to deliver at Toastmasters, although Margie fearlessly said much bolder things than this in her speeches. My trepidation ran contrary to the Voice's message and was harder for me to shake than I thought it would be. It was one thing to discuss these things with Margie in the privacy and safe confines of her own home, and another thing altogether to vulnerably stand and deliver a speech that gives everyone a blatant reason to question my sanity. I was pretty sure that anybody who ever spoke with Margie already doubted her sanity, but that didn't reflect on me. At least not like hopping aboard the crazy train myself and joyriding it through a Toastmasters meeting would.

Yet I also distinctly remember feeling that this one simple decision was discarding even more of the superfluous self and moving me closer to my truthful essence, where I really wanted to be. Perhaps this is what Margie meant when she suggested in our first meeting to undo the obstruction of the ego, because this was the false part that I had created by removing myself from God and refusing to accept what He had created. I then reinforced this falsehood by thinking it mattered what others thought of my creation. The more I realized it didn't matter, and this entire dream was just a gigantic stage production of various dream characters acting out assigned roles agreed to in advance, the less I cared. As Margie says, the dream is inconsequential. The dream is just a game we play until we learn we don't belong in this game. Understanding and implementing this mental approach acknowledges our willingness to set separation aside and end the constant human suffering it causes.

That didn't mean on speech day that I wasn't nervous as hell. I felt it was important to deliver a good, solid speech to counter any doubts that could be derived from a possible disagreement with the message. I did know that as important as this message was for me to share, it didn't necessarily mean people wanted to hear it. But I needed the practice, and if I had to practice public speaking then I wanted to do it on topics I was passionate about, and that were important and relevant to me. My willingness to share this type of message and subject myself to whatever judgment may follow was more indicative of where my mind was moving than how anyone would actually judge me. Talk about a perspective shift.

My new life was turning everything I had known before upside down, as it should since that manner of thinking had only caused suffering. But I didn't regret the suffering because it served my spiritual development by increasing my desire to alleviate it. Ram Dass once suggested that suffering is grace because it serves as sandpaper for our soul's incarnation. It does the work of smoothing and shaping our experience by showing us where we are too attached or stuck, so that we know what to work on spiritually. In hindsight, I could see that now. I finally felt I was making real and sustainable progress, rather than searching in frustration and ending up disappointed. All previous spiritual techniques I tried had failed, because they didn't address the problem at the source, but attempted to do so from within the illusion itself. Author Gary Renard likens this behavior to God waiting outside the asylum and calling you to leave and come out and join Him, but you stay inside and keep trying to drag God into the asylum with you instead.

When my name was called, I was relieved to finally take this important speaking step and put these fearful thoughts behind me. I took a deep breath and boldly stepped to the podium and into new spiritual speech territory. I titled the speech "Love or Fear."

"Fellow Toastmasters and guests, have you ever had an experience so impactful that it changed your perspective forever? I did, and it all started with a granola bar." I pulled a granola bar out of my pocket and held it up, showing its seeming insignificance, saying, "How could such an innocent little snack be the impetus for such a life-changing shift in awareness?

"One night, after having had the flu for a couple of days, I was standing in my pantry trying to decide on a late-night snack. I had finally finished retching and was feeling well enough to start snacking. I grabbed a granola bar and then hesitated, remembering this was the last thing I ate before I began vomiting two days ago." This comment gets several laughs and chuckles.

"As fear of a repeat performance gripped me, I engaged in a silent mental debate as to whether I should or shouldn't eat it. Then I heard a very clear voice interrupt this silent debate and say: *'You don't have to live in fear! You're not a body!'*" Upon saying this I spun to look behind me and hear a few chuckles as I turn back to face the group with a surprised look on my face. So far, so good.

"Startled, I looked behind me. There was nobody there. My wife and daughter were upstairs asleep, and I was the only one awake . . . inside a locked house! After looking around and confirming I was alone, the part of me that knew this statement to be true then proved it . . . by separating and elevating, allowing me to witness the silliness of this mental debate, about a granola bar, from an entirely different perspective, unattached to the body.

"This had never happened to me before, but I felt no fear, just calm peacefulness. My body took a seat on the couch as my mind repeated the words slowly and thoughtfully, 'You don't have to live in fear. You're not a body.' When I did this, the Voice spoke again, clarifying, *'One is the cause, and the other is the effect. The body causes the effect of fear. But you are not the body; you are love, so you have nothing to fear. Love encompasses all without exception, and cancels fear when it is not obstructed or denied.'*

"After allowing time for that statement to sink in, the Voice continued, saying, *'You can always tell whether you're identifying with your true Self or your false self by whether you feel love, or whether you feel fear.'* That's when it occurred to me that if I'm not a body, then I've been identifying with a wrong sense of self, and I was not really who I thought I was. I was *not* this body sitting on the couch. I was this elevated awareness apart from the body, a higher Self, and from *this* Self's perspective the entire world seemed foreign and insignificant, and so did my life. Especially all of the mental chatter constantly trying to judge, evaluate and organize everything in my life, all of the time, including whether or not I should eat a granola bar.

"From this place of higher awareness, I could easily see how debilitating, devoid of benefit, and completely mentally exhausting much of the body's thought processes are, not to mention incredibly inaccurate, and *always inducing fear*. Fear was impossible for my higher Self; it was only made possible by my belief in, and identification with, my false self or the body. Only the body can cause fear, and my true Self is not a body.

"The body is just a learning device for my higher Self, but by identifying exclusively with it, I had given it control of the curriculum, and it was teaching me fear, pain and suffering, without any resistance from my true Self. Why *do* people tolerate all of the fears of the false self, when fear itself is so unenjoyable? Because they falsely believe that is all they are, and they have not yet acknowledged and awakened their true Self.

"Life may seem complex, but it is nothing more than a simple choice between love or fear. Love is how you identify with your true Self, and fear means you are identifying with the false self. Love is what we are, while fear is a fantasy that can only be made real by illusion, misidentification, and misperception. We see what we believe is there, and we believe it there because we want it there. Perception is therefore a projection that allows us to witness our own state of mind, providing us with an outside picture of an inward condition.

"Wayne Dyer said, 'Loving people live in a loving world. Hostile people live in a hostile world. Same world.' What world are you living in? That depends on whether you are identifying with love or identifying with fear and hostility. After my experience, I now recognize fear as nothing more than an attachment to my false self. I also acknowledge love as my true Self and use it to dispel fear.

"The result of this recognition of fear and acknowledgment of love in my own life has been extreme happiness and transcendent peace. Things that used to terrify me, no longer do. Love has healed my fractured relationships and made me less judgmental and more forgiving. And that incessant mental chatter is being controlled and devalued by my higher awareness. My life has never been better since I eliminated debilitating fear by identifying with my true Self. The difference is so dramatic that it really is hard to believe it's the same world. 'You don't have to live in fear, you're not a body' was the perfect message I needed, and one that I never want to forget."

After the meeting was over, Margie immediately came up to me and asked, "Why did you take out the part about the rippling mirror?" Not only was she fearless; she wanted me to be fearless too. I might have blamed Ed for that omission.

Chapter 7

Humorous Speech Competitions

"I saw a study that said speaking in front of
a crowd is considered the number one fear of
the average person. Number two was death.
This means to the average person, if you have to
be at a funeral, you would rather be in the casket
than doing the eulogy."
Jerry Seinfeld

The Toastmasters Area Humorous Speech Contest was held on September 16th and my default victory derived from being the only club member willing to participate in the contest meant I would represent our Maui club in the Area level competition. Ann Elaine told me after my "Danger of Certainty" speech that I had mastered the art of humorous storytelling, so I wanted to see how well I could do in the competition with my newfound confidence and Ed's professional speech coaching expertise.

I had completed a few coaching calls with Ed already, so I knew he loved stories because "stories are sticky," meaning they are remembered. He shared an old Native American proverb with me that said, "Tell me the facts and I'll learn. Tell me the truth and I'll believe. But tell me a story and it will live in my heart forever." He also instructed me on a speech starting pattern that worked great for "The Danger of Certainty" speech about the Howler monkeys. It is a three-part opening.

1. You creatively break audience preoccupation and grab their attention.
2. You frame the message, in one sentence or less.
3. You jump into the content.

He had also gone into the four H's of storytelling and wanted me to consider them as I tooled with the improved speech. They are:

1. The Head makes you think.
2. The Heart connects.
3. Humor makes you laugh.
4. Heavy Hitting is the message.

A good speech should have all the above and involve your head, heart, humor, and be heavy hitting with a powerful message. I tried to incorporate all of that, but I could see I was lacking in some areas.

On September 13th, three days before the competition, I received an email from the Contest Chair confirming my expected arrival, briefing time, and seating instructions with two attachments. One was a twenty-eight-page Toastmasters International Speech Contest Rule Book, featuring a picture of Ed Tate's speech student Darren Tay on the front cover, holding his first Place World Champion of Public Speaking trophy from last year's international competition.

Arriving at the Cameron Center in Kahului for the Area contest, I knew that each of the respective Maui clubs were sending their best humorous speakers and there was bound to be some funny speeches delivered that day. Margie showed up in support, and so did Kim and Kaya. The Cameron Center was quite large but the room we were in was smaller and had about a half a dozen rows with one large aisle down the middle, accommodating about sixty audience members with about fifty people present. The first time I had given this speech I was extremely nervous, but I was a much more confident speaker now. We were briefed on the rules and procedure and told of our movement boundaries to avoid disqualification.

My speech was somewhat improved in content, but my delivery was the largest improvement. I was more energized and expressive, and I kept up the pace of delivery better and really hammed up the funny parts and got a great response. I felt confident when I finished, but there was at least one other speech that I thought was possibly just as funny, so it would depend upon the judges. Fortunately, my name was called as the winner and I stood to accept my first-place trophy, it was about two feet high and a foot wide with three pillars supporting a speaker on top of it. I got some pictures taken for the Maui News and then sat back down by Kim and Kaya and handed the huge trophy to Kaya to hold and inspect. It fascinated her. Margie also seemed as proud as a parent would be. Two days later, I received the following email:

Hi Don,

Congratulations on your first-place win at the Area Humorous Speech Contest!

You are eligible to compete at the Division Contest on Saturday, October 7 at the Central Pacific Bank in downtown Honolulu.

The top two winners from the Division Contest will advance to the District Contest on Saturday, November 4 at the Pagoda Hotel in Honolulu.

As I prepared to fly to Oahu for the Division Humorous Speech Contest, it was exciting to know my Toastmasters club would pay for my flight to Honolulu to compete. I saw it as a reimbursement for all of the crutch word fines I incurred in our meetings as penalties by the "Ah Counter." An "Ah Counter" is a designated person who listens to everybody in a Toastmasters meeting for the use of crutch words that infiltrate our speech and disrupt good communication such as, "ah, uh, um, and, so, well, you know, like, then, etc." Our club tracked them and charged twenty-five cents for each inadvertent use—up to a one dollar maximum per meeting. We even had a specific form to capture the names of the perpetrators, their most commonly used crutch words, and the number of times each crutch word was used.

I got to see my name and picture in the newspaper as the Area contest winner, and the caption stated I would be traveling to Oahu to represent Maui at the Division level. I wasn't about to make this trip alone, so I made hotel reservations and bought airfare for Kim and Kaya to also attend, which they were thrilled to do with me. On September 23rd I received an email that was sent to all Division A contestants and club presidents, thanking us for representing Area three at the Division Speech Contest, with a request for a Speaker's Bio and a Speaker's Certification of Eligibility and Originality be sent to the Division Contest Chair. It also suggested specific flights to ensure adequate time to get to the competition that day, a map to the Division Contest location, and a Speech Contest Schedule for the four different divisions that were competing that day.

We flew in the night before the contest just because I didn't want to be rushing around the airport and the city on the day of the speech. Kim and Kaya wanted to go out and walk around Honolulu that night, but I decided to stay in the hotel room and practice my speech. The next morning, I went early to watch the Division D contest at ten a.m. before Division A's contest started at one p.m. I took the rental car and Kim agreed she and Kaya would take an Uber and arrive by one for my contest. I was nervous when I arrived and saw all the commotion and activity. There were *a lot* of people here. The room was large, and it was so full that some people were even standing up along the wall. There were twice as many people here as there had been at the Area competition.

I listened to all of the humorous speeches from Division D and they were really good. It was clear the level of competition had risen. I was too nervous to eat anything, but right around the time my stomach was tying itself in knots I received a text picture of Kim and Kaya in the back seat of their Uber stating they were on their way and would see me soon. This relaxed me and anchored emotions to a calmer state. Everything else was insignificant, they were all that really mattered, and that text reminded me of this. I was excited again. I was in another room getting prepped for the competition when they arrived, but I saw them when we came out and got ready to start. I wasn't able to sit by them because the contestants had to be seated in a specific area, but I waved, and they beamed their beautiful smiles back at me.

As I delivered my speech, I got about one-fourth of the way through and I lost track of where I was, I started to panic and grabbed whatever part of the speech I could remember and got back on track. I realized later that I had left out a couple of lines in that moment of panic, but all things considered it was a great delivery and everybody laughed. It wasn't my best speech performance, but it was fine. I listened to all of the other speeches and I felt like mine was as funny as any of them, but it was a toss-up whether it would be good enough to win or not. I knew I was at least in the running.

When they announced the contest winners, they started with the runner-up who would also compete in the District competition with the winner. When they announced the person who I thought had the best chance of beating me as the runner-up, my hopes of winning soared. They made a bit of a fuss when announcing the winner, with a dramatic pause while a drum roll played, and then they called out my name as the winner! The victory music started, and everybody cheered but as I stood up and looked out at the large room applauding me, all I could see was Kim and Kaya. They were standing and cheering as families do for each other and it warmed my heart to witness their enthusiastic support. I would come back to Oahu next month to represent our Division in the District 49 competition, which covered the entire state of Hawaii. After the contest ended there were more photographs for the newspapers, and then we celebrated out on the town . . . with our six-year-old.

Word began to spread about my win at the Division competition. Ann Elaine immediately sent out this email to all of our club members:

> Hello Toastmasters,
> Congratulations to our Don McEntire for his first-place win at the Division A Humorous Speech Contest on Oct. 7! He goes on to compete at the District 49 Contest on Nov. 4th at the District Conference. We're proud of you, Don!

I was proud of myself too.

When the newspaper article and picture of the Division contest results came out in the Maui News the property manager of our commercial office building sent the newspaper link to everyone with an office in our building and told me congratulations. I didn't know he had done this so when I came to work that day a lot of people commented to me about it, a laudatory notice that was appreciated outside of the usual compliments centered on salesmanship and such.

I was on a roll. I had won three speech contests in a row with increasingly difficult competition, and had now appeared in the newspaper twice, with many accolades received from both my Toastmasters peers as well as my business colleagues. I was starting to feel pretty good about myself. The transition was subtle, but viable. I felt different, better, and more confident. I reinforced this feeling of superiority by attaching to these successes and identifying with them to feel even more special. I had uncovered a hidden talent late in life. What could possibly be wrong with celebrating such a feel-good discovery? Fortunately, I had the benefit of an excellent Teacher who would soon answer that question for me in an unforgettable way.

One of the rules in Toastmasters International Speech Contests is that every participant must present an entirely new and different speech than the one presented during that year's semifinal speech contest or any previous year's semifinal or final round speech contests. As the Division winner and a finalist in the District competition, I now had to step away from the comfortable confines of my "Safe Seat" speech to write and deliver a different speech the following month in the District finals. This required speech change is done to reward the best speaker in the competition and not just the best speech. Being required to change speeches in the final round forces you to prove that you are a good speaker and not just someone who wrote and delivered one good speech. I had made tremendous progress and put my fear of public speaking behind me due to my success in the Club, Area and Division speech competitions. I was only a first year Toastmaster who was competing against speakers who had been honing their skills for decades, in some cases. In other words, I became less humble as I continued to advance in the competition, and now that I was in the finals my humility diminished even further. Even though I had to write a brand-new speech for the

District finals, I wasn't concerned because I had Ed Tate as my speech coach.

The day after winning the Division competition, I received an email sent to all District Speech Contestants providing information regarding our briefing time, the draw of our speaking order, and the procedure for wiring and testing our mandatory microphones just prior to our speech. This VIP speech treatment was new territory for me and the requirement to be wired with a mandatory microphone magnified my feeling of self-importance.

That month I wrote and practiced my new humorous speech, returning once again to my extended Costa Rican vacation experiences. I titled the speech "Adventures in Costa Rica." I delivered it to my Toastmasters club for practice and got a very positive response. I even felt like it may have even been better than my "Safe Seat" speech. Ann Elaine was buoyant with successful expectation when she sent this email to club members just a few days before I left for Oahu to compete:

> Good luck to Don McEntire who is competing this
> Saturday in the District 49 Humorous Speech Contest
> for the title of funniest speaker in the State of Hawaii
> at the Fall Conference in Honolulu.

I liked the idea of being the best speaker in the State of Hawaii. What a great way to culminate this unlikely story, especially when considering the state of mind that I began this Toastmasters journey from.

The next few days were a whirlwind of preparations. Kim and Kaya decided, since this was going to be an all-day event with a much larger crowd, it would be best to stay home on Maui, which was fine, because it would be less to deal with that weekend. I learned Ed Tate was flying from Colorado to be the keynote speaker for the conference, which was pretty cool because I would get to meet him in person and hear him speak live.

When I arrived in Oahu, I went right to my room and practiced my speech until going to bed early, since the conference was scheduled to start at seven forty-five the following morning. When I arrived at the conference I registered, received my conference materials, and entered the ballroom. I'd never spoken to a ballroom of people before . . . and it was a huge ballroom. Seeing it for the first time clarified the Divine Mind's previous communication, "*This is My message, and it is not about contests or competitions, but about truth, no matter how uncomfortable it may be sometimes to speak it in front of an entire room full of people, or even an entire ballroom of people.*" It was awe-inspiring. No wonder they required speakers to wear microphones. There were tables stacked about five deep from one end of the large ballroom to the other, with an elevated stage at the front center. Within a short time, over 300 people were occupying these seats. I took a picture of it and texted it to Kim. She responded immediately and wished me luck.

I was able to relax and enjoy the morning session of the conference since the humorous speeches were not until the afternoon. I got to hear Ed speak live as our keynote speaker. He showed portions of coaching student Darren Tay's speeches from his run towards winning the world championship, something that Ed had also accomplished, and he discussed his coaching experience throughout that process. He was not only highly enter-taining, but it was a brilliant keynote speech because he was getting paid to deliver a speech to over 300 people that all wanted to become better speakers, and he sells coaching services. Being in sales myself, I could appreciate how easily this would translate to more coaching clients for him at 4,500 dollars a pop. The conference was busy for him between his speaking and selling his coaching services. I didn't get to talk to him too much, but we chatted a little.

After lunch we settled into the ballroom and the Humorous Speech Contest was the first part of the afternoon. I was prepared so I wasn't too nervous, although this was a new speech. It was an interesting mix of eight speakers, and I think I was the fourth or fifth speaker, so I heard a few speeches before delivering mine. They were all excellent and humorous. The delivery was the thing that distinguished them from each other. I felt bad for one speaker from Kauai who had an excellent written speech, but his nerves got the best of him in front of the big crowd and we felt for him as he delivered his speech nervously and poorly.

During the speech before mine I got up and went to the back to be wired for my microphone. I was trying to hear what I could from that speech, but the wiring and the microphone checking wouldn't allow it. I finally finished and was directed along the back of the ballroom to the far-right side of the stage, where I got to hear the last couple of speech minutes as I prepared to step up onto the stage. He closed, everybody clapped, and my name was called. This was it. I took a deep breath and walked onto the stage, taking my time on the steps to make sure I didn't stumble, although that might have played well for a humorous speech introduction. I stood in the middle of the stage and faced the audience. They were scattered everywhere and were so far away I felt disconnected from them. I was used to speaking in smaller, more intimate settings. I had practiced every facial expression, every intonation, every word inflection, every tinge of sarcasm, and I delivered my new speech with as much emotion and demonstrative grand gesturing as possible.

"My family just spent forty days in Costa Rica where I learned some very valuable lessons. Why Costa Rica? Because *I did my research* and discovered that although Costa Rica is one of the world's smallest countries, it contains about five percent of the world's biodiversity!

"Many people don't know that Costa Rica is home to over 500,000 different species. So we were excited and looking forward to our 'adventures in nature' where we would encounter all of these abundant species *firsthand*. Mr. Toastmaster, fellow Toastmasters, I learned *statistics can be deceptive.*" I said "adventures in nature" in a deep voice like I was announcing a TV program, and ended the intro sounding exasperated by statistics.

"Because what I missed in my research was that out of this *impressive number* of 500,000 species: over 300,000 of those species . . . are *insects!*' My voice intonation escalated loudly as I practically shouted "insects." There were lots of smiles, but not much laughter.

I continued, "Since there are about 925,000 documented insect species in the world, which means this tiny Central American country contains one-third of the entire world's insect species!" This got a few more laughs, but they still felt distant and disconnected and seemed to be wondering where I was taking them.

"Life is *sooooo different* when you're dealing with that many insects." I practically sang "sooooo" and they smiled again and seemed to show a little more interest. "I quickly learned bug repellent . . . was far more important than sunscreen. Being from Maui, I can handle sunburn. What I can't handle is being bullied by 300,000 species of insects for forty days." I moved from center stage to my right, directly in front of where Ed was sitting, but looking at him made me nervous so I chose someone at the table behind his to look at instead.

"I always wanted to take my wife on a romantic horseback ride on the beach, with the ocean breeze blowing through our hair. So, after arriving in Costa Rica I booked the tour. When we met our guide Meliana *the first thing she did* was hand us *helmets* to wear? The quizzical look on my face prompted her to explain that it was simply a 'safety precaution.' I admit I was disappointed by the helmet requirement. Now, instead of an ocean breeze blowing through my hair I was going to have helmet hair." As I changed facial expressions from quizzical to disappointed, I lifted my right hand and smoothed my hair from the top of the head to the back of my neck and held it there with my elbow pointed out while I paused long enough to get a laugh out of this face and hand gesture. One lady told me later this was her favorite part of my speech, and even with all my rehearsing I decided upon this gesture and dramatic pause on the spot.

"But as we made our way down to the beach, I forgot all about the helmet as I rode my horse across the white sand. It is a satisfying feeling when a vacation experience is everything you imagined it to be . . . *until* . . . I learned *why* there *was* a helmet requirement, when one of the larger, stinging members of those 300,000 species decided to sting my horse in the worst possible place to sting a *stallion!*" The slower speech from my blissful satisfaction of the initial ride was bridged by a lengthy pause after "until," and then jumped loudly to speed speaking as my horse's penis got stung. I moved back to the center of the stage as they gave me surprised and skeptical looks. I located a blurry male at the back of the ballroom and spoke directly to him.

"Suddenly my *peaceful beachfront bliss* becomes a *bucking beachfront bronco* as my horse lifts and kicks at himself to knock the stinging bug off. But horses are unable to kick themselves there, so he was jump-kicking *my* calves instead.

"I was holding on for dear life as two thoughts came to mind:

> 1. A 240-pound man is *no match* for the size and strength of a 1,000-pound beast, and

2. Helmet hair was such a trivial concern, and
    I was soooo happy for my helmet when the
    bucking started.

"I had a sinking, helpless feeling as I realized there was nothing I could do but surrender to the situation and brace myself for the worst. Then I learned *things can always get worse.*" I really animate my demonstration as I inflect the next part as the audience leans in, engaging with the story.

"Meliana sees what is happening and springs into action, racing over behind my horse, leaning low to the side of her saddle and swinging her reins up, under and between my horse's legs to swat the stinging bug off! I'm no cowboy! I don't know how horses think! But I'm *pretty sure* this horse thought she wasn't helping with all this crotch swatting." After humorously demonstrating the leaning and swatting, I pulled a crazy face as I shouted, "I'm no cowboy!" I forgot I had a microphone on, so it was a loud verbal blast, but effective. They were all laughing, and when I said "crotch swatting" they lost it. It always delighted me when I could make the entire group burst into laughter, but it was an even bigger rush with this many people in the group. Ed had already told me this was a very funny word combination, and it was his suggestion to place it at the end of the sentence rather than the middle. He wanted to make sure I didn't step on any laughs because he knew it would be a humorous trigger.

"Then my wife, who up until now had been giggling and laughing at the ordeal with my horse, gets a karmic scare of her own when her horse, which had been riding with his nose curiously close to my horse's tail, decides that all of this jumping, kicking *and swatting* is more than he wants to deal with . . . so he begins to run! As my wife's horse runs away, with her screaming in terror, it's my turn to laugh, at least until my horse does the same in order to escape Meliana's crotch-swatting.

"So now my horse is running . . . and being the novice rider I am, I never knew when the horse is running you are supposed to rise up in the stirrups so you're not straddling the horse's back while painfully bouncing . . . up and . . . down with every stride." I grimace and pretend to painfully bounce up and down with exaggerated stage jumps at each pause and land with a boom each time. The stage had seemed sturdy until I began jumping on it. I'm a large man and I felt it give as I landed each jump so I'm sure some people wondered if the platform would hold during this jump fest. It was a good thing I was fake grimacing because on the last bounce, the grimace became real when I landed and felt a shot of pain go through my left testicle. I guess I got a little carried away on the final jump. I took a tentative step to my left to gauge the testicular pain, ironically as I'm saying:

"I wasn't trying to empathize with my horse's penis pain, but I learned from this experience that *anything can happen.* Eventually our horses stopped running and Meliana dismounted to inspect *my horse.* She saw the bite mark up close and told me he would be sore tomorrow. But all I could think was, "The *horse!* What about *me?* I'm sore right now. We're gonna need cowpoke counseling . . . and a couple's massage." More satisfying laughter. The story and speech were a hit. I held up a finger and then added one as I made each of the following three points and ended with a sarcastic smile.

"I returned home much wiser. Now, I'm skeptical of statistics. I brace for the bounce when things are going wrong. And I'm aware that anything can happen, so I surrender to the uncertainty of life because I know I'm not in control. But I also know that whoever *is* in control . . . *definitely* has a sense of humor." I came off the stage, surrendered my microphone, returned to my table and enjoyed the rest of the speeches. I was content. I did my best and it was finally over. There were a lot of good speeches, but I thought mine was one of the better ones, if not the best. It was another toss up, but I really thought I had an excellent chance of winning. They brought out three trophies and started by announcing third place and called my name. I was disappointed by not winning, but I quickly went back up on stage to get my trophy from Ed and shake his hand. I had placed third out of over 1,000 members spread out over more than sixty clubs, and yet somehow, I didn't feel very good about it, and the trophy was much smaller than the winning trophy for the Area competition.

On the taxi ride to the airport I began thinking about my speech, wondering why I didn't win and feeling dispirited. Never missing an opportunity, my Teacher chimed in and quickly changed my perspective, "The ego offers a wrong minded attempt to perceive yourself as you wish to be, rather than as you are. You are love, but how can love exist when the goal is triumph?" That should have been enough said, but as I contemplated the delivery of this message and continued to struggle with feelings of failure more was expressed, "Since the ego lives by comparison it cannot survive without judgment. Equality is beyond its grasp and this makes love impossible. Fear and depression are signs of allegiance to the ego. Depression surfaces when you feel you are being deprived of something you want and do not have, but only you can deprive yourself of anything. Since your own decisions cause your deprivation, simply decide otherwise." It was clear my Teacher was referring to my choice for separation, and by choosing again I could end my feelings of deprivation forever.

He concluded with, "The ego is afraid of the spirit's joy, because once you have experienced it you will withdraw all protection from the ego and become totally without investment in fear. Leave it behind! Do not listen to it and do not attempt to preserve it. You cannot reach for Love with fear by your side because you cannot make illusions real. Leave your fearful illusions in the shabby and unsheltered home the ego has built, because it cannot build otherwise. Do not try to make this impoverished house stand. Only God could make a home that is worthy of His Son. Why then, would you choose to leave it empty by your own dispossession? The entire Kingdom is yours, and yet you wander homeless. Is it sane to choose nothing as a substitute for everything?"

Chapter 8

Struggling with Ego

"When we look at the ego, then, we are not
considering dynamics but delusions.
You can surely regard a delusional system
without fear, for it cannot have any effects if its
source is not real . . . . Perceive any part of the ego's
thought system as wholly insane, wholly
delusional, and wholly undesirable, and you have
correctly evaluated all of it."
A Course in Miracles

As a real estate broker, I particularly enjoyed my Teacher's
metaphorical ego references to the "shabby and unsheltered
home," the "impoverished house," "home dispossession" and
"homelessness." I could see how life is a tug-of-war between our
split mind's struggle to choose between "two teachers who are in
total disagreement about everything." When Jesus said you cannot
serve two masters, he made the reason clear. Because God and ego
cannot be reconciled, being diametrically opposed to each other
in such a way that partial allegiance to either is impossible.
Attempting this engenders a split mind that is constantly
confused as to what reality is. This exercise of indecision leaves us
winded by skirting back and forth between them.

I was ready for a "better way." I knew that would require
me to be honest in my evaluation of both masters, or thought
systems, in order to choose one and surrender the other. I already

knew the ego's thought system darkens and obscures the path, while the Divine Mind brightens and enlightens that same path. But why wasn't that knowledge enough? Why was I still holding onto the ego at all? We perceive everything in the world as either enshrouded in darkness or bathed in light, and our perception always reflects the guidance of the master consistent with our choice of vision. Knowing that my false perception of self had been the primary cause of all my previous suffering, I still allowed it to sneak in the back door and slip me into depression by listening to it. Now I needed to correct this temporary return to an ego-entrenched life by performing an egoic eviction and identify once again with the exciting world of spirit that my Teacher had shown me.

I had experienced spirit's joy and knew firsthand the difference between living in the shadows of fear-based thinking, and the personal peace and happiness that my sudden identification with spirit brought. The ego *is* an awful builder, and as such should never be trusted to construct anything for us, especially if it required refusal to take possession of what God built for us instead. This perspective is all that is required to make another choice and change the mind, placing it at the disposal of true authority, and all power. This reminder was effective because it was anchored to a memorable life experience, and it pulled me out of my spiritual slippage, and further distanced me from the negative emotions of fear and depression that eventually always surface from the ego's thought system. When we allow the Higher Self to interpret the dream world's activities and outcomes, then we never feel deprived or depressed because the Divine Mind mediates between the individuality of the ego and the oneness of spirit. It teaches us that our Source has already provided us with everything. Our one problem has never been about possession, only perception. If we are not aware of God's abundance we ignore the pure intelligence within and pursue false idols externally, causing split-minded confusion.

It was startling how quickly I allowed a little speaking success to wedge itself into my thought system and create a sense of specialness and superiority that supported egoic thinking. When Margie mentioned in our first meeting the need to change my mind and undo the obstruction of ego, I never fully understood the insidious nature of our inclination and susceptibility to it, nor the difficulty and importance attached to its undoing. I was beginning to understand now, and this created a sense of urgency since the "little I" was never going to stop seeking to enhance itself by external approval, external possessions, and external love. But the external searching of the "little I" only distracts us from discovering the Self that God created, which is entirely complete and needs nothing, because the Self only knows of perfect spiritual abundance.

ACIM contains a section titled "Self-Concept versus Self," which says the learning of the world is built upon a concept of the self that is adjusted to fit its reality, and that adjusted self fits the world of shadows and illusions very well. We arrive here without a self and we create one as we go along. It states, "A concept of the self is made by you. It bears no likeness to yourself at all. It is an idol, made to take the place of your reality as Son of God." This devaluation of ourselves and our true nature isn't an easy task, so we will often enlist the assistance of others.

Ram Dass described this devaluation process as entering into conspiracies with each other where we say "I'll make believe you are who you think you are, if you make believe I am who I think I am." On this concept of self, the world smiles with approval because it guarantees its pathways are safely kept and that those who walk on them will never escape.

Our created self-concept is learned and not natural. It wouldn't exist at all without our belief in it. This is not just a spiritual interpretation, but a psychological one. Psychologist Matthew Johnson speaks of "our addiction to a pattern of thinking with the self at the center of it." He says,

> "So much of human suffering stems from having this self that needs to be psycho-logically defended at all costs. We're trapped in a story that sees ourselves as independent, isolated agents acting in the world. But that self is an illusion and . . . there is no truth to it. Wherever you look, you see that the level of interconnectedness is truly amazing, and yet we insist on thinking of ourselves as individual agents."

He sounds like a Course student. Here is a Course quote that says essentially the same thing, "The self you made . . . does not exist at all. And anything it seems to do and think means nothing. It is neither bad nor good. It is unreal, and nothing more than that."

When the ego mind thinks for us we insist on believing the untrue, because all egoic thinking is characterized by the consistent combinational pattern of attacking truth and defending error. The ego's thinking is conceived "from feverish imaginations, hot with hatred and distortions born of fear." Joseph Campbell said, "The meaning of life is whatever you ascribe it to be." Self-concept is just a thought its creator provides meaning to, but it cannot ever represent the truth of what we are. I understood the human suffering that stemmed from the teachings of the "little I," and now the Divine Mind was helping me identify this lone belief as the only reason I was still suffering through this nightmarish dream of exile from God. I needed to transcend the limiting belief that I had accepted as my truth, and that was now holding me hostage to the ego instead of being a host to God. It was splitting, infecting, and imprisoning my mind and will. I wanted to rescind the ego's invitation to exist concealed within my split mind and choose a different Guest to reverse thought systems and heal this insidious infirmity. The first change the Divine Mind introduced was a change in direction.

It is worth noting here that changing direction can be a real challenge, partially because our first experience of change resulted in our apparent separation from God, and partially because of a little thing called inertia. Physicist Isaac Newton famously described inertia in his renowned first law of motion, stating that "an object either remains at rest or continues its motion unless acted upon by a force." Newton's other two laws of motion provide formulas to measure the amount of force required to overcome inertia (mass times acceleration), and the effect of equal and opposite forces applied to an object during rest or motion.

Basically, it requires a lot of force to either get moving or stop moving, and the larger the object and faster the acceleration the higher the force required, due to the influence of opposing forces. So, if you are, say, careening out of control at a rapid velocity, then the force required to stop and change direction is substantial. Thankfully, I enlisted the strongest Force in the universe to help with this change of direction, so that helps. But that still didn't mean it was easy. Inheriting God's limitless creative power and then projecting it onto our own miscreation makes the challenge formidable. The Course warns us that "Nothing made by a child of God is without power." Under-estimate this challenge at your own risk because it requires engaging in an epic battle.

Speaking of epic battles, when speech coach Ed Tate recommended that I read Steven Pressfield, I promptly bought several of his books. In them, he brilliantly dissects our opposition and labels it under the catch-all term of "resistance". He says resistance is fear that sits in the ego, and then he defines the ego as "that part of the psyche that believes in material existence" (the illusion). He also refers to resistance and ego as the second self or shadow Self. Whatever we call it, he points out that it clearly doesn't love you or care about you. It has its own agenda, which is to prevent you from actualizing your true Self and realizing who you really are, and it will kill you to achieve this agenda.

He likens it to a dragon and has a great quote that I modified by substituting the synonymous term ego for resistance: "On the field of Self stand a knight and a dragon. You are the knight. Ego is the dragon." He even details the characteristics of the dragon, in that it is invisible, insidious, impersonal, infallible, universal, never sleeps and always plays for keeps. He says the fire-breathing dragon of ego is invisible because it is a belief which cannot be seen, heard, touched, tasted or smelled, in a world that seems to only allow awareness of these external sensory inputs. But it can be felt as a repelling force that confines and distracts us. It is insidious in that it will tell you anything to deceive you. It will perjure, falsify, seduce, bully, cajole, and will even cite scripture and interpret it as a witness for itself to deceive you. It can reason with you like a lawyer or jam a nine-millimeter in your face like a stickup man. It has no conscience and will pledge anything only to double-cross you as soon as your back is turned. It is a liar and is always lying.

It may seem contradictory, but it is also impersonal in the sense it doesn't know the real you, nor does it care. It acts according to a belief system that is indifferent and applicable to everyone objectively. It is infallible and always points in one direction only (away from God). It is universal because everyone who has a body experiences its effects until it can be transcended. It never sleeps and never goes away as long as you appear to be within a body, and the battle must be fought every single day. It plays for keeps and is not satisfied with wounding or disabling you, it aims to kill. When we choose to fight it, we are in a war to the death. Pressfield then goes on to say: "The only intercourse possible between the knight and the dragon is battle . . . The clash is epic and internal, between the ego and the Self, and the stakes are our lives."

Spiritual author Jed McKenna agrees, with a nod to Captain Ahab while also speaking metaphorically of his own personal quest for truth, "The ridiculously simple realization that truth exists made me grab a six-inch knife and jump out of my rickety little boat into a churning ocean of blood and froth in a hopeless bid to slay an enormous and unslayable beast." The reason for the inevitability of this battle is because as already mentioned, the ego and the Self are diametrically opposed thought systems, uncompromising in their consistency, with each disallowing any partial allegiance or reconciliation between them. Acceptance of one requires rejection of the other. Jesus told us there cannot be two masters and he also told us why, because a "house divided against itself will not stand," so one must rule, and the other must be subservient. Which master is ruling you? For most people, the Divine Mind has been repressed and imprisoned by the ego's thought system, but we can choose again to restore His rule. If we do, our right mind gently leads us back to God and away from the wrong-minded thought system of the ego, the lair where the dragon has ensconced itself.

Intellectual understanding isn't enough. We've all wondered at times why we do the things we do, especially when we know what we know. So be gentle on yourself and remember it is a practice and anything worth doing is not going to be easy. Ram Dass knew spiritual practice is a difficult adjustment for the habitual responses of the ego, having once said, "If you think you are enlightened, go and spend a week with your family." I can't do this even now. Whatever delusion I tend to harbor regarding this ability is quickly cured within hours of any association with my dysfunctional family. I have a sister that never stops talking and will ask you a question only to interrupt your answer with another question, and she will do this incessantly for as long as you keep talking to her. My brother has no respect for personal space and constantly pulls my hair, twists my ears, or tries to wrestle me to the ground to show his physical superiority, and he's fifty-six years old!

The challenges of change are not just limited to spirituality. I used to tell my Spanish students in High School that they would need to really apply themselves if they wanted to learn Spanish, because it took me years of dedicated study and practice to learn, and I didn't even speak it all that well. I thought I did, until I went to Mexico and spoke with native speakers that spouted syllables like they were shooting a machine gun. Add a native accent to their verbal barrage and it was all over. I didn't want to discourage my students, but I felt it was important to be realistic with them regarding the challenge that awaited them, and I still do, which is why I don't want anybody to underestimate the difficulty of attempting to undo the ego.

What is this obstruction of Self that forces our alliance with fear and forges a forgetfulness of Love? From a spiritual perspective it is nothing and cannot even be defined. Assigning a definition to the unreal and undefinable implies it must be something real, and making it real ensures its illusive nature is concealed behind the words that make it appear to be such. In reality, the ego is nothing but a belief about ourselves, presented deceptively enough to make it seem real. Nothingness forms a dream of what we think we are, and the dream seems real as we dream it, but it isn't, and the cost of carrying this belief is the source of all our suffering. There is no definition for a lie that can ever make it true, just as there is no truth that lies can ever completely conceal.

According to *ACIM*, when the mind made the ego, we threw knowledge away in favor of perception, and since perception is a choice, we are still choosing this same error today. But it needs to be corrected if we are to unite with God, because error cannot enter God's Mind, where we are. By choosing this error we create a false perception of separation from God and deny His reality in favor of our own illusion. God knows, He does not perceive. Perception always involves uncertainty, and since perception was not God's Thought, it does not belong to Him. When God extended Himself to His perfect creations, He imbued them with His same will to create. Our likeness to our Creator means we cannot ever lose this creative ability, although we can misuse it by projecting into a perception of separation rather than extending His perfect oneness.

When I read this, I was confused by the difference between projection and extension, so I asked the Divine Mind to explain. His answer, "Projection involves a thrusting forward that attempts separation from the source of the projection. Extension refers to a lengthening or expansion that remains attached to the original source. God creates by extension, but the ego makes by projection. Your creation by God was an extension of the Mind of God, and your subsequent creation of the ego was a projection that seemingly separated you from your Source, thus removing His creative power from your creations and causing them to wither in sickness and death because they were projected away from Love instead of being extended as Love."

Projection occurs when we believe that some emptiness or lack exists in us that we can fill with our own ideas instead of truth. The projection process requires several things. First, we believe what God created can be changed by our own mind. Next, we pretend what is perfect can somehow be rendered imperfect or lacking. This distorts the truth of God's creation, and these devious distortions represent what occurred in the separation, or our "detour into fear." All distortions are misperceptions that we don't have to believe in the existence of; and when we don't believe in them, they won't exist. The world touts a healthy self-esteem or self-image as a positive, but our belief in the separate self, or the ego, can only limit and diminish the Self. Our acceptance of and belief in the "little I" is a pledge of allegiance to fear, anxiety, and death, and causes unnecessary suffering.

By siding with the ego, we choose to believe we can change what God created, make the perfect imperfect, and distort the creations of God. These inappropriate projections caused a tiny aspect of God's mind to fall asleep and experience itself fragmented as separated beings, instead of as the same Being, forcing the mind to split and requiring a choice between the ego mind and the Divine Mind. The ego creates convincing illusions to reinforce wrong mindedness, but it needs constant defense precisely *because* it is defending error.

The Course goes so far as to say the ego "is the anti-Christ; the strange idea there is a power past omnipotence, a place beyond the infinite, a time transcending the eternal." It is rather insane to think that a part of God, a part of the All that includes everything, could somehow split off and separate from everything. Only insanity could grant an illusory power past omnipotence, a place beyond the infinite, and time that interrupts eternity. Only in an insane world do "the deathless come to die, the all-encompassing to suffer loss, and the timeless to be made the slaves of time." Only here can the changeless change and the peace of God give way to chaos. Only here do we hold onto beliefs that split the mind and force us to choose between Heaven and earth, real and unreal, or fantasy and Reality, according to the voice we listen to.

While we cannot define nothingness, we can define what it is not. It is not God. It can temporarily obstruct our sight as a blindfold would, but it cannot darken our actual path or make the way itself grow darker. Reality is awash in luminous light as soon as we remove the blindfold of illusion that obstructs it. The ego is an attack on God because it deceives us into believing we dwell in the darkness of separation, rather than within the unified Mind of God. It convinces us we are somehow apart from our Creator, causing us to arrogantly appear to be what God didn't create. But God created everything eternal, just as the ego created everything perishable.

Of this *ACIM* says,

"However ridiculous the idea of attacking God may be to the sane mind, never forget that the ego is not sane. It represents a delusional system and speaks for it. Listening to the ego's voice means that you believe it is possible to attack God, and that a part of Him has been torn away by you. Fear of retaliation from without follows, because the severity of the guilt is so acute that is must be projected. Whatever you accept into your mind has reality for you. It is your acceptance of it that makes it real. If you enthrone the ego in your mind, your allowing it to enter makes it your reality. This is because the mind is capable of creating reality or making illusions."

The ego's survival depends on our willingness to tolerate it. Its greatest weakness is our own spiritual strength, which is why it fights so hard to keep us unaware of who we really are. When we identify with the ego's smallness and insignificance, we embrace weakness within us and perpetuate it by lying to ourselves about our own strength, and thus we are lulled into a sense of complacency, powerlessness, and mindlessness. "The ego arose from the separation, and its continued existence depends on your continuing belief in the separation." Correcting this belief is our primary purpose in this world, and our disbelief in our own spiritual power is the only thing that keeps us trapped in the darkness of delusion and denying our divinity. The ego knows if we ever stop believing in its existence it will have no existence, since nothing unreal exists, so it holds tightly onto our chains of perceptual imprisonment to ensure this doesn't happen.

Our release requires we change our minds and withdraw our belief in the ego's delusional thought system.

> "Faith can keep the Son of God in chains as long as he believes he is in chains. And when he is released from them it will be simply because he no longer believes in them, withdrawing faith that they can hold him, and placing it in his freedom instead."

In his book *40 Days*, Alton Gansky relates the following story: Harry Houdini was a master escape artist who escaped every imaginable confinement, from straightjackets to multiple pairs of handcuffs. He boasted that no jail cell could hold him and no matter how difficult the escape was, he would always reappear minutes later. It happened every time, except one.

Once, he accepted an invitation to demonstrate his skill. He confidently entered the jail cell in his street clothes and they shut the cell door. Once alone, he pulled a thin piece of metal from his belt and began working the lock. But something was wrong. He couldn't get it open. No matter how hard he tried Houdini could not disengage the lock. After two hours, he was exhausted and drenched with sweat. Frustrated, he admitted a rare defeat. Then someone walked up and simply pulled the cell door open. They tricked him. It had never been locked. The only lock placed on the door was the lock his own mind had created.

This story reinforces the idea that we are the only obstacle to our spiritual liberation. The dream may only be an illusion, but it is a very convincing one if we believe in it. But by looking more closely we realize the cell door is not locked and our journey to

God spans no distance, but awakens our Divine Mind to the knowledge of where we are and what we are. This is the miracle of awakening; it reminds us that we have a choice and that our power is not outside of us, but our problem is. We keep making the same mistake we made in the beginning, repeatedly. When we let go of God's hand, we coupled with the ego instead. But God never left us and is still walking with an extended hand in case we change our mind and let go of the ego's hand and take His instead. This is what the miracle does, it switches hands, changes masters, restores our right minds, removes mindlessness, and allows us to choose again from an entirely different perspective which makes for an easy choice.

This dragon is conquerable, yet it defeats nearly every opponent it faces on this earthly battlefield. The odds are not in our favor if we engage this battle on the ego's terms. We must be willing to engage in this battle on our own terms, not from a mindless egoic state, but from our place of power which is the grandeur of God. *ACIM* has a section titled, "Grandeur versus Grandiosity," but it may as well be titled "How to Slay the Ego Dragon." It says,

> "Grandeur is of God, and only of Him. Therefore, it is in you. Whenever you become aware of it, however dimly, you abandon the ego automatically, because in the presence of the grandeur of God the meaningless of the ego becomes perfectly apparent . . . The ego is immobilized in the presence of God's grandeur, because His grandeur establishes your freedom. Even the faintest hint of your reality literally drives the ego from your mind, because you will give up all investment in it."

And *that* is how we slay the dragon, by placing our awareness on the grandeur of God within us and abandon the dragon to restore the power we gave away when we chose to make ourselves tiny, vulnerable, and afraid. Incidentally, Pressfield tells us the slain dragon regenerates while we sleep, and when we wake up each morning he'll still be there, and he'll fight just as hard with just as many nasty tricks. However, if you slay the dragon once he will never have power over you again, because by beating him once you'll know you can beat him again. And that's a game changer that will transform your life.

While I obviously enjoyed Pressfield's dragon metaphor, I also like the Course's metaphor of the ego as the devil,

"The 'devil' is a frightening concept because he seems to be extremely powerful and extremely active. He is perceived as a force in combat with God, battling Him for possession of His creations. The devil deceives by lies and builds kingdoms in which everything is in direct opposition to God . . . . The mind can make the belief in separation very real and very fearful, and this belief is the 'devil.' It is powerful, active, destructive, and clearly in opposition to God, because it literally denies His Fatherhood. Look at your life and see what the devil has made."

As the Holy Spirit already told me after my Humorous Speech Contest defeat, the ego builds a shabby and unsheltered home for us because it is a bad builder and cannot build otherwise. We needn't try to make the ego's impoverished house stand. Let it fall. We will never be homeless.

Sometimes when selling real estate, a brokerage firm will encounter a client that has substituted reality for a dream and is dwelling within the domain of delusion. I call this scenario "commission impossible". This term denotes a seller who wants to enlist our services but completely ignores our market knowledge and expertise, assuming they have a better grasp of current selling conditions and fair market value than we do. The result of this blatant disregard for our professionalism is to request an asking price far beyond what any reasonable buyer would ever consider paying. In the beginning, this doesn't seem to matter to the stubborn seller, and if we want our services employed then we must obediently comply with their delusion. But some brokers won't comply. They deny the listing, making comments such as "Prosperity comes from being the second wife or the third realtor." This means they only accept listings that are "commission possible," which usually happens only after the seller has already tried unsuccessfully to sell an overpriced listing, and then consents in abject frustration and agrees to end their suffering by swallowing the bitter pill of reason.

Reason's goal is always to make something plain and obvious, and the introduction of reason into the ego's thought system is the beginning of its undoing. This is because reason and the ego are contradictory and cannot coexist within our awareness. How can the segment of the mind devoid of reason possibly understand what reason is? Reason is as foreign to the ego as suffering is to God. The term I use to describe this process of eventual arrival at reason is "seasoning". The longer a real estate listing languishes on the market with no showings and the only feedback from other Realtors being inquiries as to what the seller is smoking (and if I can get them some), the more likely the seller will wise up and correct their pricing if they really want to sell their property.

Spiritual awakening is no different. It eventually becomes an inevitable and unavoidable conclusion, since "God will not fail, nor ever has in anything." It is God's Will for us to be with Him, so His Will can only be denied temporarily. I loved the

Course's description of spiritual "seasoning", which inevitably results in the same unavoidable conclusion,

> "You can temporize, and you are capable of enormous procrastination, but you cannot depart entirely from your Creator, Who set the limits on your ability to miscreate. An imprisoned will engenders a situation which, in the extreme, becomes altogether intolerable. Tolerance for pain may be high, but it is not without limit. Eventually everyone begins to recognize, however dimly, that there *must* be a better way."

Realization of a better way will ultimately end our futile attempt to attack truth and defend error, causing us to succumb to reason and part ways with the ego. The introduction of reason to the split mind becomes a turning point that shifts our perspective and awakens spiritual vision. The Divine Mind has infinite patience and will allow as much "seasoning" as necessary for this to occur, but God's Answer prefers we find reason sooner rather than later, to avoid unnecessary suffering.

Of course, my unwillingness to continue to tolerate the ego now had to be tested, in the form of an unexpected pop quiz by the Universe. Shortly after making this commitment to go all-in, and undo rather than outdo, I began having a recurring dream. I've had lots of dreams in my life, but this was the first time I could ever remember having the same dream more than once. But it also seemed like more than just a dream, because after I started having the dream, with perfect clarity of recollection the following day (which never happens) then the same imagery from the dream started showing up during my meditation sessions, raising the obvious question, "What was my subconscious mind trying to tell me?"

In the dream, I am walking through a dry and dusty wasteland. I am alone and it is a desolate place. I don't really like it but I do what I must to survive. Although there is nothing to really see, I am looking for something, but I don't know what. I am lonely, and feel small, powerless, and vulnerable, but I keep walking. My path eventually leads me to the edge of the wasteland and a bridge ahead. I cannot see anything but darkness below the bridge or behind me but there is light on the other side. In fact, light appears to be everywhere across the bridge but somehow, I'm still standing in darkness. How can it simultaneously be day and night?

As I near the bridge, I notice a kindly gentleman on the far side of the bridge as if he is waiting for me. He seems excited to see me and asks me if I would like to cross. He smiles warmly and I sense his devotion to me. I feel compelled to cross the bridge, and I tell him this. He is pleased with my decision and tells me before I can cross, I must leave everything else behind. Although I was standing in darkness and wanted to cross into the light, I was surprised that I was not willing to abandon everything for this crossing quest. I am saddened by my decision because I really feel like I belong on the other side. I ask the man what is on the other side and he replies, "Truth and completion."

I ask if there is any way to obtain this from my side. He shakes his head and says, "No, on that side is only bleakness and illusion, where nothing is certain, and everything fails to satisfy."

I disagree with this statement as I think of Kim and Kaya, and how certain I am of my love for them and the satisfaction they bring to me. I could never just leave them behind forever and cross this bridge, as much as I wanted to. He tells me that as long as there is anything outside of me that keeps me on that side then I am not ready for a crossing into a union with truth. I ask about the love I would leave on this side and say surely that must be true. His reply is that this type of love is a barrier to truth and a substitute for true love.

This is confusing to me because I value their love so highly, which I always felt was a good thing. He points out that on my side of the bridge there is far more fear of love's lack than a true knowledge of love. He waits silently with an extended hand to assist me in the crossing if I so choose. Then the bridge itself speaks to me, acknowledging its purpose to assist my crossing whenever I am ready. I still don't understand, but the bridge tells me that when I do cross, I will understand completely, and the crossing will direct me straight to Love. The bridge tells me it will always be there if I ever want to return and take the extended hand of the man on the other side. I do feel his love, but I am just not prepared nor willing to leave the love of Kim and Kaya in exchange. That is simply too big of a sacrifice since my attachment to them is too strong to give up.

The bridge and the man know I am not ready to cross, but neither am I leaving. We are silent but it is not awkward, it is quite peaceful. The bridge then informs me that the love keeping me from crossing is a weapon disguised as a gift because it exists on the side of the bridge with hate, a bizarre state that only seems natural from my side, while only love exists upon crossing. The man seems to understand my hesitation and encourages me to return when this form of love no longer seems natural and sufficient, for that will mean I am ready to leave a form of love that believes in attack and battles its opposite, and unite with only love and nothing else. I am torn by disagreement with this statement yet know the truth in it. My split mind knew it was true, but didn't want to believe it, preferring instead to value a dreary world that often opposes love but still made it feel valuable enough to stay for.

The value of love from my side was confusing because it excluded all but a few, and then placed conditions on the love those few were offered. The man tells me this form of love frequently produces guilt, which belongs on my side of the bridge. He is not angry or disappointed, but he states that my choice does not change the truth that is on his side. He reminds me that my fear won't allow me to recognize truth for what it is because I have chosen what I wish to be true rather than what is true. He said I have decided not to know truth and have learned to carefully place obstructive barriers to ensure that I value what is not truth, placing myself in bondage rather than being free. He assured me that once I crossed the bridge, I would see things differently. The dream ended after he finished explaining that what I see on my side is a stigmatization of smallness, where what is strong and powerful is diminished down to appear small, weak, and powerless.

In recurring dreams, I noticed an increasing desire to cross the bridge each time, but whenever it was time to decide, I always opted to stay put for the same two reasons: Kim and Kaya. I knew I wanted to cross, but I stubbornly resisted because of the value I placed on love for my family and my unwillingness to ever willingly leave them behind. But each time was a little different, and I felt more and more drawn to cross, only to ultimately decide against it in the end. I was unwilling to cross, but not crossing was also becoming more and more intolerable.

Chapter 9

An Unexpected Tragedy

"We are not human beings having a spiritual
experience; we are spiritual beings having
a human experience."
Pierre Teilhard de Chardin

When it comes to spiritual instruction, you could do a lot worse than having Margie in one ear, Ocean in the other, and *ACIM* in front of you. I was almost complete with my 180-degree change of direction turnaround. The only thing remaining to finish this transition perfectly was to end the marital separation and restore unity to our family. I felt confident that was close, but I had no idea what we would have to go through to get there.

Thomas Partyka was a Christian who found Jesus in his late twenties and never let go, carrying his faith all his life without wavering, and instilled this faith in his children by example. Regardless of any possible differences in ideology, it is admirable to see people grab something positive, be changed by it, and then hold onto and practice it faithfully in a quest to improve and become the best possible version of themselves. Tom was like that. Another thing I admired about Tom was that he put love before judgment. His three kids did things he didn't approve of, but he made the decision long ago to love them first and foremost, and then deal with their behavior. His parenting priority was love, and that trumped any judgment or verbal attack, and all three of his kids loved him for it. They may have all had issues with their mother, but none of them had any issues with Tom.

Not only was Tom a great father, but he was also an amazing grandfather. He only had one grandchild, and that was Kaya. Tom's eyes sparkled whenever he was around Kaya, and Kaya had her grandpa wrapped around her little finger, and they both knew it. Because Tom supervised grounds maintenance at resort property accounts in South Maui, he had a flexible work schedule and often stopped by our house during the day before Kaya started attending school to play matching games, board games, assemble children's puzzles, and pretty much anything else Kaya wanted to do. Believe it or not, Kaya always won. We always knew he was throwing the games, but it wasn't until Kim and I started playing matching games with Kaya ourselves that we learned she was really good and could often beat one of us. Not every time like she did grandpa, but sometimes.

On November 5th, the day after my District speech competition, Tom had some extra time, so he went for a walk. On that walk he came to a crosswalk and paused before entering, and upon seeing he had the walk signal, he went. As he did, a car that was looking left to turn right did not see him in the crosswalk and struck him going only 5 miles per hour. Tom put his hands down on the hood to brace the brief impact and after the car bumped him, he fell backwards onto his behind, with his momentum carrying his head back to also bump the road. But Tom hopped right back up and as the driver got out and apologized Tom told him he was fine. The police arrived, and after they completed their police report Tom just wanted to go home. But the police told him because he fell and bumped his head then he should go to the hospital to be checked out, and that is where they took him. On the way to the hospital, he notified his kids that he was heading there but assured them he was fine. He told them they were just going to run some tests as a precaution, and he was planning to leave soon. One son visited him briefly, but Tom told him he was fine and could leave, so he did. The other son arrived after the first had left, and he saw something entirely different.

Apparently, Tom was on medication for high blood pressure which thins your blood. So, when he fell and bumped his head on the road, although there was little external blood, there was significant internal hemorrhaging around his brain. The blood thinning medication only made it worse. The second son was visiting with his father when he suddenly got woozy and then a flurry of activity surrounded them as his father slipped into unconsciousness right in front of him. A nurse quickly escorted this bewildered son from the room. One minute they were laughing and talking football, and the next his dad was unconscious, and he was being escorted to the waiting room. There was a long night of treatment that included an extremely late emergency surgery, lots of waiting, and then more waiting. Early in the morning the doctor emerged and informed us that he was out of surgery but had still not woken up. He was in a coma. They knew the hemorrhaging around the brain was bad and the surgery helped clean much of it out, but they honestly didn't know what would happen from here. He could go either way.

The kids went home to sleep for a while, and when everybody came back later that day there was no change to his condition. Kaya did not like seeing her grandpa with all those tubes and a respirator in him. She cried and told us that she didn't want to go back to the hospital again. Kim told her she did not have to. But Kim returned to the hospital every day, which meant I stayed with Kaya. I communicated with Kim a lot during this time, about her father, Kaya, and how she was holding up. Every day was emotionally grueling for her as she sat with him, talked to him, read to him, and prayed over him. I remember her coming home from the hospital in the evening, exhausted and in shock.

On November 8th after she returned home from the hospital, we put Kaya to bed and stayed up late to watch the results of the presidential election. Just two days into the ordeal of her father's coma, I could tell Kim was still in shock. This same sentiment registered upon the rest of the world that night when Donald Trump surprisingly lost the popular vote but still won enough electoral votes to become our next President. Kim obviously felt somewhat disconnected from it all, but I do remember her going to bed confused and highly surprised by this surreal election result.

The following day as thousands of protesters in cities nationwide marched against Trump with signs and slogans like "Not my president," with some even resorting to smashing windows and setting fire to garbage bins, David Remnick of The New Yorker, wrote an article about the election result titled "An American Tragedy" that began like this, "The election of Donald Trump to the Presidency is nothing less than a tragedy for the American republic, a tragedy for the Constitution, and a triumph for the forces, at home and abroad, of nativism, authoritarianism, misogyny, and racism. Trump's shocking victory, his ascension to the Presidency, is a sickening event in the history of the United States and liberal democracy. On January 20, 2017, we will bid farewell to the first African American President—a man of integrity, dignity, and generous spirit—and witness the inauguration of a con man who did little to spurn endorsement forces of xenophobia and white supremacy. It is impossible to react to this moment with anything less than revulsion and profound anxiety. There are, inevitably, miseries to come . . . ."

It was hard enough having Kim's father in a coma, but the rampant anger and national division that followed this election was unlike anything we'd ever seen before and was difficult to not be concerned about. But Kim stayed focused and kept the same hospital routine every day for a week, with no change to Tom's condition. The only hopeful thing that happened was once when Kim was holding his hand and talking to him, he squeezed her hand. She told the doctors about it, but they disregarded it as a muscle spasm. The doctors felt like the longer it took for him to exit the coma the more brain damage he would have from the internal hemorrhaging if he did return. After twelve days, the prognosis was grim. The doctors said although he was still alive, it wasn't likely that he was going to come out of the coma, and even if he did he would never fully recover, and at this point he would need a full-time caretaker based upon the amount of lost brain tissue and activity.

Tom had told his kids on more than one occasion, that if it ever came down to it and he was going to be incapacitated or on life support, he would not want that, and they should do whatever they could to avoid it. It almost seemed like his soul knew this would happen someday because he delivered this premonition to each of his kids on more than one occasion. Which meant when his kids met that day to decide what to do, as difficult as that decision was, they unanimously agreed to let him go. As the oldest child and the one that was at the hospital the most, Kim had become the family spokesperson and point of contact for the doctors. It was heart-wrenching for Kim to make that decision with her brothers, and then have to tell the doctors at the hospital to go ahead and take her father off life support and let him pass.

On November 17th, after almost two weeks of immeasurable emotional turmoil for Kim and her brothers, they decided to meet at the hospital and remove him from life support. But once they saw Tom's bodily reaction to being removed from life support, they could not bear to stay in the room with him and had to go to the waiting room until the doctors informed them a little later that it was over, and he had passed. There were tears and hugs, of course, and everybody went home in a stupor. Kaya was only six years old and really loved her grandpa, so it was an exceedingly difficult day for her also, being the first time anybody she loved had ever died. I remembered the confusion and inability to grasp the concept of death the first time I was introduced to it, when my mother and grandmother were killed by a drunk driver when I was only four years old. I was pretty much in denial at that age and always believed my mother would come back some day, but of course she never did, and I eventually got used to not having her around.

During that difficult period, my strategy to just love Kim and Kaya unconditionally no matter what could not have been applied at a better time. Kim was clearly devastated by this tragic and unexpected loss, and I was there to love her and let her lean on me and she did. We had been making progress in our relationship for months and she could see I was no longer the same man she separated from. We had been dating and attending Couples Communication classes together and were pretty much as close as we had ever been before the separation. She knew my recent awakening and decision to identify with a different perception of Self was genuine and would be a permanent part of me forever. She had enjoyed having me around for the past couple of months, and especially now that she was struggling emotionally from the passing of her father. One day in the car she just blurted out that she wanted me to move back home. There was no discussion about it beforehand, no fanfare or any explanation of conditions and expectations, just a clear and simple directive to correct the only thing left to correct within our relationship, the restoration of our family unit. I was both happy and sad at the same time. I was happy to be reuniting with my family, but so sad for Kim and what she was going through with both her father and her daughter, who was similarly struggling.

Ocean contacted me during the time Tom was in a coma, so she knew what was happening with us personally. She was sensitive to the issue, but I welcomed the distraction, so we discussed switching from looking at homes to vacant land, since she had exhausted all the existing home inventory. We started walking large land parcels together with her same meditative showing procedure. Soon after Kim's dad passed, I had a showing appointment with Ocean and Kim decided to come along because she felt she needed Ocean's spiritual perspective. When we met Ocean at the property, Kim jumped out of the car and Ocean got out of her truck, and without saying a word to each other they embraced in a tight and enduring hug. People like Ocean and Margie can shift your spiritual perspective without even saying a word.

I called Margie the day Tom died to give her the news. She was very compassionate, and we chatted for a while. Since the presidential election was such a hot topic of concern, and I knew she had daily communication with higher wisdom, I asked for her take on the matter. She was, as always, very peaceful, and unconcerned, and confided that the reason she was not worried was because she had been receiving messages from the Holy Spirit about it, the latest one coming that very morning. As I probed for more information, she simply said everything was in divine order. Then she explained how the political well had become dirty and a social and spiritual revolution was needed to cleanse it, and the Holy Spirit would use all of this as a catalyst for a mass awakening. I told her that sounded a lot like Trump's campaign promise to "drain the swamp," but she had no idea what I was talking about. Since she didn't take the bait, I pressed her to tell me if that meant Trump was going to be a good or a bad president, meaning was his election going to start this revolution by the people as was happening now, or was he going to initiate it himself as the president. She didn't know and didn't care, she simply iterated that he would be a catalyst for a great awakening and didn't understand my desire to know more than that. She asked if I would like to see her recent dictation from the Holy Spirit on this matter. I replied affirmatively and asked her to please email it to me. As soon as I read the comments from the Holy Spirit, I immediately felt more at peace.

Margie sent me three of her daily dictations from the Holy Spirit. The first was dated <u>November 9, 2016</u> and mentioned the election was now over and although new leaders are installed as instruments of the ego in the "consensual reality" of the dream, God will never change. He told her, "I have assisted every dreamer to use this election to ultimately come to the Election of the Holy Spirit as the Leader of their life." He said the history of mankind is composed of a series of rebellions, starting with the Son's departure from God and attempt to bring order through his own means. But all change is an aspect of that system and no choice made by the ego is ever a choice for God. It is always a choice for the "betterment of life in the world of bodies." He said to "step aside from the dream and watch the show. Do not take sides. I am the Peace that exists in you, as you. Listen to no one." He expressed that "the new president has his mission, but this is not the deletion of the ego thought system which is our focus. Let the world unfold as it does. Be unaffected. Accept what is true—All are One."

On <u>November 12, 2016,</u> He reminded her that everyone she meets is a projection of her own mind, placed by Him. "Everything you see in this world was constructed by Me, arranged for your viewing to wake you up." With the presidential election over she only sees the unfolding of His Divine Will, which puts her at peace and accepts His Will as hers, meaning "loving what is." He spoke of a United Sonship, iterating there is only One Son. "Know also that the president-elect is being used as an instrument of change, stirring the nations to look below the surface for solutions that will eventually lead to the awakening of a world asleep. Ultimately, the energetic experience of wanting a better way will lead to a change of mind, releasing man from enslavement to his egoic perceptions." He admonished her to look deep inside because only by turning inward will man become aware that he is dreaming his whole world, and that as peace is found internally, the desire for conflict vanishes. He requested she let Him live her to become One with God, so He could bring peace.

November 17, 2016 was the day Tom passed. The Holy Spirit told her that day He never leaves her side as her right hand and right mind, even when she is not aware of Him. He said when fear arises, she should release it to Him and know He will carry her through all storms and troubled waters, since nothing in a dream is to be feared. "An election, a threat, both express the insidious nature of fear—passing phantoms. The ego mind loves to rally around a frightening event to keep man entrenched in the fear of life itself. Look at it as a TV drama, a soap opera, a silly show. This world is either an out picture of fear or a symbol of love. I have told you that the president-elect will bring a revolution of awakening to the planet. He is being used to open new channels in the mind for humanity to see more clearly." He also warned that living in fear stymies the enjoyment of life and that no harm can come when you know We are One. He finished by saying He will release her from all pain and suffering within the dream and that each experience man needs to awaken to His Presence will be given, and that will open the pathway to peace.

Once again, the right message showed up at the right time to aid me during a difficult period. I was touched by the Holy Spirit's messages of love and peace that replaced the fear, sadness, and anxiety of everything else going on in the world. Not only was Margie's connection to the Holy Spirit able to keep her incredibly calm during a time of turmoil, but she was able to extend that effect to me as well. For the first time since Tom's accident and the presidential election that so effectively divided our country, I felt hope and greater trust in the divine intelligence that supports us.

Tom had been involved in divorce proceedings for years at the time of his accident, which was part of the reason his kids had issues with their mom. She had separated from Tom and left Maui and was now living in Texas, but the divorce was still not final due to delays on her end. Since Tom had no will at the time of his death this meant all of his assets would legally pass to his estranged wife, even though he had been attempting to divorce her for years and none of the family was on speaking terms with her. Although Kim was the one who sat with him every day and had to make the difficult decision to remove him from life support, and was now planning his memorial and cremation, she had no access to any of his financial resources to cover these necessary expenses. All of that was taken by her mother, who incidentally refused to contribute anything for the expenses. She didn't even attend the memorial but had the audacity to tell us that any sympathy money we received at the memorial was also to be forwarded to her. Kim and I talked about it and decided we would take whatever expenses were needed from our real estate business. The company could cover it and we'd deal with it later.

The next few weeks were a challenge to coordinate the funeral preparations while communicating and arranging lodging accommodations with travel plans for family on the mainland that were coming out for Tom's memorial. Kim enlarged and framed some of her favorite pictures of her dad with his children and granddaughter. The memorial was held at his church. Kim's brother Tommy spoke, and I also stood and tearfully honored him. Kim arranged a very soothing and symbolic release of white doves after the service, and their elevation and disappearance into the Maui sky resembled purity ascending to heaven. After the memorial there was a potluck at the same church. We came home late and emotionally exhausted, but glad to have closure to it all.

Kim and Kaya went right to bed and I carried in the framed photographs from the car and set them on the kitchen table. I closed the garage and was locking up the house and turning off lights in preparation for bed when I suddenly felt a presence.

It was both a feeling and a knowing that there was life energy around me. As I looked at the pictures on the kitchen table, I felt the spirit of Tom move through me, which identified the presence I had felt. I discovered we could speak telepathically when he said to my mind, "Take care of my girls." I assured him that I would and reminded him that they were my girls too. He communicated his peace to me, and he left, leaving me full of gratitude for yet another confirmation that we are not these physical bodies, and we didn't begin at birth and we definitely don't end at death.

The next few weeks were hard on Kim and there were lots of condolences and sympathy cards and gifts. One gift she put on top of the piano without paying much attention to in her state of grief. During one of the rougher days that followed Kim was sitting on a chair by the kitchen table and looking out the window, missing her father. I had told her about my communication with him on the night of his memorial and she enjoyed hearing it, but now she wanted her own sign of living. Her dad loved butterflies for the symbolism represented by the metamorphosis. He felt he could really relate to that concept from his conversion to Christianity. I could relate to it too after my experience changed me. So, Kim decided to ask for a butterfly sign, something to know he was okay. I wasn't there when this happened, but this was a bold request because butterflies were not that prevalent where we lived and I'd never seen any on that side of the house by this window, since it is a narrow, somewhat enclosed walkway with areca palms and stepping-stones, but no flowering foliage.

Just then, something metal on the piano slightly twists and catches the outside sun and glistens. She looks closer. It is a butterfly. She set this sympathy gift down on the piano and never even noticed that the little metal piece that hangs from the stand was shaped like a butterfly. Not only that, but it turned to catch the sun and glisten in her eye right at the precise moment that she asked for a butterfly sign from her father. Message received. She felt at peace, and part of a much bigger spiritual reality. She progressively felt better after that calming experience and was able to continue to find peace within this temporary separation, knowing that love binds eternally so they would always be connected. I felt like Margie's message from the Holy Spirit on the very day of her father's death may have actually been for Kim so I shared this part with her: "You are with me and nothing can sever our relationship. I never leave your side. I am your right hand, your right mind . . . even when you are not aware of me. Day to day, moment to moment, I am there."

Moving home was a happy day. I didn't have much stuff to move so it was over within a couple of hours. As I was putting things away in the bedroom it struck me that my new spiritual perspective had not required any sacrifice at all. The entire idea of sacrifice belongs to the ego, and only by letting go of the illusion of sacrifice did I make room for another thought system begin to take hold in my mind. It is not a sacrifice to give up the things of the world, because how can the sacrifice of nothing mean anything? Is it a sacrifice to give up pain? Once your spiritual vision has glimpsed the perfection of Heaven would you look back with longing on a slaughterhouse? My decision to become right-minded had been nothing but positively beneficial for me in every way imaginable. There was not a single area of my life that had not improved due to my recent shift in perception, and the miraculous effect of this perception shift was undeniable. "Decide for God, and everything is given you at no cost at all. Decide against Him, and you choose nothing, at the expense of the awareness of everything." Even my business was doing better than it had done in years. It seemed like the loss of stress and anxiety in favor of personal peace was good business, and the less I worried about money the less reason I had to worry.

Kaya came into the room to talk to me while I was putting my things away, and it was as if I had never left, even though I had been gone for many months. Not only were Kim and I closer than we had ever been, but now Kaya and I were also. Unconditional love is the only way to love. There used to be so many things that set me off and damaged my personal relationships, but now I just let that stuff go, realizing the importance of following Tom's example of applying love first. When suffering a major life tragedy like the one that Kim and Kaya were going through now, it helps to lead with love and let everything else fall where it may.

Within days of moving back home I received some sad news from Ocean. She told me now that Donald Trump had been elected, she was going to stop looking at property with me and withdraw her spiritual energy work for a time and really focus on assisting to end the manipulation and brainwashing that was going on in our world today. I had no idea what she was referring to but wondered if this had anything to do with the revolution of political and social institutions that Margie's messages had mentioned. Margie had said these changes would be a disruption that would serve as a catalyst to cause people worldwide to question their beliefs and pursue peace and unity instead, stimulating a great awakening. Ocean simply said the Universe told her she would be needed in the coming years. At the time I was completely oblivious to the political activities of the world, but it didn't escape my attention that the two most spiritual people I knew were treating Trump's election as anything but just another four-year election. The old me would have been fearful of their dramatic responses to this specific election event, but the new me was somewhat apathetic since I knew it would all bring about a positive outcome in the end.

In my last conversation with Ocean she told me she would no longer be answering any phone calls or emails, but it was important that I know she had been selected by the Universe to deliver me a personal and very specific message that provided guidance during my critical spiritual transition. She affirmed that the Universe wanted her to communicate this message because I had been selected for a particular purpose with a timeline that needed to be set in motion at this time. She asked me if I understood, and through moist eyes I said that I did, while remembering Margie's similar message for me from the Holy Spirit. Whether this message came from Ocean's higher power of the Universe, or Margie's higher power of the Holy Spirit, it was obviously the same message coming from the same Source. Receiving this confirmation independently from both of my spiritual teachers was humbling, and mind-boggling.

Ocean's final words to me were threefold: peace, love, and trust. She asked me to live by these words. She requested I always be vigilant to maintain personal peace under all circumstances. Personal peace is evidence of union with the oneness of the Universe. She then said love should always be applied unconditionally, to my family as well as everyone else. Love should never be limited or held back for any reason because love is what we are and limiting it will limit our true nature because only we can deprive ourselves of anything. She said you do not have to do anything to find truth because every loving thought is true, and everything else is just a call for love. Lastly, she said to trust the Universe, and surrender to It knowing that It knows much better than I do how everything should be organized for the greater good. She repeated a phrase she had told me often, "Thy will be done." She said this is the ultimate way to realign our mind with the Will of the Universe and transcend any limitations we accept as our temporary truth. She admonished me to remember that since we are all one then there is only one Will that we share with the Universe. Since this Will always seeks the greatest good it is pointless to try to push the river, wanting something to be otherwise and outside of this one Will by thinking the small "I" knows better or is better able to judge what is happening or how things should flow. This non-acceptance will only create turbulence and choppy waters by destroying my personal peace and limiting my expression of love, which will cause suffering.

When I returned home, Kim was at the pool with Kaya, and I pulled her aside to tell her of my final conversation with Ocean. We sat at a table by the barbecue grill as I shared with her everything Ocean had said. Kim began to cry immediately and said how sad it was and what a great influence she had been on me. I knew exactly what she meant, because Ocean showed up in my life shortly after my awakening experience and without me even telling her about it, she confirmed it to Kim, who didn't think it was authentic. Ocean then stayed in our lives until just after our family was reunited, and I was enjoying the complete love and harmony that I had seen on the white screen of my mind at the very beginning of this spiritual journey. The remainder of my life pivoted on that epiphany, and now it identically matched my present life situation. I felt like Ocean's ruse of a real estate rental or purchase was nothing more than an excuse for the Universe to provide her an inroad to my life so that she could influence my spiritual transition as she did, at the specific time that she did. I was, of course, flattered and grateful for the special effort the Universe made on my behalf.

That was the last time I ever saw or spoke to Ocean, and I have really missed her at times. But her association with me had served its purpose and now I was back home with my family, and even closer to them than I had ever been before, just like I knew would eventually happen after seeing that vision on the white screen of my mind during the most difficult moment of my life six months ago. Peace. Love. Trust. Kim purchased and mounted these three memorable words across our long living room wall and we each hung a Christmas stocking from them. We were the only ones who understood their special significance, and how they held a symbolic meaning we would never forget.

There was only one Toastmasters meeting in December due to Christmas. Tom's memorial had only been three days earlier, but I wanted to get back into my routine. I also knew Margie was speaking and that is always a treat for me. So, I attended the meeting and sat at the back. Margie was our club's sergeant-at-arms, meaning she was responsible for meeting room preparation and hospitality. It was not uncommon to arrive and have her greet you and answer any meeting questions as she set out the forms and supplies.

But this time I arrived before she did, and as I watched her enter, I immediately noticed she had on a long and pretty Hawaiian dress. I had never paid much attention to Margie's wardrobe before, but this dress really stood out. She was at the front and I was at the back, but I heard a familiar Voice tell me to compliment her on the dress. I lazily agreed to do so when she brought the speech voting ballots and pencils to my table. As she made her way to the back, she began talking to somebody, and they were fully engaged in conversation when she was at my table, so I didn't want to interrupt her to compliment her on the dress. I was sure she already knew it looked nice anyway. But as she walked away from my table the Voice told me again to compliment her on the dress.

She finished the conversation, but she was not coming back near my table and the meeting was about to start. The Voice told me a third time to compliment her on the dress. I didn't understand why it was so important, but I got up and approached Margie's table where she was talking with someone. I waited until their conversation ended and then I leaned down to Margie and told her I just wanted to compliment her on the beautiful dress and that it looked nice on her.

I expected a cursory thanks and that would be the end of it. But she stopped cold when I said this, turned and locked eyes with me, and said contemplatively "Thanks. Thank you for saying that. You're going to hear about this dress in my speech tonight." That was an interesting response, I thought as I went and sat down. Just after the meeting started, a guy a little older than me, that I'd never seen at a meeting before, came in late and slipped into a seat at one of the back tables by me. A few minutes later, Margie was introduced and delivered this emotionally stirring speech.

"Fellow Toastmasters, two years ago at Christmas, Jay, a visitor on Maui, rented the condo next door to mine. One night during his stay he commented on the pretty string of Christmas lights on my lanai railing. A little later that evening he came back out with his own strand of lights and stretched them out on his lanai and then connected them together with mine and said we were now linked. I told him they looked beautiful and I was happy to be linked with his lights. He then told me that his birthday was the very next day.

"At eight the next morning, after finishing my morning walk, I saw the screen door to his condo open when I returned home from my walk on the beach. Although I couldn't see Jay inside his condo, I stood outside his door and briefly sang him Happy Birthday before entering my own condo. Soon Jay was at my door in tears. I invited him in, and we sat on my couch so he could regain his composure before talking. Through his tears he told me that six months ago his eighty-nine-year-old mother died. He went on to say that he was dreading this birthday because it would be the first time in his entire life, she would not be able to call and sing him Happy Birthday at precisely eight a.m., as was her annual ritual. He choked back tears as he told me he felt the hand of God in meeting me the day before his birthday and then to have me sing Happy Birthday to him at exactly eight, just like his mother always did. Jay has called me 'mom' ever since." Some of the women in our Toastmasters club got teary eyed, and even I felt a lump forming in the back of my throat.

"After Christmas he asked me if I could store his lights for his return again next Christmas. But before he returned to the mainland to begin the emotional chore of selling his recently deceased mother's house, he noted that I was about her same size and that she had some beautiful vintage Hawaiian dresses. His mother grew up in Hawaii and was the sixteen-year-old daughter of the admiral in command at Pearl Harbor the day it was attacked. She vividly remembered watching the Japanese pilots drop the bombs from their planes that day.

"Jay insisted that I have all of her beautiful Hawaiian clothes and he knew they would fit me since we were about the same size. He said she had many beautiful Hawaiian prints which would be perfect for my upcoming speaking events after the release of my book. After he returned to the mainland, he emailed me photos of the joy he experienced taking pictures while his partner tried the dresses on and modeled them for me to provide a preview before he shipped them. That year I received Christmas in May, when a heavy box arrived with thirty-five pounds of clothes in it. I felt like a princess dressing for the ball.

"A month later I was fifteen minutes away from being picked up to go to the airport for my very first book signing in Denver, when I decided to check my mail before leaving and opened the mailbox to find a rumpled envelope. I opened it up and inside was this beautiful dress." She steps away from the podium and strikes a pose. The dress really was beautiful, and very elegant.

"I couldn't believe my eyes. I guess there was one more dress that he found that didn't get shipped with the others. The absolute perfection of this dress arriving at that very moment was an incredibly clear sign that the Holy Spirit had arranged it all. I ran to my room to try it on before leaving. It was a perfect fit! I slipped it into the suitcase, overwhelmed with gratitude, and then I heard my Inner Voice say it was His gift to me for our first book signing. Of course, this book was written after hearing His Voice resulting in the publication of *One With God: Awakening Through the Voice of the Holy Spirit, Book 1*. This was His way of saying He is always with Me through the love shown to me by friends like Jay.

"I felt such joy arriving at My Favorite bookstore in Denver dressed in this beautiful Hawaiian dress and feeling clothed in love from Jay, his mother, and the Holy Spirit about whom I would be speaking that night. Last week Jay returned to vacation on Maui. We visited in my living room while looking outside as torrents of rain poured from the heavens onto the Christmas lights on our lanai balconies that brought us together two years ago and connected us in more ways than just Christmas lights can. And now today we celebrate our island dressed in brilliant, lush verdant green. I would also like to say that I am delighted Jay has asked to come and hear my speech this evening in honor of his mother, and our new friendship."

With this she gestures towards the guy sitting at the back by me and adds, "Thank you all for welcoming him," and she sits down. After the meeting everybody wanted to meet and say hello to Jay after such a heartwarming story. This time it was my turn to tell Margie, "Now I know why I was told to deliver you that message." I just didn't tell her it took the Divine Mind three separate requests to get me off my duff to do it.

After Tom's memorial we began to get ready for Christmas, which is Kim and Kaya's favorite holiday of the year. I was planning on something special for Kim this year. I figured if there was ever a time to go a little overboard at Christmas it might just be the year that you get separated, spiritually awakened, heal your soul and your relationship, and then get reunited better and stronger than ever before. That checks a lot of boxes for reasons to splurge on a special Christmas gift. So, I did. I bought the biggest and most expensive diamond ring they had . . . in Costco.

We were grocery shopping one day and with two girls I always must stop and look at anything shiny. They were looking at diamond rings in a display case and Kaya pointed to the biggest and most expensive one and told her mom that is the one she liked. Kim hadn't noticed that one yet but when she did, she ooohhs and aaahhs all over it. She agreed with Kaya and we continued grocery shopping. I'm sure Kim never thought in a million years that she would someday be wearing that very ring Kaya had selected for her. I definitely had the element of surprise going for me with this gift because I'd never spent that much money on anything I'd ever bought Kim, and I'd shelled out some serious cash in the past.

But I didn't want to just give it to her under the tree, that seemed too boring of a presentation for such an expensive oval diamond ring. Kaya kept asking me what I was getting mommy for Christmas, but I was afraid to tell her because I wasn't sure if she could keep it a secret. She was awfully young. But the more she pestered me the more I got her to commit to secrecy until I finally told her, because I wanted to anyway. She remembered the ring and was so excited that I actually bought it, especially after I had complained so much at the store about the price of it. I told her that was just to get mommy to think I wouldn't buy it, but I did, and now she needed to help me present it to her. I told her we were going to wrap a bunch of presents for mommy and hide them in various places around the house with rhyming notes attached to them that would give the clue for the next present, like a treasure hunt for presents, with the ring being the final gift. Kaya didn't need to know the reasons. As long as it made mommy happy, she was game for anything.

We wrapped the gifts together and then I thought up the rhyming clues and we wrote them on each of the gifts. We had to remember which gift was in each hiding place because the gift itself had to be found to receive the clue to the next hiding place. We waited until closer to Christmas to do the actual hiding. We invited Margie over to our house for a Christmas music ukulele concert on the 23rd. Margie had learned to play the ukulele since moving to Maui and Kaya was only six but she had already taken a strong interest in music, excelling in piano but also taking ukulele, violin and singing lessons by that age. She was strongest in piano and singing, but she also enjoyed the ukulele. However, the violin was not something she wanted to continue taking lessons for.

Kaya loves any company at the house, but especially company that plays music with her. She was so excited! When Margie arrived, we started playing and singing Christmas songs together. If Kaya knew how to play the song on the piano, then she would leave the sofa and go play the piano while Margie played the ukulele. It wasn't anything we could have sold admission tickets for, but it was a lot of fun and provided plenty of laughs. It was nice to see Margie bonding with Kaya over something they both enjoyed. When the evening was over both Kaya and Kim gave Margie a big hug and wished her Merry Christmas and thanked her for coming over.

The next day, Kaya and I waited until Kim left for the gym and we spent that time hiding all of the gifts in the proper sequence and location for their clues. I think Kaya was more excited to escort her mother through the present hunt than she was to open her own presents. The ring itself was hidden in Kaya's room in her stuffed animal net and the clue was Minnie Mouse, who happened to be holding the gift-wrapped ring. The present hunt was a blast for all of us and Kim liked the clever rhyming clues. Once she got the final present, she ran downstairs to open it and when she did, she could not believe her eyes when she saw the beautiful diamond ring Kaya picked out for her, which made it all the more significant. She put it on her hand and looked at it all day. It was so large it was kind of hard to miss. For years now she has enjoyed looking at it every day, and she always feels naked without it.

My firstborn son Jordan returned to Maui to visit between Christmas and New Year's. He also brought his fiancé, now wife, whom I had not met before. It was great to see them, but they were together all the time and I really wanted some time with him alone to share my spiritual awakening experience with him. The last time he visited us, me and Kim were just a few months away from our separation and things were not great between us. I wanted him to not only see the difference but also hear why everything had changed for the better with me. I asked him if we could go out to dinner alone so I could talk to him. Over dinner I told him that I had missed the purpose of my life until recently. I told him nothing is more important than love, and that if he really wants to find happiness in a relationship then he will need to let go of his attachment to his ego and always defer to love, as that is the only path to true happiness. It was an awkward lecture in some respects, and I'm sure he wasn't expecting it and probably felt a little ambushed by it, but I didn't want him to reach my age before realizing there *is* a better way. He was receptive and very cordial, despite the awkwardness of my ambush. Young men see the world differently than older men, but I felt like he understood the intent of what I was trying to say and seemed to appreciate it. That Christmas remains one of my most memorable to this day. I finally felt like I was right where I wanted to be.

Chapter 10

Applying Forgiveness

"You dream of a desert, where mirages are your
rulers and tormentors, yet these images come
from you. Father did not make the desert,
and your home is still with Him.
To return, forgive your brother,
for only then do you forgive yourself."
Jesus speaking to Thomas in
Disappearance of the Universe

After the holidays ended Jordan and his fiancé returned home and
I continued englutting the Course. I had read about ninety percent
of it when I came across a section titled "The Hero of the Dream."
It was only three pages long, but it stood out to me as particularly
profound, so I read it again. Then I read it a third time and still
wanted to go deeper, so on January 9th I emailed Margie and
requested a meeting to discuss the rich content within these
pages. She enthusiastically agreed and said she would review that
portion of the text prior to meeting on the afternoon of the 11th.
On the 10th she sent me this email:

> "You are the Holy Spirit's impetus for us both to
> achieve CLARITY. I am so grateful and have been
> writing with Him, rereading "Hero," and feel a new

sense of clarity! I started *ACIM* 33 years ago—and
today it makes sense.
We are One."

This was obviously an exciting email and it had me looking
forward to our meeting. By the time I arrived at her condo the next
day I had typed out those pages so we could each have a hard
copy to reference during our discussion. I asked if I could start by
reading it aloud and stop when I had questions. She agreed and
we began. It started out by making clear that in the ego's dream
of separation the body is the hero and central figure that makes
the dream possible. As long as we appear to be within this dream
of separation, the body will constantly pretend to be real and
relevant, in an attempt to prove to the world that its existence is
real. It will do anything to be seen, heard, and believed. The
body's purpose within the dream will never change, as it tries to
teach it is cause, and you are its effect. When in reality, the
singular Self is the cause of the dream, and the body is just an
inconsequential effect of that dream, but causeless effects within
a dream are not real and don't exist.

I stopped reading as I remembered a Toastmasters speech
that Margie began with the line, "This world is an illusion." It was
a shocking opening statement and she smiled when I reminded
her of it, adding, "Illusions are investments that only last as long
as they are valued, but we can dispel illusions at any time by
withdrawing all investment value from them. We give life its
meaning by ascribing it ourselves. But when dream figures are
seen as they truly are, they cease to have any effect, because only
within the dream do these false effects appear real."

I agreed and we read on as the Course asked if we were
willing to take a closer look at these effects posing as cause, and
stop allowing them to operate as cause so we can escape these
worldly dream-like effects. If we don't repossess this power then

we continue to empower the dream by ascribing it cause, instead of inconsequential effect. By looking at the dream's beginning it becomes much easier to see and understand the ascribed cause, and how dream figures are merely an effect of that cause. But dream figures don't remember their initial attack upon themselves, when they attempted to separate from everything that is, nor do they believe there really was a time when a world of separated bodies could ever have been conceived as real. Being One with God, it should have been easy to see this idea of separation as an illusion too ridiculous to be seriously considered for anything except laughter. But we did not laugh these ideas away, and now look at how serious this illusory idea of separation has become. I read slowly and thoughtfully one of my favorite phrases in all of *ACIM* about the illusion of separation and how we should respond to it, "Into eternity, where all is one, there crept a tiny, mad idea, at which the Son of God remembered not to laugh. In his forgetting did the thought become a serious idea, and possible of both accomplishment and real effects. Together, we can laugh them both away, and understand that time cannot intrude upon eternity. It is a joke to think that time can come to circumvent eternity . . . . "

I love the perspective shift that comes from reading the Course, and even more so when reading it with Margie. This phrase stood out to me, "It is a joke to think that time can come to circumvent eternity . . . ." I paused, and then read it again with more levity.

Margie sensed what I was doing and seemed pleased, adding, "The problem was not the thought or idea of separation, the problem was that we took it so seriously. We simply listened to the wrong teacher and made the wrong choice. God is not mad at us for this. How could He be when it never really happened? God is the only cause, so the causeless must be an illusion. For God to be angry He would have to acknowledge this illusion and make it real. Jesus is telling us to laugh away the non-existent effects of this error just as we would a joke."

I chuckled and replied, "The next time somebody asks me if I've heard any good jokes lately, I'm going to say 'Yes, it is a joke to think that time can come to circumvent eternity,' and I laughed out loud at my own joke.

Margie laughed too, and said, "The Joker has been un-masked, and it is the ego." She was still smiling when she added, "But this Joker wants you to take the world too seriously, when it should be met with laughter and disbelief instead, because this world was made by the ego as an attack upon God. This is not a cause for fear, it is grounds for laughter, which is the only appropriate response to such foolishness. Imagine the delusion and insanity necessary for the ego to puff up its puny chest and attack the perfect, all-encompassing, and all-powerful. How silly is it to accept a false belief that can only exist within the realm of illusion, and that appears to usurp God's power? No wonder we feel guilty for believing such rubbish. As Shakespeare said, 'It is a tale told by an idiot, full of sound and fury, signifying nothing. Nothing will come of nothing.' That is an appropriate response to the tiny, mad idea of separation, because nothing cannot ever be anything."

I nodded and smiled at her description of the ego's insane logic. She continued, "Without a proper perspective and consid-eration of the cause of this error, the effects do seem dire. But they only follow the cause, and effects of effects are just illusions piled upon illusions, all amounting to nothingness from an idea that never should have been taken seriously in the first place, and still shouldn't. The dream of our false identity appears real to us, but it is laughable from an eternal perspective, where the reality of perfect oneness encompasses all. An insane world appears to trap the timeless Self within time, creating an illusion where God can attack Himself, where a separated brother can appear as an enemy, and where one infinite mind can appear separated and restrictively contained within a finite body. All of these effects are caused by valuing ridiculous ideas that are nothing more than a joke to be laughed at. Don't let the Joker deceive you." Margie helped me see that no matter how much we may appear to be victims of effects; we are clearly their cause. As strange as this idea had seemed to me at first, I now knew the dream world did not really exist, and our experience here was just a way to depict our own internal frame of reference.

I read further about how our subconscious sense of loss that derived from losing and then forgetting our perfect oneness with God created unconscious guilt, which now insidiously accompanies us on this unhappy journey and is what makes separation appear real. The effect of this internal guilt is then projected to a place outside of us, within a body on a dream world. That body houses this guilt but attempts to get rid of it by projecting it onto other dream characters. That way this guilt appears to be outside of us rather than within our own mind. This confinement of guilt to a body requires us to accept the illusion of sin and separation when we are pure, innocent, and guiltless. This projection of a false belief into an illusion has not changed our reality at all, and our distorted perception only causes guilt-ridden effects to manifest suffering.

"We continually project this illusion of self, because if we don't then the illusion of self will disappear. Truth lies beyond this illusion." Margie said during a break in the reading. "Projection makes perception. We look inside first, decide the kind of world we want to see and then we project that world outside, making it the truth *as we see it*. We make it true by our interpretation of what it is we are seeing. If we are using perception to justify our mistakes, we will see a world of evil, destruction, malice, envy, and despair. It is this world we must learn to forgive, because we are seeing what is not true. We've distorted the world to see what is not really there. As we learn to recognize these perceptual errors, we must also learn to forgive them. This forgiveness of others is actually just forgiveness of ourselves, and that is achieved by looking beyond our humorous projection of distorted self-concepts to the Self God created in us and as us."

I read on about the body being a learning device that communicates the extent of guilt that needs to be healed, allowing us to witness it and then demonstrate our transcendence of it as we heal it with forgiveness. This restores the perfect innocence and guiltlessness that has always been ours. Eternity has not been disrupted by the tiny, mad idea that resulted in seemingly causing these effects. The Course says, "Not one note in Heaven's song was missed." Nothing has changed in God's reality. Yet this impossible idea of separation, which was corrected within the Mind of God without missing a single note in the song of Love, is believed and played out here as if time could somehow circumvent eternity. Margie explained it is our unconscious guilt that continues to engage this insane idea, so that is what must be healed, and our lessons will repeat until they are learned. We appear to be stuck in a time warp of repetitive lessons until they are learned and transcended, until we correct our false perception and convert it to true knowledge. That graduation removes our need for earth school and restores our unity with God. As the Bhagavad Gita says, "every creature in the universe is subject to rebirth, except the one who is united with Me" (8:16).

Even though it appears we have no power within the dream, we do. This is precisely because we are the cause of the dream and not its effect. This power is based solely upon our perspective, and whether we identify with the ego's false idea of separation or with God's reality of spiritual oneness. Any expression of guilt that surfaces upon our judgment and condemnation of others is our own guilt being displayed externally so that we can identify it and isolate it for the perception correction that is required to heal it. Thus, the external guilt we ascribe to anyone becomes evidence of internal guilt we need to forgive in order to heal our own mind and restore our true power of perfect Oneness with God.

Once again, Margie added some insight to help me understand. "Judgment you taught yourself. Vision is the means of salvation and vision is learned from God, Who is trying to undo your own false teaching. God does not limit, so you can only be deprived by yourself. Thinking otherwise only serves to justify your placement of guilt on others in an attempt to establish your own innocence. But innocence cannot be acquired by giving your guilt to someone else. Whenever this game of guilt projection is played it always results in loss. Someone else must lose their innocence so that you can take it from them and make it your own."

We paused to briefly discuss how we delude ourselves into judging, blaming, and condemning others without being aware that the cause of this guilt comes from our own minds. We do this because we don't want the guilt, so if our judgment justifies the condemnation of others then we can project it away and make it appear to rest on them instead. This allows us to retain our own innocence at their expense, when in reality we are already innocent and this judgment only serves to ascribe unconscious guilt that can only be released through forgiveness, or non-judgment. This is the paradoxical illusion of our distorted perception of seeing others as separate instead of as a resonant image of ourselves, while our actual reality of oneness with Source has never changed and is only one corrected perspective away. To make this perception correction we must laugh away the initial cause of separation, rather than dwell on the seriousness of its effects that we now appear to see. The cause deserves to be laughed at, rather than the effects to be judged or feared. Why bother judging effects when judging their cause removes them entirely?

The Course simply asks us to take a closer look at the idle dream that created time and witness how none of this can be the truth about what we really are. We need to notice how the dream marches on as we judge, blame, and condemn others to hide this unconscious guilt, when others are merely serving as the mirror from which we see ourselves. Margie explained how healing and restoring our perfect reality of being One with God requires acceptance and forgiveness, rather than judgment and guilt which only reinforces feelings of victimization. "It is a dream of separation that is made possible by judgment. Whenever you're judging, you are seeing separation and guilt, instead of acceptance and forgiveness. The transcendence of duality requires our acceptance of all experiences without judgment. Acceptance also develops trust in the divine intelligence that surrounds and supports us, while judgment demonstrates our disbelief in Oneness with God. Just remember that all is as it should be because all is not as it seems. When you refuse to judge and choose forgiveness instead, you will wake up from the dream world and enter Reality. Forgiveness is the source of our spiritual healing, and the messenger of God's Love."

It is only with this perspective that we will escape imprisonment and return to where we belong. The secret of our salvation lies in one simple truth; that we are doing this to ourselves. We are keeping salvation at bay by blaming instead of forgiving. No matter what the perceived form of attack is, or how that attack seems to cause our pain or suffering, this is always true. You cannot maintain your innocence by blaming others, because there is only one Self. Would you attack yourself? Of course not, and neither would you react to figures in a dream if you knew you were dreaming. They can have no effect on you unless you fail to recognize it is only a dream. These dream figures are only displaying your own unconscious guilt. Once this singular lesson of deliverance is learned, it frees you from all suffering. Until then, salvation remains a secret you are keeping from yourself. So, let this be your mantra: "I have done this thing, and it is this thing I will undo." This mantra withdraws all value from illusions and undoes suffering caused by a belief in separation. This is salvation, and how differently we will see and perceive the world when this truth is recognized.

If our entire dream and all the dream figures within it are the effect of our own unconscious guilt, then how is this guilt removed? Through forgiveness, of everybody for everything. If all guilt is representative of our own guilt, then every time we place blame anywhere, we are only placing it on our Self, condemning ourselves as guilty, and safely harboring and retaining that guilt within us, imprisoning ourselves as well as the one we judged guilty. Every time we find fault and blame another it proves guilt's existence within our own mind. Only forgiveness can heal this guilt. When we recognize that the very existence of blame anywhere indicates personal guilt, it becomes clear that everyone must be forgiven for everything. "Others" are only acting out for our own benefit, to show us our own unconscious guilt, and provide us with an opportunity to forgive them and thereby heal our own mind. Only this perspective results in the reduction and eventual elimination of judgment, blame and condemnation. This forgiveness perspective allows our awareness to be healed and restored to perfect innocence within the one mind of God, which is our inescapable reality, regardless of how convincingly we delude ourselves with serial dreams to the contrary. When we forgive the world, we are forgiving our mind of unconscious guilt. Once healed, we are free of it, having released it forever. It will no longer be part of our perception, and our awareness will be of oneness, without separation or suffering.

Margie had been letting me read but she interjected here to anchor the importance of this lesson, saying "Always remember that whatever you see in another, exists in both of you because what is the same cannot be different. All dream figures share an infinite and undifferentiated oneness that makes it impossible for them to be unlike each other. Whatever is in one is in both. You are either both guilty, or both innocent, but you can't be different when you share the same Self. It's important to realize that true forgiveness is not accomplished by first establishing the sin so that it can be forgiven. Doing this only makes the illusion real. You can't claim injury through identification of wrongdoing just to forgive the hurt and show you are the better person. This violates their innocence by forcing their retention of the sin, while elevating yourself to higher ground and disrupting your inherent equality. True forgiveness isn't forgiving what they did, its forgiving what they didn't do, by realizing that what happens within a dream doesn't *really* happen at all. The pardon and the sin cannot exist together because one denies the other and makes it false. Instead, you must attest the sin has no effect because the dream state isn't real, or else you imprison you both. As you see others, you see yourself."

This was definitely a different lens to look at the world through. I remember feeling resistance and discomfort because there was so much I still unconsciously judged and condemned within this guilty world. Only by becoming conscious of those judgments as seen in myself could I get better at forgiveness. This had always been a challenge of mine. I'd gotten better as I aged, but all my life I'd been a world-class grudge holder. Anybody who knew me could attest to this. I don't need to mention specific examples but there were many times that I went days without speaking to Kim. Holding the grudge was so much more work than forgiveness was. Sometimes I even forgot why I was holding the grudge in the first place. I only knew that if I was still holding it, then there must be a damn good reason. Little did I know back then that holding onto the grudge was nothing more than a confirmation of ego-identification and a reminder that I had forgotten who I really am.

Margie sensed my discomfort and stopped speaking, looking at me expectantly. "I don't think I've ever thought of guilt and forgiveness in that way," I said.

"In what way?" she asked.

"In the way that we are one mind and one spirit that has fragmented itself, so that every time we judge and find guilt, we are only finding it within our own mind, no matter how much we try to externalize it outside of us."

"Yes, and that is why forgiveness becomes so important. You can't just intellectualize the concept of oneness and leave it at that because you will not be healing the mind of the unconscious guilt caused by the separation, which is the only reason we are still appearing as separated. Without healing guilt through forgiveness, you continue the separation, and the devil wins."

"The devil?"

"There's no such thing. That's just a metaphor I use for the ego. Did you know that you can substitute ego for devil in virtually every reference in the Bible and it makes even more sense and becomes easier to understand? Try it sometime." This did sound like a fun experiment to me.

"It's just that forgiveness has always been hard for me, but I guess that was because I was seeing it from the ego's perspective of reactivity and guilty judgment. I'm definitely on a better track now, but it is still a struggle sometimes."

"Most people do struggle with this, but the miracle-minded understand forgiveness reverses the world's thinking and replaces it with God's thinking. God's reality is oneness, and since oneness implies uniformity of thought then our thinking must not be contrary to God's or oneness is not possible. How can you be One with God and think differently from Him?"

It was a rhetorical question, so I didn't bother to answer and asked a question of my own, "By miracle-minded you mean those having the thought system of the Holy Spirit?"

"Yes, it means the miracle is affecting your mind and healing it by restoring the reality of oneness instead of opposing it with the joke of separation, and the only way the miracle heals is through forgiveness. I cannot emphasize enough the importance of this because your spiritual practice and everything else you learn in the Course will be ineffective if you do not practice true forgiveness. Forgiveness reverses the ego's thought system and demonstrates a diminished belief in it, and thereby heals the split mind of the effects of the separation that caused the split in the first place. Everything hinges on forgiveness."

"And if miracle mindedness sees this world as an illusion because we instead identify as being One with God, then forgiveness should be easier because none of it is really happening within God's reality anyway."

"That's right. Forgiveness proves your belief in the innocence and oneness of Christ. If Christ is one mind, then everything you see is within that mind. Therefore, if you see guilt, that guilt is from your own mind. It is never outside of you because you are one. As such, all guilt you see anywhere is your own, and when you forgive it you are healing your own mind of it and thereby restoring oneness."

"Wow, that is such a mind-blowing perspective to think that everything I see in the world is within my own mind, and everything I condemn is just evidence of reflected guilt within my own mind."

"It is an expanded perspective rather than the limited one the ego offers. Which is why forgiveness of everybody for everything is the only way you will ever see your own innocence.

When you see your own innocence, then you will know your mind has been fully healed of all guilt. You can only heal and restore your own mind of guilt by not seeing it in others because we share the same mind. Think of it this way, you each carry salvation within you, but salvation is not selfish and cannot be attained alone. Giving is receiving. Salvation is achieved by sharing, and you receive yours by giving it to another and liberating their innocence through your forgiveness, rather than imprisoning you both in the guilt of your judgment. Forgive, be healed, and find your own salvation by freeing it within others. Forgiveness is the paradox of all paradoxes."

"I sure have a lot of forgiveness to do, because as much progress as I have made and as much as I've already reduced and eliminated judgment towards others by now seeing them as an extension of the oneness of Christ, I also still see so much guilt in the world. I need to forgive it and heal it from my mind."

"You always will see guilt before you are fully awakened to the oneness of Christ, but eventually you will come to know that your brother is just the mirror within which you see an image of yourself, and to deny him forgiveness is also to deny it to yourself. To forgive is to heal, and to judge is to make an inconsequential dream real for you. Remember that it is just a dream, and there is nothing you need to do within the dream except forgive it."

That's easier said than done, I thought to myself. Sensing my resistance to this all-important step towards salvation, Margie continued her encouragement: "A forgiven world is an entirely different world. You cannot imagine the difference this one simple concept will make in so many areas of your life. Do you want peace? Forgiveness offers it. Do you want happiness, a quiet mind, certainty of purpose, and a sense of worth and beauty that transcends the world? Forgiveness offers it. Do you want a quietness that cannot be disturbed, a gentleness that can never be hurt, a deep abiding comfort, and a rest so perfect it can never be upset? All of this forgiveness offers you. The entire purpose of this world is to correct our unbelief. Our only responsibility here is to learn how to accept the Atonement by undoing the projection of separation, and the means to do this is forgiveness. As I said, forgiveness is the source of our spiritual healing and the messenger of God's Love. Allow it to heal separation and lead you back to the Oneness of God."

After leaving Margie's condo I almost floated along the exterior walkway to the elevator. This whole experience of life was becoming such a lucid dream. I really felt like my awakening within the dream was transforming it to a happy dream, and not one to be taken so seriously because "it is a joke to think that time can come to circumvent eternity." Ocean had already explained to me that signs from the Universe are everywhere if we will just look for them and pay attention. As I approached the elevator leaving Margie's building, I spotted a white rectangular paper just outside the elevator door. Imagine my surprise when I got close enough to see that it was a Joker card, steps away from Margie's condo, in front of the only elevator available for me to depart the building, and right after the conversation we just had. Coincidence, or pennies from Heaven?

Jed McKenna, in his book *Spiritually Incorrect Enlightenment*, proposes that the universe often delivers probability-defying experiences that are "so utterly, preposterously, and incalculably unlikely that the only conclusion you can come to is that . . . the universe is really just a big, playful puppy." I rather like that metaphor. For me it symbolizes smiles, fun, laughter, excitement, happy acknowledgment, joyful interaction, loving engagement, complete love, unlimited acceptance, and an ability to interrupt anything else going on at the moment to get our undivided attention and adoration for one brief transcendent glimpse into eternity, in which we surrender to a perfect love that cannot be explained but is entirely understood. This was one of those transcendent moments. The puppy was playing with me, and it made me feel loved. I laughed out loud as I bent down to pick up the Joker card and shook my head and chuckled to myself on the elevator while staring in amazement at the Joker card in my hand, allowing a message from the eternal realm to speak to my Divine Mind in a familiar voiceless Voice, "Only the ego regards the function of time as a means of extending itself in place of eternity." This was followed by gentle, loving laughter and a repeated punchline that never gets old: "But it is a joke to think that time can come to circumvent eternity."

The following week, as if on cue to test my spiritual progression, the Universe gave me another pop quiz to test my ability to forgive according to my newly aligned thought system by providing me an extremely challenging forgiveness opportunity. Since I mostly maintained perfect peace within a daily context lately, I rarely felt the surge of anger that used to frequently rise within me and demand to be projected onto others. This was apparently a good reason for life to turn things up a notch and see if I could handle it and forgive it. The Course says we are always teaching, by demonstrating our beliefs through our actions and reactions to others.

During the week's reading I was moved and inspired by this passage in *ACIM* about the meaning behind Jesus' crucifixion,

> "I was persecuted as the world judges and did not share this evaluation for myself. And because I did not share it, I did not strengthen it. I therefore offered a different interpretation of attack, and one which I want to share with you . . . . As you teach so shall you learn. If you react as if you are persecuted, you are teaching persecution . . . . You are not asked to be crucified, which was part of my own teaching contribution. You are merely asked to follow my

example in the face of much less extreme temptations to misperceive, and not accept them as false justifications for anger . . . . I elected, for your sake and mine, to demonstrate that the most outrageous assault, as judged by the ego, does not matter. As the world judges these things but not as God knows them, I was betrayed, abandoned, beaten, torn, and finally killed. It was clear that this was only because of the projection of others onto me, since I had not harmed anyone and had healed many."

Armed with that perspective, we met with our dentist because Kaya had been losing her baby teeth as new permanent teeth grew in, and she had some issues with one in particular. It was an impacted baby molar that never pushed through her gums and now as her other permanent teeth were coming in around it, that impacted baby molar needed to come out to make room for new teeth. We got X-rays and discussed it and our dentist referred us to a pediatric oral surgeon that was supposedly the best on Maui. We met with him and set an appointment for the removal of the impacted tooth.

Kaya was understandably very apprehensive but we talked extensively to her about the simplicity of the procedure and why it was important to get that tooth out so the others could grow in, but she still entered the dental office for her extraction appointment very clingy to her parents. After we waited a while, they took us back to the surgical room where we met the recommended surgeon who would do the extraction. He went through the entire procedure with us in detail, showing us the impacted tooth on the X-rays while explaining the extraction process. It was the same stuff we heard before. Afterwards, he told us only one parent can be in the room with him while the extraction is performed. I didn't understand why I couldn't also be there when the room was plenty large enough, but he said it was not allowed. So, I went to the restaurant across the street and left Kim with a very worried Kaya.

As I was eating, Kim texted and told me the tooth was not coming out and it was really hurting Kaya, even with the localized anesthetic. I felt bad for Kaya and didn't understand why that would be the case since it was just a baby tooth. Shortly thereafter, I received another text from Kim demanding I get over there right away. She seemed terribly upset about something. I responded to her text right away but got no reply, so I hurriedly paid for my uneaten food and left. Her text tone and lack of response filled me with dread as I quickly headed back to the dental office. When I arrived, the receptionist sent me right back and I saw the doctor talking to Kim very intently and apologetically . . . and she was physically shaking as he spoke. Kaya was standing nearby and seemed to be in extreme pain and traumatized. Kim saw me and didn't want to say anything in front of Kaya so she told me, visibly upset, that he could explain it to me, and she stormed out with Kaya. I was a little freaked out by now, and it was about to get worse.

The doctor seemed pained to have to explain this all over again, but he hesitantly told me that instead of extracting Kaya's impacted baby molar he instead extracted her very visible, non-impacted first adult molar that was right next to it. I felt myself swoon, but when the blood started flowing back into my brain, I felt like my head was going to explode! I asked how he could do that when he knew and explained the exact tooth and procedure to us right before the extraction. He assured me that this had never happened before in his forty-year career as a dental surgeon. Oh, I felt much better knowing my daughter was the only person's mouth he had screwed up in over forty years of extractions. I was livid!

I asked why his assistant didn't stop him or correct him or say doctor why are you pulling out the first adult molar instead of the impacted baby tooth. It didn't seem like if you had your eyes open at all you could possibly make that big of an error. He told me when his hands are in the mouth it is hard for the assistant to see anything. I didn't like any of these answers and I had so many more questions. But I wanted to know solutions. How do we fix it? Can we put it back in? He says he tried that, but it wouldn't go back in and she was in too much pain to continue trying. He said we can do an implant but there are complications with that too. He informed me we could move her other teeth around to fill this one spot in. None of these solutions sounded appealing. I just wanted her first molar back. I still couldn't believe anyone who called himself a dental professional could make such a mistake.

As we walked to the front, I was maintaining my composure pretty well, and then he commented that a big guy like me could really do some damage if I decided to get physical. I'm thinking there is still time for that as I briefly considered putting him in a cross-face chicken wing or a cobra clutch bulldog. This enjoyable mental image temporarily appeased the anger welling up inside of me, but then it came right back. It had been a long time since I had felt this much anger. I met Kim in the lobby, and she was still steaming, and doing her best to comfort Kaya who was in a lot of pain from her molar, roots and all, getting violently and unnecessarily ripped out of her mouth. The office gave us a prescription for children's pain reliever, and we went right to the pharmacy to pick it up. When we got home with it, their office called and told us not to give her that prescription because they made a mistake, and it was too high of a dosage. Lucky for us we waited until we got home to administer it. So, they gave us another prescription and had to call it in to a different pharmacy closer to our house. I rushed over and picked it up right away since Kaya was still bleeding, crying, and complaining about the pain. I did so with absolutely no confidence at all in this doctor.

Neither Kim nor I slept much that night, and when Kaya woke up in tears and with blood stains all over her sheets from the nighttime bleeding, whatever brief sleep-induced calm I did enjoy was immediately gone, and I wanted to find and physically harm that doctor. His incompetence made me so angry! And then it happened. I began to hear thoughts pushing forward from somewhere deep in my mind that my anger had been repressing. "Anger is always the projection of separation, so it is never justified, and must be accepted as one's own responsibility rather than being blamed on others." I tried to repress this thought, only to have another one surface, "This guilt you see is your own. Forgive it to heal it." I tried to argue it is not, and then I realized that I was arguing on behalf of the ego, for the justification of blame and externally projected guilt.

Once I recognized the ego's thought system at work, I slowed my roll. But a large part of me also felt like right now I really wanted to be on the ego's side because . . . because . . . because of the guilt in my own mind that the ego can use to maintain the projection of the tiny, mad idea of separation from God. I could suddenly see it clearly within my own mind, I was passing on peace to make room for blame and guilt which obscures God and keeps me separate from Him. It was definitely not easy to do, but this is where I had to apply my spiritual practice. I understood it intellectually, but could I apply it pragmatically? I took several deep breaths and a few minutes later I managed to get my hateful thoughts under control. I did it. I forgave him. I did not want this anger, guilt, and ugliness in my mind any longer, so I forgave him. What in the past would have taken weeks, months, or even years to eventually forgive was forgiven within twenty-four hours. Peace returned and I was able to share that peaceful presence with Kim and Kaya who also needed it right then.

Forgiveness has many components, and much can be said about it, but I had to see the unreality of this world for myself before I could believe its illusory nature was enough of a reason to give forgiveness a fighting chance. Had I not been shown that this life is not at all what we think, then my stubbornness would never have allowed forgiveness a chance to become a part of my spiritual practice. But once my perception shifted away from this deceptive unreality then forgiveness flowed more easily and further reversed the world's thinking, as it simultaneously healed my mind of unconscious guilt.

Forgiveness is extremely difficult when ego-identified because the ego demands wrongs be retaliated. But when you realize that none of what appears to be happening is really happening from a spiritual perspective, then it is so much easier to look beyond the actions occurring within physical form and see the innocence of spirit instead. The body is the lower order, the perfection of spirit is God's higher order, and the mind is in the middle, willing movement in either direction according to our choice of identification. The Voice of the Divine Mind is now a constant part of my internal communication and interpretation of this world, and He is such a great Teacher. He makes corrections to my perception with questions that always contain the answers I need for me to understand and interpret the dream correctly.

That summer we went to Eastern Canada to attend the Quebec Music Festival, because I have a young daughter that is a music lover and because Shawn Mendes would be performing there. Although I've heard every Shawn Mendes song at least a hundred times, it was a great event and Kaya loved being there and attending all of the concerts. Maui boy Lukas Nelson was also there and was amazing, with little Kaya thinking his cuteness computation was a close second to Shawn's. There were hundreds of thousands of people attending so we rode the bus to the musical events and back, which was often an arduous process with so many people being transported. One night after a long night of music and then waiting extended periods in lengthy lines for a bus, we were finally moving up to get on the bus when a teenage boy cut the entire line without waiting at all. I had been waiting over twenty minutes to board the bus, so this act of rudeness made me angry, irritated, and annoyed.

The Divine Mind says "forgive him" so I do, and my peace of mind is restored. As we board the bus it is filling up fast and I end up being the first person getting on the bus that won't get a seat, and it is a fifteen minute bus ride to where we parked our car. Guess who jumps back into my mind and body slams my personal peace? That's right, the line cutter, because now he has got *my seat*. I begin to look for him and my inner Voice asks me, "You have already forgiven him, so why look for him to judge him?" It's a good question. I don't answer but I stop looking.

He isn't finished teaching though, and says, "Would you retract your forgiveness?"

"No." I answer immediately.

"Then let it go, because judgment cancels forgiveness and also retracts the peace that forgiveness brought."

"I wish I had a nickel for every time You've told me to let it go."

"That would be a lot of nickels," He agrees.

The Divine Mind also taught me that the emphasis on forgiveness, to heal our seemingly separated mind, must extend to the entire Sonship, which includes yourself. One night Kim came home late from the gym and was hungry. She had something specific to eat in the refrigerator, but I thoughtlessly ate it when I came home from work, which made Kim cry when she discovered it was gone. I felt terrible and apologized profusely.

It really bothered me, but she wouldn't let me go get her anything else. After a couple of hours of feeling bad, my inner Voice spoke.

"Forgiveness restores peace by bringing truth to all situations. That truth is the innocence of the Son of God. By forgiving others you acknowledge their innocence. But of what good is their innocence if you can't also see your own?

"I need to forgive myself?" I ask.

"Especially yourself. You are often much less forgiving of yourself than you are with others because as blame is withdrawn from without, there is a strong tendency to harbor it within. But if any judgment is present at all, then so is the ego. Perfect love doesn't judge. It looks on everything that is real with love and accepts only love from every situation. It filters everything else out as distraction and illusion, leaving only love to give and love to be received. Innocence in the Sonship must include the entire Sonship. Your spiritual practice to forgive others must also include forgiveness of yourself. Let it go."

"Another nickel . . . ."

"If only . . . . "

If you didn't know the Divine Mind has a sense of humor, then you should. I already mentioned His joviality, but humor and fun seem to go hand in hand with laughing away the tiny, mad idea of separation, and treating this world as it deserves to be treated; risibly, because our only reality is One with God. By not making this illusory world real, we can more easily laugh at it, until we forgive it enough to completely laugh it away.

Which is why I'm going to tell a story that makes me laugh, because it seems eating other people's food is a genetic inheritance. Growing up we called my father "Bear" because of what bears will do to your food supply if they wander into your campsite or cabin. Once I bought my dog, Scruffy, some dog jerky. Even though I usually hid my food, as the youngest of seven children, this was dog jerky, so I didn't bother and just left it on top of the refrigerator. There was a cartoonish drawing of a dog on the package, with his salivating tongue out as he looked at a strip of jerky with writing in bold, capped yellow letters at the top of the package that said, "Dog Jerky." How can you possibly mistake that? It is either jerky made *for* dogs, or jerky made *from* dogs, but either way it wasn't meant for human consumption. However, hunger must make us dumber because somehow Bear's selective perception only saw the word "jerky" and filtered out everything else.

I discovered this when I went into the living room and found him sitting on the couch chewing while watching TV. He looked up at me when I entered the room and said with a full and happy mouth, "Hey Donny, there's some beef jerky in the kitchen and it's really good." I knew immediately what he was eating, but Bear had a short temper, so I didn't know whether to tell him and risk getting him angry, or not tell him and let him go ahead and finish eating Scruffy's dog jerky. After all, he really did seem to be enjoying it. How much harm could it cause? Right then Danny enters the hall from his bedroom and hears Bear's happy declaration and immediately heads into the kitchen for some jerky. At least now I wasn't going to have to be the one to tell him.

Danny grabs the package and immediately starts laughing and brings the package out into the living room, but he is laughing so hard he can't speak. The laughter escalated until he finally fell to the floor in a fit of laughter as my dad eyed him curiously. The cat was about to escape from the bag as soon as Danny regained his speaking composure. I knew exactly why he was laughing so I began to giggle too. He finally shouted between bursts of laughter that he was eating dog jerky. I'll never forget, for as long as I live, the look on my dad's face as he pulled the corners of his mouth back and made a toothy grimace of disgust with large chunks of well-chewed dog jerky wedged between almost every tooth in his mouth. Seeing the dog jerky in his teeth as he made this grimacing face got me laughing uncontrollably too, and I fell to the floor rolling in laughter beside my brother as he held up the bag to provide my dad a better look at the package he was dining from.

What followed was a quick (for a 350-pound man) rise and run (ok, fast walk) to the kitchen sink to loudly and emphatically spew the nasty stuff from his mouth in dramatic fashion, although just a moment ago he extolled the flavorful treat. I've made this story my metaphor for battling the ego about the idea of separation. I was quite enjoying certain aspects of it, until I realized what it actually was and then hurriedly and disgustedly spewed it out. If only undoing the ego were that easy.

With my practice of forgiveness being top of mind, I decided to deliver my next Toastmasters speech about it. So, me and Ed huddled up and created something that we both liked. I sure enjoyed having Ed's professional assistance and I could tell it was paying dividends and making me a better public speaker. The ideas and writing were not that difficult for me but forming it into a speech that could powerfully make the point in five to seven minutes was sometimes a real challenge, and that was where Ed shined. I called this speech "Life's Greatest Lesson" and I recorded it and posted the link on Facebook and YouTube afterwards and got a lot of views and positive comments.

"Fellow Toastmasters, a new form of entertainment has recently emerged where you pay a significant sum of money to get locked in a windowless room with the task of figuring out how to escape within a certain time frame by solving a sequence of riddles and puzzles. They're called escape rooms and there are now about 2,300 of them in the United States, and the number is growing rapidly.

"When my daughter and I tried it recently at the Maui Mall, our only communication with the outside world was by making a clue request which then showed up on the video monitor in the room. Sadly, our time lapsed, and we never escaped. They had to come and let us out after our time expired and we walked out frustrated and defeated by the challenge." I didn't think this was funny, but it got a few laughs anyway. I guess being rescued from an escape room can be humorous.

"As we left, it occurred to me that life often feels like an escape room experience, in that we become trapped or imprisoned in our own psychological identification with physical form and thought content, and we don't know how to escape and liberate ourselves from the structural dysfunction of the conditioned human mind. We pursue the wrong clue, or we suffer the anxiety of trying to decipher the complex puzzle of life while under a mortal deadline, and we often get frustrated.

"But if life were an escape room, there would only be one clue necessary to guarantee escape and liberation from the frustrations of this mortal experience. This one clue or concept trumps all others and is so universally applicable that it is not only the best lesson I ever learned, but it is also the *only* lesson that we really need to learn. This all-important clue or life lesson may surprise you in its simplicity, but don't confuse simple with easy. However, the practical benefits it delivers are beyond question. Do you want to know what it is?" I had really built it up so I could see the eagerness in their eyes and faces. "This clue is forgiveness." I paused for effect, and I noticed a few club members were expecting something more profound after that buildup, apparently not yet sold on the benefits of forgiveness.

"Forgiveness is often only considered a religious or spiritual practice, and it may appear to be something we do to and for others, but it is really done for ourselves, for these reasons:

1. Forgiveness severs our connection to the ego or false self and automatically connects us with our true Self instead.
2. Forgiveness frees us from judgment and the projection

of guilt onto ourselves or others.

3. Forgiveness removes emotional burdens that would otherwise obstruct our happiness.

4. Forgiveness is the fast track to personal peace."

Ed was big on giving the reasons or benefits and then expanding on them with stories. I liked the structure it gave to the speech.

"Forgiveness forces us to identify with our true Self because forgiveness is an act of love. If we identify with love, then the expression of that love will naturally result in forgiveness. If we identify with fear, which is derived from the false self, then we will only perceive the threat in others, and threats require judgment, condemnation and the projection of guilt.

"This judgment may seem personal, but it is really just structural. It is simply a function of our conditioned human minds. It is how our primitive brains are wired, to constantly assess the world around us and analyze threats. Judgment is what our brains default to as a protection mechanism for our body, or false self. Just like an escape room, judgment keeps us trapped, incarcerated in a prison of our own choice and making.

"This choice to judge instead of forgive means we will perceive *everyone* as worthy of and deserving of judgment and condemnation, including *ourselves*. We will not be free of our own judgment because the same judgment that we apply to others will also be applied to ourselves, and that judgment will inevitably bring guilt.

"We don't like the guilt that our judgment causes, so we will attempt to project it onto others to get rid of it. But just as we didn't want the guilt that resulted from our judgment, others don't want it either. So, we end up playing a vicious game of guilt hot-potato by redirecting and projecting guilt onto each other. But forgiveness breaks this vicious cycle of guilt projection. We simply decide to let go and drop the potato. We forgive instead of judge. We love instead of fear. We release guilt through forgiveness instead of holding onto it. We don't have any judgment or guilt to project because we forgave it all, and the slate is clean.

"Judgment invites a guilt monkey with long claws to climb onto our backs and cling to us, forcing us to carry an unwanted burden. Forgiveness is like using mace on that monkey, quickly and efficiently ridding us of that burden completely. Sometimes we become so accustomed to carrying the burden that we don't even realize it is there.

"Recently Kim and I were invited to a BBQ on the beach with a client I had sold a condo to. Kim had a sore hip, and his wife was an energy healer and asked Kim if she could clear her energy. Kim agreed, but I was skeptical as she began to distribute invisible energy around Kim's body without touching her. Although she got my attention when she told Kim the problem with her hip originated in her foot, because Kim had hurt her foot in a gym class the previous week. She also said there was an energy blockage involving Kim's mother, and forgiveness was required to clear it. I was shocked, because Kim and her mother were not speaking, but this lady didn't know that. When she finished, I asked her if I could be next, and soon she was doing the same air movements around me as she told me I had arthritis in my knees, and that my left knee was worse than my right, which was true. She then told me that I also had some blocked energy towards my father that likewise required clearing by forgiveness.

"My father and I had a nasty fight near the end of his life, and I stopped visiting him before he passed . . . twenty-six years ago. I didn't even know I was still carrying this emotional burden. That night, I decided twenty-six years was long enough. I laid in my bed and thought of my father. I immediately recalled all of his hurtful words from twenty-six years ago like they were yesterday, and then simply said in my mind, 'All is forgiven and released.' I continued to bring up and then release any other negative memories with the statement 'all is forgiven and released.' I did this until I could not think of anything else to forgive. When I finished, I felt as if I had walked out of a self-imposed prison after a twenty-six-year sentence. No longer burdened by my own lack of forgiveness, I felt much lighter, happier, and more peaceful.

"Have you ever heard someone say, 'I'll never forgive them for what they did' as if they were somehow punishing that person by denying themselves the personal peace derived from forgiveness? What an unfair trade. Peace is never found among the regrets or grudges of the past, or anxiety towards the future. Peace is always anchored in the present moment of forgiveness.

"A story is told of two monks who were traveling together and arrived at a high river. They were about to cross when a woman approached them and asked for assistance crossing the river. Knowing that it was a monastic vow not to touch a woman the younger monk turned away and refused to help, after which the older monk stepped forward, picked up the woman, carried her across the river and set her down on the other side.

"The two monks continued on for several hours without speaking, until the younger monk just couldn't stand it any longer and blurted out, 'How could you do that? You know it is against our vows to touch a woman.' To which the older monk replied, 'I put her down on the other side of the river hours ago. Why are you still carrying her?'

"What are you carrying that is obstructing your personal peace and happiness? Peace is only five words away, 'all is forgiven and released.' Make these five words your mantra anytime you feel dissatisfied, unhappy or lack peace. Use them to identify with your higher Self, escaping emotional bondage and making the world a better place by ending judgment and the subsequent projection of guilt onto yourself and others. Let it go and find peace through forgiveness. This is life's greatest lesson, and you can start learning it by asking yourself one simple question, 'Who do I need to forgive?'"

I was happy with my speech about forgiveness, and even Ed enjoyed my metaphor of life being an escape room. But later I read Jesus' description of the benefits of forgiveness in *ACIM*, and nobody says it with quite the same authoritative flair,

> "Your relationship with your brother has been uprooted from the world of shadows, and its unholy purpose has been safely brought through the barriers of guilt, washed with forgiveness, and set shining and firmly rooted in the world of light. From there it calls to you to follow the course it took, lifted high above the darkness and gently placed before the gates of Heaven . . . . The messenger of love [was] sent from beyond forgiveness to remind you of all that lies beyond it. Yet it is through forgiveness that it will be remembered. And when the memory of God has come to you in the holy place of forgiveness you will remember nothing else . . . Forgiveness removes only the untrue, lifting the shadows from the world and carrying it, safe and sure within its gentleness, to the bright world of new and clean perception. There is your purpose now. And it is there that peace awaits you."

Chapter 11

The Pursuit of Peace

"God is not the author of confusion, but of peace."
1 Corinthians 14:33

As confident as I felt about my ability to speak in front of a group now, my frustration at times was that I didn't feel I could convey the indescribable feeling of peace that accompanied my spiritual practice. I wished I could just hold up my life and say "Look" because ever since my awakening life had become so positively peaceful. But communicating this effectively within a five to seven-minute speech was a challenge.

Then I had an idea. One of the speaking assignments to achieve my Competent Communicator award was to use visual aids in a speech. This was typically done with computer-based visuals, overhead transparencies, flip charts, whiteboards, and props, but not people. Kim would never stand up in front of an audience with me anyway and couldn't understand my strange new fascination with public speaking, something that held absolutely no appeal for her. But little Kaya loved a stage, and at six years old she was not yet self-conscious enough to turn down an opportunity to deliver a speech with me.

Kaya had already attended a few Toastmasters meetings, once to hear Margie's final speech and a couple of other times when I was speaking or competing. One time Kaya attended, and we were short on members and needed an "Ah Counter."

Remember the "Ah Counter?" It is a designated person who listens for the use of crutch words such as "ah, uh, um, and, so, well, you know, like, then, etc."

Kaya volunteered for this task and loved it! She listened carefully and was thrilled each time she heard a crutch word used and could mark someone down and charge them a quarter. She may have been the best "Ah Counter" we've ever had. By the end of the meeting she had the tracking form all marked up and everybody owed money. It was a good thing they capped it at a dollar because Kaya had marked one poor lady down for seventeen crutch words. I've even heard of Toastmasters clubs that use a tiny bell and will "ding" you upon each use of a crutch word. I didn't struggle with crutch words like some did, but I'm glad our club didn't use a bell because being "dinged" in the middle of your speech would have been distracting and annoying, and Kaya would have been dinging that bell all night. After that meeting, Kaya often asked if she could come to Toastmasters with me just to be the "Ah Counter" again.

Anyway, I ran the idea by Ed to use Kaya in my speech and he loved it. He said he had never heard of a person being used as a prop before and he praised my creativity. I wrote the speech, we practiced it for him, and he enjoyed it and made his usual suggestions. Then I practiced it with Kaya several times to make sure her timing was perfect. I only had her saying a few words, but her timing, tone and enthusiasm was critical. I also had her holding a bag of props that I would walk over to and get one by one as my speech called for them. I thought it was adorable and both of us were excited as we practiced and prepared for the upcoming meeting.

The name of the speech was "Pura Vida" and when we arrived, we were both dressed in matching red "Pura Vida" T-shirts that we had bought on our trip to Costa Rica, a trip I had already used stories from in several other speeches, such as the

Howler monkeys supposedly peeing on me, and the bug stinging my horse's penis and providing me with a wild ride. Everybody was super friendly with Kaya as they greeted and welcomed her, but they had no idea she was part of my speech that evening. Kim came, of course, and wanted to record the speech for her own enjoyment. I used her recording for Ed's evaluation and suggestions later.

We were ready, and when I was called to speak I put a chair to the side of the room, facing both the podium and the audience, and I sat Kaya down in it with her bag of props, wondering how she would respond to the pressure of public speaking. I started my speech by explaining Kaya's presence.

"My daughter Kaya is sitting in that chair because I told her it is a Toastmasters rule when you have a child that cute, you must use her as a visual aid. Thank you, Kaya." Nobody heard me thank her because they were all laughing and chuckling as soon as they heard I was using her as a visual aid due to her cuteness. My speech just got a whole lot more interesting to everyone once they discovered why Kaya was up there with me. It was a pretty effective opening line, even though I unexpectedly stepped on some laughs when I thanked her.

"Just as Hawaii has Aloha, Costa Rica has . . . Pura Vida. Madame Toastmaster, fellow Toastmasters and guests, Pura Vida. The direct translation is 'pure life.'" I turned a page on a white flipchart that had the definition written on it, trying not to limit my visual aids to just Kaya.

"But to Costa Ricans it means much more. It's a popular phrase that is used as a greeting, a farewell, and generally any time you feel good and have a sense of well-being. Sound familiar?" In Hawaii, the word "aloha" is used similarly in that it is used for hello, goodbye, love, goodwill, etc.

"We had a waiter who said it every time he cleared a plate from our table, which is usually where I taught Kaya Spanish. I would say, 'Kaya, go tell our waitress we need . . . .'" This was rehearsed and Kaya was ready, she finished my sentence with perfect timing when her sweet little voice said, "Más vino," which means more wine in Spanish. Everyone laughed heartily. I paused so as not to step on Kaya's laughs and let her enjoy this moment, knowing full well the absolute adrenaline rush of delivering a punch line and then hearing the entire room burst into laughter, Kaya was adorably beaming at their risible response. ~M is u jod

"And whenever Kaya wanted anything from the waitress, she would ask for it herself, in Spanish, by first asking me 'How do you say bread, or butter . . . or dessert.' She got so accustomed to this ritual that even the day after returning home when she went to request more ice from a waitress she came back and asked me, 'How do you say ice in Spanish?'" They laughed again. Kaya was sitting so cute and innocent, and everybody seemed to be enjoying my different speech idea.

Ed and I had practiced how to do dialogue in a speech, and he recommended it for humorous effect and other reasons. We determined that I would deliver the following dialogue by slightly turning my upper body to one side or another to show who was speaking and to keep it rapid. I practiced in the mirror to get the speed right so that it was quick but didn't look like I was stealing Kevin Durant's free throw shoulder shimmy.

"I was a Spanish teacher over twenty-five years ago, but my Spanish is rusty, and my fluency has faded. Once, just after being seated in a restaurant, Kim said:

'Let's leave.'

'Why? I thought you were hungry.'

'I am, but everything on the menu is in Spanish. I can't read any of it."

'I can translate it for you.'

'Are you sure?'

'Don't worry'

"She was skeptical because I'm always telling her *not to worry*, but then constantly doing things that cause her *to worry*. But I translated the Spanish menu, she made her selection, and when the waitress came, I gave her our food order entirely in Spanish, and Kim was impressed . . . until the food came." More laughter. I expanded the story to even more laughs.

"My fish was delivered as chicken, and somehow Kim got eggs for lunch. She glared at me to fix it. I responded, 'The last time I spoke Spanish we got chicken for fish and breakfast for lunch! What do you think my chances are of realistically correcting this food order in Spanish?'

"Kaya has a nickname for me that she loves to share with people, even strangers, and it is: I gesture to Kaya and she responds with perfect timing, exuberantly shouting, "The weird daddy!" Everybody laughs again and I pretend to be disappointed by my nickname. Kaya is loving this, and my laugh ratio is through the roof because of her.

"Because I don't think or behave like other daddies do. For example, one night in Costa Rica I'm sound asleep in our villa and Kim shakes me awake and says:

'Kill it!'

'What?'

'Kill it, kill it.'

"I've mumbled one word from a dead sleep, and I've been told to 'kill it' three times. I notice Kim has the blankets pulled all the way up over her head so all I can see is her worried eyes as she shouts, 'kill it' one more time. Then I hear the flapping. It must be one of those giant jungle moths. So, I get up, get out of bed, and stumble over to pick up . . . my kill slipper." My feigned sleepy stumbling from the podium to Kaya's chair ends with her handing me a size twelve flip-flop, which I hold up to more laughter as Kaya smiles enthusiastically. I groggily walk to the other side of the room to act out the following narrative:

"The flapping stopped but I know the general area where it stopped. After turning on the light, I approach the area with my slipper and see it on the floor. I hold my slipper up to strike and move closer, and then I freeze.

'Kill it!'

"The combination of sleep fog and what I was seeing temporarily paralyzed my mind so I couldn't respond.

'Kill it!'

"How do I tell her it wasn't a giant moth . . . but a giant *bat*?" Nobody saw this setup coming and they all roar with laughter. I love that feeling, when their humorous response is even better than expected and they are completely engaged with my story and gleefully laughing without inhibition.

"With my slipper still in strike position, I notice the wingspan of the bat was longer than my size twelve slipper . . . so I drop the slipper." After holding up my slipper sideways so they could see how long it was, I drop it on the floor, and it lands flat and makes a loud splat sound on the tile.

'Kill it!'

"Before I can respond to Kim's incessant death chant, the bat flies up off the floor and circles my head about three times, obviously trying to get out. But of course, all the doors and windows are closed." Here I used exaggerated physical humor and crouch as I move my hand in a wide arcing circle around my head to mimic the flight path of the bat as I fearfully bob and weave below my own hand. They continue busting a gut laughing.

"If you're asking yourself how the bat got into the villa with all of the doors and windows closed, I was thinking that very same question. I even asked that question to the owner of the hotel the next morning.

"After orbiting my head, the bat touches down on my daughter's bed, who is amazingly still sleeping even though her mother is now frantically screaming. At least my response is no longer required, because Kim now clearly sees the bat walking on its wings across our daughter's bedsheets . . . and she is hysterical. So, what does *'weird daddy'* do? I grab my phone to film it, of course!" I hold up my cell phone as I say this and receive a loud eruption of laughter. After it subsides, I explain.

"Nobody would have believed me otherwise. So here is that short video: Note Kim pleading with me to kill it while I'm filming." I had previously set up the visual aid equipment to play the short video quickly upon saying this. As they all saw a dark, grainy image of a black bat crawling across a white bed sheet with Kaya's legs under it they cringed, scowled, and whimpered.

"I wasn't sure how Kaya would feel about the video, so I waited until we returned home to show it to her. She watched it calmly and then said, 'It's not scary.'" Once again, delivering her speech line right on cue as everyone smiled in acknowledgment of what a brave sleeper she was.

"After boarding the plane to leave Costa Rica, Kaya watched her portable DVD player as Kim and I placed our neck pillows and cuddled up in a blanket for a nap. Surrounded by my beautiful family, with my wife's hand in mine as I dozed off to sleep, I felt completely happy, peaceful, and relaxed. This moment was absolutely perfect, and I was one-hundred percent content."

I begin to make one last trek towards Kaya who is holding my almost empty prop bag and say, "I may be Spanish challenged, but I know the exact Spanish phrase to describe this feeling. That's easy: Pura Vida!" I say as Kaya removed and handed me a Pura Vida hat, which I put on as I smiled wide. I finish standing by Kaya, and as everyone clapped and cheered upon completion of our speech I bent down and whispered to her, "You did great! Do you see how much they loved your speech!"

Kaya was now bitten by the public speaking bug, and this experience gave her a very real public speaking desire, and she asked me if she could be in another one of my speeches. I explained to her that my speeches are meant to chart my progress towards a specific goal, and that I was only able to use her that time because my speech called for the use of visual aids. This didn't stop her. Whenever we had company or Kim's brothers were visiting, Kaya would sit us down in the living room and deliver a speech, which was really just her telling us a story. We would all listen intently and then clap and cheer when she finished. My little Toastmaster.

After moving back into my house, I was so happy, grateful, and peaceful that I made a personal commitment to never be a source of anxiety or stress for Kim ever again. But this commitment to only bring peace to my wife was tested under some rather humorous situations. Once, shortly after we had reunited, we went to the infinity pool and hot tub at our complex for a sunset swim and soak. As she swam a few laps I relaxed in the hot tub with the jets on and leaned my head against the lava rock wall behind me and closed my eyes in complete relaxation. I heard a sound and opened my eyes to see a much older lady enter the hot tub. I briefly acknowledged her and then closed my eyes again.

A couple of minutes later I felt the lady's fingernails groping my inner thigh, fairly close to my crotch, as I sat with my eyes closed. I was obviously shocked by this aggressive sexual maneuver from a horny older woman and my eyes shot open to see exactly what she was attempting to accomplish with this scandalous crotch-grab. But when I opened my eyes, I saw she was all the way across the hot tub with her eyes also closed in peaceful relaxation. But wait . . . I definitely felt fingernails on my inner thigh. Puzzled, I looked in the foam and bubbles caused by the jets. I flinched when I saw a huge rat swimming next to my leg and groping for something to hold onto to climb out of the hot tub!

Kim saw me sit up and widen my eyes and knew something was wrong. She asked me from the pool what it was, but I knew if I told her she would freak out, start screaming, and make a scene. Being committed to not disturbing her personal peace, I decided not to answer her and kept my watchful eye on the swimming rat as he paddled towards the older lady, in search of a way out of the hot tub to avoid drowning. As he moved away from me, I slowly moved away from him, realizing I had an important choice to make. If I didn't shout out a warning it might climb onto the lady as it tried to do with me. But if I did then my wife would overreact to the situation and it would definitely disrupt her peace. Either way, somebody would be screaming soon. I decided it would not be my wife.

The rat moved towards the older lady who had now immersed her shoulders and neck in the water, leaving only her head from the chin up exposed. Watching the rat swim towards her face with her eyes closed prompted me to change my mind and shout out a warning, but just then Kim asked again what I saw. I didn't like being trapped between disturbing my wife's peace of mind or staying silent and letting this scene play out. It was all happening so quickly. I stood up and then froze with indecision as I morbidly watched the rat swim within a foot of the woman's peaceful face. My standing caused a disruption in the water, causing the woman to briefly open her eyes to see what I was doing, and see me staring in frozen horror at a brown blob that she now noticed out of her peripheral vision on her right side. She quickly turned her head and fearfully locked eyes with the already fearful eyes of a drowning rat less than a foot away, struggling to keep his black, beady eyes above the bubbles and foam as he swam right towards her face.

She then demonstrated what true fear looks and sounds like by contorting her face and opening her eyes so wide that I could see the curvature of her eye sockets as her entire face elongated and her jaw dropped as she opened her mouth so fully I'm surprised her jaw didn't lock as she released an eardrum-piercing, blood-curdling scream. For a brief moment, the proximity of the swimming rat to her widely opened mouth just inches away made me wonder if the rat might try to somehow swim inside. But I quickly dismissed that possibility because even as wide as her screaming mouth was opened, it still wasn't nearly wide enough to fit *this rat* into. This rat was almost the size of a cat with a tail that was longer than its body. After she had expelled all of the air from her lungs with an impressive scream, this old lady then sprung out of the water with such dexterity that it made me wonder if she was really as old as she looked. She shot upwards like a lightning bolt, or a boomerang video in reverse, in one quickly coordinated and highly adrenalized jump.

I wish the story ended there, but once she safely landed her jump onto the edge of the hot tub, she turned to me dripping wet, as I was slowly getting out on the other side, without saying a word but communicating her thought to me quite clearly with an expression that said, "What the f*** is wrong with you!" She knew I had seen the rat before it got that close to her and she couldn't figure out why I hadn't said anything. She placed her hand over her heart to signify that she was having difficulty breathing, and then bent down with her other hand to pick up her towel on the chaise lounge nearby and stormed off in an angry huff, leaving me to deal with the rat still swimming in the hot tub.

My wife was now aware that something was desperately wrong, so she started moving to the far end of the pool and away from the hot tub as she shouted, "What is it?! What is it?!"

It was just the two of us now, so I tried to calmly tell her there was a rat in the hot tub. She screamed anyway and hurriedly jumped out of the pool and went as far away from the hot tub as possible, shouting, "Kill it! Kill it!" Obviously, she likes me to kill things that don't belong in the house, villa, or in this case, the hot tub. I grabbed the long pool net that removes leaves and bugs from the pool surface and carried it to the hot tub to extract and then dispose of the rat. Without thinking it through clearly, I scooped the rat into the net and lifted it out of the water. But the frantic rat simply took advantage of the traction of his claws on something solid and quickly climbed out of the net and landed with a loud, wet splat on the patio that surrounds the pool, and then started running in the direction of my wife. Fortunately for her, it didn't get too far before splashing into the pool. I scratched my head as Kim continued to scream, realizing I just successfully transported the rat from the hot tub to the pool, where it commenced swimming again.

"Kill it! Kill it" Kim screamed as fear-laced tears moistened her eyes. It wasn't a peaceful look. I didn't know what to do, and her screaming sure wasn't bringing me any clarity of thought. I usually only had to kill cockroaches, spiders, centipedes, or moths. Even the bat she wanted me to kill in Costa Rica wasn't this large. I don't think I'd ever killed anything this large before, and even though it was a rodent the sheer size of it made being the executioner seem so much graver. Obviously pulling it out with the net didn't work, so maybe I should keep it in with the net. I decided to net it, rotate the net to hold it under the water and drown it. This would alleviate the risk of another splat and run to "who knows where." So I did, and then dropped it in the garbage can with a heavy thud and left a note for the on-site manager that I had killed a rat swimming in the hot tub and left it in the garbage can by the pool for him to dispose of properly.

I left the pool that evening with the understanding that peace is not always possible in all situations, especially those that combine rodents and women, but if you try to make the right choices to protect peace you can enjoy it more often than not.

In all seriousness, peace is an important word to me, because it was one of the last three words Ocean left me with before parting. It was also one of the first things I noticed about Margie that shined through everything else my ego-identified mind was using to judge and separate. Peace is a game changer. Once we find it, we'll want to keep it and be vigilant of anyone or anything attempting to separate us from it. The presence of peace is proof we are prevailing over the ego and remembering God, and the absence of peace is evidence we have succumbed to the ego and forgotten God. Peace is God's unique vibrational frequency, so when we feel peaceful, we align our own vibration and energy to the Source of all that is. When we don't feel peaceful, we cannot possibly be in alignment with God. Peace is a byproduct of true forgiveness and cannot exist within judgment. Peace is powerful, peace is personal, and a peaceful mind signifies identification with the Divine Mind. This is why I mounted this word on my living room wall, because I want peace to be at the top of my awareness as my daily objective, and my constant choice.

Since my family moved a lot when I was young, we spent a fair amount of time in the car. My dad had a unique form of narcolepsy that only triggered while driving. He said it was due to a hypnotizing effect from the dotted lines in the road. All we knew was that somebody always had to be on watch whenever he was driving, or else we would be in for a rude and potentially painful awakening, if we woke up at all. He once fell asleep at the wheel and rolled his vehicle three times down the side of a mountain. He and my sister Eve were forced to crawl out of the broken windshield to escape the vehicle because the doors were too crumpled to open. He even somehow survived an airplane crash in the Air Force before they realized he had no business attempting to fly airplanes with his condition and they clipped his wings.

Several times while driving on long trips I was awakened by the sudden transition from smooth highway to the rough rumble of being off road. Once he went off the road and hit a highway marker with his window down and I was awakened in the "safe seat" behind him to the spray of glass from his rear-view mirror hitting my face. We understood how difficult it was for him to stay awake during long car rides, but we also figured it was a reasonable expectation that you would stay awake if you were the one driving the vehicle. With our dad, that *never* happened. If we all fell asleep then our dad would also fall asleep and eventually, we ended up off the road. Whenever this happened there was somebody to blame besides my father, because we always assigned watch duty to make sure he would not fall asleep, a duty which was obviously shirked by someone if we ever ended up off the road. As we got older, various kids took turns driving, even if we did not have a driver's license yet. My brother was a pretty good driver by the time he was fourteen, and I was allowed to take my first turn behind the wheel at age eleven, but only on the most isolated highways when there were very few other cars around. That may sound risky, but it was actually a lot safer than letting our narcoleptic dad drive.

We didn't say anything to our dad about it because it pretty much happened every time, so we knew it was our responsibility to watch him closely whenever he was driving. When I was on watch duty, I would see him fading and I'd prod him or shake him to keep him awake. Constant vigilance was required, just as constant vigilance is required to maintain our peace in this world. If personal peace is not monitored constantly then before we know it, we've lost it and we're rumbling through rough terrain, wondering how we transitioned so quickly from a smooth journey to a perilous one. Just as falling asleep at the wheel can be disastrous, so is the casual monitoring of peace because we will be quickly absorbed into and identified with an anxious, threatening, stressful and challenging world; a sure sign that we have lost our perspective of Self.

When Ocean told me to never let anything take my peace, I sensed the tremendous spiritual importance of the lesson she was

243

trying to teach. When Margie seemed completely crazy to me, it was her personal peace that still drew me in to learn more, and my own lack of peace is what pointed me towards my own awakening and caused me to surrender to a better way. Peace is both the purpose and the desired result of all spiritual practice because it accesses God within you, cleanses any egoic illusion or misperception, and allows a much deeper wisdom to flow through peace and infuse our creative expression and personal relations in a magical, synchronistic and divine extension of immanent unity as it shines from us like a beacon. Personal peace gets quickly noticed and responded to by others. After my awakening, comments about my personal peace were prevalent, from anybody who had ever known me. Until inner peace is accomplished, world peace will never be possible. Peace has been willed for us by God Himself, and peace will eventually prevail precisely because it is God's will. Once peace is found, it is understandable why it is worth the commitment to maintain it. Until then, these are just meaningless words. Peace is a foreign commodity in this world because peace can only come from transcending the everyday perception this world operates from, which is mostly misperception.

One night on one of our long road trips with my family, my sister Eve got out of the car barefoot to quickly use the bathroom at a rest stop while my dad took a driving break and tried to regain some alertness to continue driving. When we all got back in the car to drive off, Eve ran from the bathroom and stepped in mud running back to the car. As we drove away Eve grabbed a popsicle stick in the back seat and started to scrape the mud from between her toes and wipe it on a napkin she was holding. It didn't take the rest of us very long to realize it wasn't mud she was scraping from her toes, as the entire car filled with the stifling scent of dog poop. Her mistaken perception disgusted her and everyone else riding in the car. This is another reason why peace is so important to monitor because the presence of peace denotes our veracity of perception. Of all the various ways we can perceive something, the truest perception will always bring the most peace. Thus, peace becomes a benchmark for our spiritual progress that serves as a true indicator of how we are faring on this mortal journey, and acts as an effective compass for our journey home. One of my favorite phrases from *ACIM* says: "How can you know whether you chose the stairs to Heaven or the way to hell? Quite easily. How do you feel? Is peace in your awareness?" If it is, use it as a handrail while climbing the stairs to Heaven and you can't stumble.

Peace also gauges understanding because we cannot have peace without understanding. Peace and understanding fit together like love and forgiveness, as the cause and effect of each other. If one is missing then so is the other, which means our perception must be wrong and we've forgotten who we are. Wrong perception is why we spin our wheels in conflict and chaos, mistaking "mierda" for mud, and lacking peace and understanding. Just as true perception fosters unconditional love because that is what we are and how we were created, misperceptions foster misunderstandings which cause fear. Just as we can tell whether we are on the stairway to Heaven or hell by how much peace we feel, we can likewise gauge the accuracy of our perception by how much love or fear our perception elicits because fear is always evidence of misperception. Sometimes these fearful misperceptions can be quite humorous, and when they are it is fine to laugh at them. In fact, laughing at them may be the best way to correct them and restore the love and peace we temporarily lost by misperceiving. Since misperception is inherent in a world that originated from distortion, we should have a lot to laugh about. Here is a humorous example of one of my early misperceptions that my family still laughs about even though it happened over forty years ago when I was only eleven years old.

One Sunday afternoon my sister and her husband came over to take my brother and I bowling. During the drive to the bowling alley her husband made an illegal turn as we entered a side street to the bowling alley parking lot, and a cop noticed the maneuver and signaled for us to pull over. The cop was a few cars behind us, so we were temporarily obstructed by the building on the corner when we turned into the parking lot. My sister and her husband looked at each other and both seemed worried. I may have only been eleven, but due to an extreme lack of parental supervision my older brother and I had already experienced being chased by cops on numerous occasions, so I was ready to run if the situation required it. Nobody said a thing but as soon as they put the car in park, while still out of sight of the cop car, they both quickly opened their doors and jumped out. There was my cue, and although I had never seen anybody flee cops from a parked car before, I was game. I opened my door just a split second after they did and bolted down the nearest alley, sprinting as fast as I could. I heard them yelling as I ran, but I wasn't taking any chances. I was already gone.

At the end of the alley it opened onto another road, so I turned right and headed around that building in a frantic panic. When I got to the end of the building, I peered around the corner to look back towards them to make sure it was safe to keep going. They got caught and didn't make it. I could see them talking to the cop by their car and pointing in the direction that I had run. I couldn't believe they were ratting me out. While the cop was distracted and asking them questions about the one that got away, I crossed the street out of their view and disappeared behind another building, and then another, further distancing myself from the long arm of the law. I hid in a parking garage for a while before venturing home, steering away from main roads, and staying in residential neighborhoods as much as I could with my eyes peeled for the police.

We were several miles from our house, but I made it back home about an hour later. When I walked in the front door, my entire family all started yelling and laughing at me simultaneously and it was so loud I couldn't understand what they were saying. Finally, their laughter and shouting subsided enough for one of them to ask me what I was thinking running away from the cops on a routine traffic violation. I told them I was just following their lead; they started to run, so I did the same. This brought another round of raucous laughter, and when it finally subsided, they told me they were just switching seats because my sister's husband had so many traffic tickets that if he got another, he could get his driver's license suspended. They figured if they switched drivers while the cop's vision was obscured by the building, they could have the ticket written in my sister's name instead.

I was a scared eleven-year-old troublemaker who'd already formed an unhealthy fear of police and there was no way I could have known any of that, since they never said a word between them before quickly jumping out of the car. I just figured we were making a run for it. They said it took them three times as long to get the ticket written because the cop wanted to know why a young kid sprinted away from the car and down an alley after he pulled us over. My sister said it was her little brother who just got scared but the cops were, of course, highly suspicious. It probably didn't help that my teenage older brother was laughing so hard during their explanation of the event. It wasn't the first time I'd had to ditch a cop, nor would it be my last.

My point is that perception is just a choice tied to a belief, it is not fact. Everybody thinks their beliefs are correct and their perceptions are accurate, but what we believe is just what we believe, and the truth is usually far from the beliefs that we often allow to form our perceptions. But since we make decisions based upon what we believe, then we should at least verify the accuracy of our decision by determining whether the choice we're making will deliver a peaceful result. If not, then we should choose again.

As funny as a young kid abandoning the car and fleeing a routine traffic pullover is, if we are honest, we can all produce a similar story of gross misperception. This is because once our mind attaches to a fixed belief then it directs our perception to create the world it believes we *should* see. This becomes a problem if the belief is false because then that belief forms a false foundational base from which we color our perception and co-create the outcome we are looking for and want to see. We do this because we want to maintain psychological consistency and have our internal beliefs coincide with the external world, as we see it. Our perception doesn't form our beliefs, our beliefs form our perception, and then our perception creates our reality, even if that reality is different from everybody else's because they don't share our same beliefs.

This is why we can't underestimate the importance of peace as the litmus test of spiritual direction, accuracy of perception, alignment with love, presence of true forgiveness, and choice of master or guide. In *ACIM* , Jesus says, "The ego's qualifications as a guide are singularly unfortunate." That's just a polite way of saying the ego knows nothing, and if we choose according to its dictates then suffering, misperception and fear are inevitable, and so is our loss of peace. Our Self will always remain in peace because our reality is One with God, but our free mind can also choose to create a false reality of separation and conflict if we allow the ego to be our guide. Our objective is to elevate our mind until it aligns with peace because that is proof of our unity with God. But if we let our mind sink to the lower order of the body or the ego where fear and chaos reign, we will succumb to the delusion of separation and appear distant from God. *ACIM* paints a clear picture of the ego's thought system and what true perception reveals about it. "Perceive any part of the ego's thought system as wholly insane, wholly delusional and wholly undesirable, and you have correctly evaluated all of it." Singularly unfortunate indeed.

ACIM also states there is no such thing as neutral thoughts because all thoughts produce an effect. Everything we see is the result of our thoughts, without exception. All thoughts are either true or false, and those that are true create their own likeness, while those that are false make theirs. What gives rise to the perception of an entire world can hardly be called neutral or idle. Every thought we have contributes to either truth or illusion, and this thought contribution extends truth or multiplies illusions. This is yet another reason why we must be vigilant for peace because the presence of peace proves we are contributing to truth and not multiplying illusions. One excludes the other, as stated in ACIM : "Conflict and peace are opposites. Where one abides the other cannot be; where either goes the other disappears."

There is a story about a young Cherokee speaking to his grandfather about the dual nature of his thoughts. The youngster says, "I feel like there are two wolves inside of me which are always at battle. One is a good wolf which represents things like kindness, bravery, joy, peace, serenity, love, hope, humility, benevolence, empathy, generosity, truth, compassion, and faith."

His grandfather nodded his head as he listened, and then he asked, "And the other wolf?"

"The other wolf is evil, he is anger, envy, sorrow, regret, greed, arrogance, self-pity, resentment, inferiority, lies, false pride, and superiority." His grandfather nodded.

The young man then asked his grandfather, "Which wolf will win this battle?"

The wise grandfather replied, "Whichever one you feed."

We relate to this story because we each have the same battle going on inside of us. It may seem at times like it is beyond our control, but we are the only ones supplying nourishment to each wolf. We get to decide which one feeds, and which one doesn't. We may lose every other personal freedom we have, but nobody can ever take away our right to choose our response to whatever appears to be happening within this world. That is, and always will be, uniquely ours to decide. Viktor Frankl calls it the "ultimate freedom" in *Man's Search for Meaning*, and this all-important decision determines whether we choose conflict or peace, and once one is chosen the other disappears from our conscious awareness. With two opposing thought systems constantly in complete disagreement, the only way we can ever have peace is if we consciously choose it and relinquish the conflict consistently raging on the ego's battlefield. Beyond this senseless battle lies the memory of God, ready to be remembered when we choose peace.

Peace proves our unification with the Divine Mind and diminishes our belief in the ego's tiny, mad idea of separation which cannot understand peace so it cannot deliver it. Peace is invoked by true forgiveness which heals unconscious guilt, turning us away from judgment that attempts to place guilt outside of us, but which only ends up back on us because we are one. Peace is the state where love overrules fear and seeks to be shared instead of buried or hidden. Peace comes from choosing forgiveness over judgment and seeing innocence instead of guilt. Peace brings the presence of God into hell. If you have peace, hold it with both hands as tightly as you can. If you don't have it then make a decision to find it, and when you do, maintain it, protect it, guard it, keep it, but also extend it to strengthen it, because to the hand that extends peace is the gift of peace given, ensuring it remains constantly present. How can it be otherwise with oneness? When you are united you receive as you give, because oneness unites the giver and the receiver as the same. But you cannot extend or share what you do not have. Allow the Divine Mind within you to guide you to the peace of God that is your inheritance, which was willed to you by God upon your creation. "When God gave Himself to you in your creation, He established you as host to Him forever. He has not left you and you have not left Him." His peace is our peace, and it is a peace that passes all understanding. Allow it to constantly remind us that God is.

Chapter 12

Transformation

"Everyone thinks of changing the world,
but no one thinks of changing himself."
Leo Tolstoy

I recently watched The Matrix again and this time it seemed more like a documentary than a science fiction movie, as I realized just how similarly Neo's experience within the simulated reality of the Matrix correlates with our life experience on earth. Neither experience is real, but both are so effective at blurring the lines between illusion and reality that it is almost impossible to determine the difference. I asked Margie if she had ever seen it, but she said she hadn't. I briefed her on the idea and told her it is a movie that really makes you question the nature of your reality by opening a psychological door that exposes the deception that has always been hidden from us. I also shared with her a few of my favorite parts.

One of them was when Neo (an anagram of One) enters a training program for the mind with Morpheus and although he knows he is sitting in a chair and plugged into a program, he can't believe how seemingly real everything is. He looks at Morpheus and skeptically asks, "This isn't real?"

Morpheus replies "What is real? How do you define real? Real is simply electrical symbols interpreted by the brain." In the training simulation, he tries to free Neo's mind and get his belief to transcend the simulation. Neo gets hurt in the simulation and when they return, Neo's mouth is bleeding.

He says, "I thought it wasn't real."

Morpheus replies, "Your mind makes it real."

In another part, Neo has a meeting with the Oracle (symbolic of the Divine Mind) and he sees gifted children doing amazing things. One little boy is making spoons bend with his mind. Neo is fascinated, so the boy hands him a spoon and Neo studies it.

The boy then tells him, "Do not try to bend the spoon, that's impossible. Instead, only try to realize the truth."

"What truth?" asks Neo.

"There is no spoon. Then you'll see that it is not the spoon that bends, it is only yourself."

Since the spoon only exists within the Matrix, a simulated reality, that means it doesn't really exist at all. This is a lesson to help Neo realize that manipulating the Matrix isn't about changing anything within it. Since the Matrix objects don't exist in reality, then the only way you can change the Matrix is to change yourself, especially your mind and the perception that governs the way you think. Since the mind created the Matrix, the mind is the only place any real changes to it can be made. This also coincides with the miracle that *ACIM* says comes from shifting your perception. Staying consistent with my passion for writing speeches about current topics of spiritual interest, I wrote and delivered the following Toastmasters speech and called it "Changing Your Perception."

"Fellow Toastmasters, I love a good movie. One of the things I love about a good movie is how I can get completely absorbed and lost in it. As the sights, sounds and images begin to flash across the screen in a synchronized fashion, and as part of a compelling story, I often forget that I am just watching it all from my soft seat, in a safe, comfortable place. The reason I forget is because my heart rate increases; I feel tension, anxiety, or even adrenaline. I may feel happy, sad, mad, scared, shocked, confused, concerned, or a multitude of other emotions. I lean forward and sit on the edge of my seat, sometimes even speaking out loud to the characters on the screen and trying to resolve their problem or help them escape from imminent danger." I get several chuckles because everybody has done that before in a movie.

"I am no longer aware of who I am or where I am. I am not even sitting in the theater anymore. I am up on the screen, and I have so strongly identified with the actors that their world is now my world. I allowed my perception to slip from being a casual observer to somehow being an active participant, even though what I am participating in is not real and doesn't even exist. None of what is happening on the screen is really happening . . . yet my body and mind seem to disagree." Once again, hard to argue with, and several heads are nodding as I speak.

"This happens because our perception can trick our minds into believing what isn't true, and once we believe something then it becomes true for us. By allowing our perception to change, we are then able to change the real to the unreal and make what is false true. In other words, we can delude ourselves, and we are deluding ourselves if we have forgotten who and where we really are, and instead believe we are somebody or someplace we are not. Who and where we actually are is beyond question, except within our mind, which believes the untrue and thereby makes it appear true for us by raising our heart rate and engaging our emotions. Perception cannot change our actual identity or location, but it can seem that way within our own belief and perspective.

"A Course in Miracles describes the miracle referenced in the title as being a simple shift in perception to a different thought system, one that is true and not false, and based upon an accurate perception. Can that really be a miracle? It's a miracle because exchanging self-delusion for true perception has a miraculous effect that moves us from illusion to reality, just as the movie experience can temporarily remove our reality and allow us to step into an illusion. All we need is a believable movie, one that we can identify with enough to shift our perception, and that altered perception creates its own experience of reality in our minds, even though it is far from our actual reality. This movie experience is one we can all relate to, but just imagine if we further enhanced the movie experience so that we not only see the images and hear the sounds, but we also smell the aromas, taste the foods, and even feel the same physical sensations the actors do. What if we also listened to the actor's thoughts and felt the emotions generated by those thoughts? In *this* enhanced movie experience, how much easier would it be to completely lose yourself and have no idea whom or where you really are?

"So, let's ask some questions. Who are you? Who sees when you see? Who hears when you hear? Who is aware of the difference between calmly sitting in the theater observing, or identifying with and participating in the human drama occurring up on the screen of life? These are all questions of perception, and there are only two choices. You either perceive yourself in the theater, detached from the movie experience, but still able to enjoy it, or you perceive yourself up on the screen, as a character or personality within the story, a victim of circumstance within a predetermined plot that you have no control over and are helplessly subject to. Once you recognize that this perception is a choice, then the world you always allowed your perception to pull you into is seen for what it is; nothing. It has no meaning at all because it does not exist, which means it cannot be justified and therefore cannot be made meaningful. There is only one reality and anything that opposes it means nothing at all because it is not real, and if it is not real then it must be an illusion. The convincing movie is just seen as a temporary illusion experienced within your actual reality.

"In the Matrix movie we see an example of this, when the reality that appears to exist is exposed as an illusion and shown to be nothing more than a simulated reality or an unrecognized delusion that has nearly everyone trapped within it. In the very beginning of the movie, Neo, played by Keanu Reeves, asks a telling question: 'Do you ever have that feeling where you're not sure if you're awake or still dreaming?' When you are dreaming and yet you are aware of the dream, that is referred to as a lucid dream. We should all evaluate and question our current perception to make our present dream a lucid one. In the movie, Neo arrives at the point of decision regarding whether he stays in the illusion of the simulated reality, as a slave to those who created it, or learns the truth of his reality. He is told by Morpheus that "The Matrix is the world that has been pulled over your eyes to blind you from the truth. No one can tell you what it is. You have to see it for yourself." He then offers Neo two choices. A blue pill that keeps him within the illusion, or a red pill that delivers the truth of his reality and exposes the illusion he always thought was real. Well, are you all ready to be "red-pilled?" Some nod nervously, while others seem skeptical, and absolutely nobody is smiling . . . except me.

"Ok, here it is. You are the projector, and not the projection on the screen. The mind is not inside the body, the body is inside the mind. The body that seems to surround you, is actually outside of you, encompassed by the mind. You are not within a body, because what is within cannot also be without. We are not separate selves; we are the same Self seeing through the eyes of different observers. Your projected body is an avatar of the mind, and your mind's projection of this body has caused this unique perception as an effect, making what is the same appear as different so that it can show you an outside picture of the inner condition of your mind. As we think, so we perceive, but when we look at the world through our perceptual apparatus that world is an illusion just like the Matrix. You don't need to change the world; you only need to change your perception of the world and doing so will change your experience of reality.

"I personally discovered this phenomenon through meditation, because whenever I meditated and went inward there was so much expansiveness. I always asked myself after meditating: 'Why does going inward cause such expansiveness?' The answer is because we are not really the body, we are outside the body, projecting the body with a very narrow bandwidth that creates an illusion of separation. This bodily projection is limiting, but when I go within, I transcend this limitation by unplugging from the Matrix and realizing that the mind is outside the body, and my consciousness extends far beyond any physical limitations. By believing otherwise, I was placing an unnecessary limit on otherwise limitless power and dissociating from reality, simply because I did not believe I was part of it when I really am. Madame Toastmaster . . . ."

Ann Elaine didn't want us to ever leave the podium unmanned, so after I finished as I waited for Fiona, our Toastmaster for the evening, I felt a little vulnerable about the radical nature of my speech. Some of the audience members seemed lost in thought, while others looked like they were sizing me up for a strait jacket. This made me wonder how much I may have overshot the message. I focused on those that didn't appear confused, that looked deep in thought, and tried to imagine what they were thinking. I would soon find out during the mandatory evaluation period that follows each speech. Fiona herself seemed flustered and a little slow to adjust to me calling her name to come back up front. Even after I passed her the podium and left for my seat, she took a moment to get her mind back on the Toastmaster task and explained her delay by looking right at me while saying to everyone, "That was intense!" Intense? I'll take that as a compliment, although I was aiming for fearless.

As mentioned, every Toastmasters speech has a formal evaluation from a club member, in front of the club, and then several informal written ones that club members circulate to you after the meeting. I haven't shared any of these from my previous speeches, but this speech's evaluation comments were too amusing not to share. It seemed club members either didn't understand and didn't like my speech, or else they didn't understand it but liked where I was trying to take it. Here were some of their comments:

> "Deep thoughts need time for them to sink in and absorb or understand. Use pauses after a key idea."

> "You need to balance examples and anecdotes with philosophy. Help us grasp the concepts."

> "A very esoteric and complex topic that you got into in an interesting way. Your analogy of the movie was apt."

> "A tough subject to follow."

> "Great subject—a difficult one to fit into five-to-seven minutes though."

> "Very intriguing content—a good challenge to audience!"

> "Deep topic—very thought provoking!"

And my personal favorite, "Very trippy." Which was pretty much my same summation of Margie the first time I heard her speak. I guess that means I'm in good company, but I still would have preferred to see the word "fearless" somewhere in my feedback.

One of existential philosopher Jean-Paul Sartre's most famous quotes is, "Hell is other people." What he meant is that when we perceive ourselves through the eyes of others, our existence is subjectively dependent upon their perception, which places us at their mercy. This effectively makes them just like my older brothers, torturers and tormenters able to lock us into a state of being that deprives us of our freedom and imprisons us. He makes a valid point; in that we are damned by the perceptual limitation of others if we agree to accept their perception as our reality. *ACIM* would say our truth is changeless, but our perception varies and tilts toward distortion because of this illusory dream. We need help escaping the dream because our primary identification is with the body, and the body censors spirituality to protect the illusion of separation, while exclusively allowing sensory perception to be our only source of perception. But the senses will only witness for the reality of the dream and force us to be a captive of it.

Thankfully, God has provided a Helper to awaken us from this hellish dream. "The strength in you will offer you the light and guide your seeing so you do not dwell on idle shadows that the body's eyes provide for self-deception." The strength referred to here is the Divine Mind or the Holy Spirit, which illuminates our escape path and exposes the idle shadows of self-deception. God's Answer is His Voice, speaking to us from within the Divine Mind and bridging the dream world of perception with our actual reality of perfect oneness, love, and truth, which lies beyond perception and unifies us with our Source. The Voice for God may be dormant in our Divine Mind, as mine was before I met Margie, but it can be awakened and released by our choice to do so and is ready to commence guiding us home. This I know experientially.

After this awakening happens the Voice for God will tell us how to correct our perception and change our thought system to align with the Divine Mind. The paradox we encounter is that restoring our awareness of reality relies on Self-perception that can only manifest itself through our perception of others. The Course tells us, "As you see him you will see yourself. As you treat him you will treat yourself. As you think of him you will think of yourself." It also says, "Projection makes perception. The world you see is what you gave it, nothing more than that . . . . It is the witness to your state of mind, the outside picture of an inward condition. As a man thinketh, so does he perceive. Therefore, seek not to change the world, but choose to change your mind about the world." But how do we do that? How do we heal our mind's errant projection so that it only reflects true perception? I can only tell you what worked for me.

Often when reading *ACIM* I will come across a passage that jumps off the page and into my expanding awareness in such a way that I can feel my perspective shift, immanently correcting my perception. Here is one of those passages, and it started a transformation within me that eventually restored true vision, seeing Heaven where I once saw hell: "Think how holy he must be when in him sleeps your own salvation . . . . However much you wish he be condemned; God is in him. And never will you know He is in you as well while you attack His chosen home, and battle with His host. Regard him gently. Look with loving eyes on him who carries Christ within him, that you may behold his glory and rejoice that Heaven is not separate from you. Is it too much to ask for a little trust for him who carries Christ to you?"

Read it again, if necessary. Truly understanding this passage could change your mind forever, as it did mine. How does my salvation sleep in him? It sleeps in my perception, and when I judge him my salvation stays asleep. When I don't judge to project guilt then salvation awakens to both our benefit. Salvation is freedom from guilt, but you cannot be free of guilt unless you are free of judgment.

In the movie "Who Framed Roger Rabbit?" Roger's bombshell human toon wife, Jessica, is renowned as the most celebrated sex symbol in animation. The following dialogue occurs between her and private investigator Eddie Valiant, who was hired to investigate rumors of Jessica having an affair.

Jessica: "You don't know how hard it is being a woman looking the way I do."

Eddie: "You don't know how hard it is being a man looking at a woman looking the way you do."

To which Jessica replies with her most memorable line of the movie, and one which most people are already familiar with: "I'm not bad, I'm just drawn that way," affirming an innocence that somehow got obstructed by our judgmental perception.

If salvation is freedom from guilt, which requires freedom from judgment, then we can only obtain it by perceiving others as innocent. It is only when we see their guiltlessness that we can restore true vision by reversing and correcting judgmental perception, so it liberates rather than imprisons, because it was guilt that got us here to begin with. "The acceptance of guilt into the mind of God's Son was the beginning of the separation, as the acceptance of the Atonement is its end." Atonement is the undoing of the separation guilt caused, and it ends the delusion and self-deception. Once we look deeper, beyond the surface differences we tend to dwell upon to justify our judgment and guilt, we can begin to see this innocence. When we do, an interesting transformation commences, which will end in liberation and Atonement. Just how important is our perception of others? Here is the Course's answer, "When you accept a brother's guiltlessness you will see the Atonement in him. For by proclaiming it in him you make it yours . . . . His guiltlessness is *your* Atonement. Everyone has a special part to play in the Atonement, but the message given to each one is always the same: God's Son is guiltless."

Just as we cannot know God unless we first perceive Him in others, we also cannot achieve Atonement unless we first perceive others as guiltless. It is our perception of their innocence or guilt that establishes our own, and we either bring them within the circle of salvation and Atonement along with ourselves, or else we leave them outside in separation and join them there. Their innocence is spiritual truth, so when we project guilt onto them instead, then we have separated ourselves from truth and sided with the ego and for guilt. Guilt is what hides God from our awareness, while guiltlessness reveals Him. Whenever guilt is present, then salvation and Atonement can't be. What a tidy paradox, we heal our own guilty minds by not projecting guilt onto others in an attempt to defile their innocence, because our perception of them is merely a reflection of how we actually see ourselves.

This was a game-changer for me. As soon as this light of awareness shined through my perception onto others it changed everything. A new vision surfaced that exposed the pervasive guilt shadows lurking deep within the dark recesses of my mind, waiting to replicate and lethally project themselves in order to keep me unconscious and perpetuate the ego's illusion of separation, imprisoning us both by my misperception. I had found the main obstruction that was keeping me separated from God, and now it was time to release it. "Can you to whom God says, 'Release My Son!' be tempted not to listen, when you learn that it is you for whom He asks release?" I used this Course quote to remind me not to be judgmental when looking upon others: "In the name of my freedom I choose your release because I recognize that we will be released together." This vision clearly delineated how large of a perception correction was needed. Now I knew the only way I could ever truly know God, because "He cannot be known without His Son, whose guiltlessness is the condition for knowing Him."

I decided to practice perceiving guiltlessness immediately and took a shortcut by starting with my family. I would hold my gaze on them a little longer than usual, resisting any judgment, seeking to change nothing and accept everything. The results were phenomenal. I did see their innocence, but I also made them a little uncomfortable in the process. It reminded me of how Margie looked at me the first time we met. Kim would ask me why I was staring, and Kaya would just catch my prolonged gaze and say "Whaaaat?" I did see them differently, and there was definitely a union of our minds that I could feel. So, I decided to try it on strangers, and I got the same result. But I was more cautious and less creepy about staring at strangers, to save their discomfort. It was like stepping into their perception briefly, and with the same non-judgment and union I felt with my family. Sometimes I would pick up something non-verbally that I never would have known or noticed, just as Ocean had done with me. I had never paid this much attention to others because I was always wrapped up in my own egocentric perception. This was an entirely different vision, and the results were unbelievable. One day, as I pondered the strangeness of this perceptual pheno-menon, I read in *ACIM* , "Is it not strange that you should cherish still some hope of satisfaction from the world you see? In no respect, at any time or place, has anything but fear and guilt been your reward."

Sorry Sartre, but salvation is a collaborative venture that is dependent upon our choice of perception. "The ego is the choice for guilt; the Holy Spirit the choice for guiltlessness." We are "guilty or guiltless, bound or free, unhappy or happy" according to our perception. We decide which is true for us. "Hell is other people" can only appear accurate when we engage in misperception that imprisons us *both* in hell. I chose to be liberated by truth instead, deciding to change my mind and end judgment and guilt projection. So, I choose to believe "Heaven is other people," because only that perception awakens salvation within my brother by restoring his truth, which is also my truth. If giving is proof of having, then I give Heaven to you to prove I have it myself, because we are one. Either statement may appear correct, depending upon our perception, but only one of those perceptions is true.

Here are the specific benefits that came from my true perception. Every encounter now offered me another chance at salvation from guilt. Each person offered me an opportunity to withhold my judgment and thereby heal my own unconscious guilt. I was no longer using judgment to chain them with guilt and imprison us both. I was abandoning it to free us both by seeing that their "sinlessness is guaranteed by God." Each social situation was a perceptual opening to replace darkness with light, weakness with strength, separation with unity, and fear with love. Every day I demonstrated the strength of my new thought system by aligning it with the Divine Mind, identifying with reality rather than illusion, and looking beyond separation to the purity of the Christ Self that binds us all in perfect, identical spirit.

Once this mindset is adopted and adhered to, we can only imagine the impact it has on every encounter and relationship in our life. I already mentioned being at a swimming pool and seeing a tube or cylinder of light extending from the top of each person's head up into the sky. As more vision was restored my perception became better. Even short glimpses behind the veil of illusion were enough to make me want to keep looking, and when I did, I noticed that the Christ Self remains completely pure even though it may dwell in impure things. But if we do not choose to identify with spirit to see this purity then we will never see it. Christ's vision dispelled the ego's belief in a separate self and canceled all of the judgment and conflict that used to define my perception, leaving only peace remaining.

In abiding peace I now reflect back upon my feelings and emotions of the past year, from the angry period when I was cussing out old ladies who objected to being on my postcard mailing list, to when I met Margie and learned I was somehow selected by the Universe for a crash course in spiritual transformation. It seems like I moved closer to God in the last year than I did during the previous thirty years. My previous life seemed like a dream now. I was finally awake, and a byproduct of that awakening was a mindset of unshakeable equanimity and profound personal peace. Now I know how to end the psychological suffering associated with the ego's spiritual siege. "The guiltless mind cannot suffer." If I did wander into the guilt trap, I would quickly allow my new thought system and spiritual awareness to free me of it. I saw others as part of the same innocent Being, together forming the one face of Christ, God's only Child. This not only caused me to regard them gently, but to look upon them with love instead of fear. "There is no fear in love, for love is guiltless."

I now understand and apply forgiveness to every person and situation (eventually), thereby healing my mind of unconscious guilt and restoring to God what never should have been separated from Him in the first place. I have learned to let go of grievances that only confirm a belief in separation. I can clearly see the delusional thought system of the ego and how it had trapped and imprisoned me without my conscious consent. Now my perception-healed Divine Mind immediately senses when judgment and condemnation are attempting to disease it with ideas of separation, disrupting my healing of unconscious guilt by attempting to project it externally. I see judgment, condemnation, and guilt exactly as it is, viewing it from the perspective of spiritual oneness.

A year ago, I engaged in it regularly, and was miserable due to the prevalence of unconscious guilt that harbored within my mind and manifested into my materiality. The difference is seen whenever guilt surfaces through another's perception while in my presence, as my immediate thought and inclination is to remind them, "You are the Christ." It seems like if they could just be reminded of that by someone whose vision sees the same Self in everyone, who knows the delusion tactics of the ego, and feels truth all the way through their Being, then maybe they'll remember too, and want to return to peace, restore oneness and end the suffering caused by their belief in guilt and separation, as I did.

You are the Christ. I challenge us to look at anybody while thinking this about them and see if it doesn't immediately shift our perspective. Knowing that only by acknowledging the Christ Self in others can we recognize His presence in ourselves, I use this phrase whenever I catch myself in a judgmental thought. It is like using a nail gun to attach the Divine Mind's thought system. You can't possibly look at anybody in the same way once you have considered your spiritual oneness with them, and you won't treat them the same either, since action is derived from perception. Seeing spiritual oneness also arouses compassion, and since our perception is an outward reflection of the inward condition of our mind, then our dream becomes a happy one.

That is what truth does, it changes our perspective so that smallness and separation are no longer our reality and cannot satisfy us because we see the unnecessary and undesirable limitation that we're placing on ourselves. We finally understand, as Rumi did, that we are not a drop in the ocean, but the entire ocean in a drop. This is the truth that wants to be expressed. It wants to be laid alongside illusion and given a fair comparison since it is the obvious choice. An illusion is an attempt to make something real that is untrue, and the only ones who will choose illusions over truth are those who have never known truth and always known illusions. We can't make a valid comparison between everything and nothing.

If we are the Christ then we don't belong here, and we should return home. True perception will take us there, and when we "reach the gates of Heaven, God will open them. For never would He leave His Own beloved Son outside them, and beyond Himself." Like Margie, I wanted to fully identify as being One with God, completely undoing the ego and accepting the Atonement to eliminate or diminish my belief in the flawed, tiny, mad idea of separation. When I first heard this concept from Margie, it was difficult to get my head around it. Now it is simply a part of me, has brought me unimaginable peace, and is the miraculous tangible benefit of incorporating this truth into my spiritual practice.

When I changed my thought system to align with the Divine Mind, I discovered the Mind of God isn't divided, leaving me on the side that experiences scarcity. That was just a perception that needed correction. As abundance became my only eternal reality, I wondered why we insist on holding nothing at the expense of everything. Can this really be a difficult choice? It can't be. But then I remembered. I was there. It seems like another lifetime ago, but it was only a recent previous mindset. It is flabbergasting how far one can travel on a journey without distance. It is the same journey we will all make to restore the oneness to which we belong. Delaying this decision only prolongs unnecessary pain and suffering. The Divine Mind can easily interpret the false world for us, telling us what each symbol means, and how to use those symbols as a compass to guide us home.

I like that the journey is an interior one, and that nothing need be done externally. Not needing to pursue anything outside of myself makes me feel in control of the only thing that matters, which is my mind. I do not need to worry about changing my external behavior, because all behavior is derived from the internal thoughts and beliefs where choice is exercised. Every decision we make stems from what we think we are, and what is done always follows what is first thought. This is the fundamental law of cause and effect. There is no need to pressure or concern myself with changing behavior, the effect, when I can change my mind, which is the bedrock of all causality for behavioral effects. Changing the mind only requires a willingness to do so. When I changed my mind and brought it into alignment with reality instead of attempting to make reality from an illusion, a lifetime of suffering from separation ended. When the problem is corrected at the cause, a corrected effect must follow.

Until that happens, it is impossible for us to ever be satisfied by the ego's Barmecidal buffet of nothingness, because the Divine Mind will always know that the ego, or the idea of separation, is a lie. It may be believed now, but on an unconscious level the truth is already known, and that truth within will needle and wheedle until it is recognized, and the error corrected. Until then, it causes enough cognitive dissonance to make separation convincing, and allow fear to trump love. There are only two choices, and there have always only been two choices. We choose between fear and love. If we choose fear then life becomes confusing and complicated, obfuscating the simple and obvious. But if we choose to love a different world unfolds according to the perspective shift this choice elicits.

I choose which world I see, and I am bound by that choice, whether blinded by belief in fear, or illuminated by a belief in love. "The world began with one strange lesson, powerful enough to render God forgotten, and His Son an alien to himself, in exile from the home where God Himself established him." I had chosen the ability to learn and gave it to myself as a way to uphold a wish that God's Will could be opposed by my choice to do so, in order to make a will apart from His appear more real than His. This errant belief taught me incorrectly and now stands unrelenting between the Voice of Truth, making reality appear false and illusions seem real. But God did not will for His Son to forget Him, so His Voice is also unrelenting, and will not stay quiet amidst these senseless sounds that have no meaning.

Just as there are only two choices, there are only two lessons to be learned. Each lesson has its outcome in a different world, and each world flows from its source. The lesson that God's Son is guilty is the world I used to see. It is a world of terror and despair, with no hope of happiness in it. There is no plan for peace or safety that will ever succeed, nor is there any joy I could ever seek and hope to find. However, when I learned the lesson that God's Son is innocent, I saw another world. A world that holds no fear and is lit with hope, love, and kindness. Between these two lessons I can see which one is mistaken, and which one I must learn to restore wholeness. The Christ in me remembers God and is certain of His Love, but only when I see His Son as innocent can it be so.

When I still my mind through meditation, I release and forget errant learning, and unlearn the thoughts and preconceptions which created inflexibility and obstructed truth. So, I continue to release and forget these ideas and let them be swept away with the judgment I used to hold them together with, leaving only innocence remaining. This is my birth into a different world, where innocence can live free, and where learning may be born again without judgment, and without any restrictions on truth. This transition is not unlike Rumi's poem which says, "Out beyond ideas of wrongdoing and right doing there is a field. I'll meet you there. When the soul lies down in that grass, the world is too full to talk about. Ideas, language, even the phrase 'each other' doesn't make any sense."

Recently I assisted Kaya with learning her times tables and other basic math. Some of it was difficult for her to learn, but we both realized right away how simple working with the number one is. Everything that is multiplied or divided by it remains itself. That makes it easy even for a small child to learn. Complexity only surfaces when we depart from simplicity, but this complexity is not necessary nor does it come from God. As *ACIM* states so clearly:

"Complexity is not of God. How could it be when all He knows is one? He knows of one creation, one reality, one truth and but one Son. Nothing conflicts with oneness. How then, could there be complexity in Him?...The truth is simple; it is one; without an opposite...What is everything leaves room for nothing else...Here is the meeting place where thoughts are brought together, where conflicting values meet and all illusions are laid down beside the truth, where they are judged to be untrue...Here is every thought made pure and wholly simple. Here is sin denied, and everything that *is* received instead. This is the journey's end."

This is our point of entry into the real world, where perception confronts knowledge and is told that only one is allowed where Oneness is. It is here we decide to let go of perception after making one last comparison, a final judgment between truth and illusion, between knowledge and perception. The choice is only difficult from the perspective of this world. In the real world our choosing is greatly simplified by acceptance of one simple fact: God is.

Whenever Kim returns home and her cell phone comes within the range of the blue tooth speaker in our house it says, "The connection is complete." That is how I feel after going through this awakening process over the past year. The connection is complete, which means my correction is also complete. Connections can be lost or severed by separation and distance, but what was lost was found when I discovered who and where I really am. I stay close to my Source in awareness now because I know how to think like Him, and I know that because I *am* part of Him. In reference to this completion *ACIM* states, "We thank our Father for one thing alone; that we are separate from no living thing, and therefore one with Him. And we rejoice that no exceptions ever can be made which would reduce our wholeness, nor impair or change our function to complete the One Who is Himself completion."

We are separate from no living thing, especially God. Any separation we see has only occurred within the mind's perception, by choosing to believe something untrue. While that choice of belief did not make me happy nor bring my peace; I found joy, peace, unity and connectedness with everything when I abandoned separation in favor of oneness with God. My connection with the Divine Mind bridges my connection with Source, and it is a strong and sturdy bridge that brings peace, love and trust into a place where Christ has forgotten who He is and desperately needs these reminders. As we share them, light spreads, gratitude grows, and Christ remembers. This is the end of the ego's arrogance that believed Christ could be divided, and separated from His Source, or be anything other than the one Child of God.

The transformation complete, there was only one topic I could possibly consider for my final Toastmasters speech. The one word that most described my attitude as I looked at the improbable progress I'd made, and how I felt about it all, was gratitude. As the Course says, it is "insane to fail in gratitude to One Who offers you the certain means whereby all pain is healed, and suffering replaced with laughter and with happiness." How could I ever fail in gratitude to the One Who healed all my pain and replaced my suffering with laughter and happiness? I couldn't. So, I did some research, applied some personal experience, and wrote my final speech for the Competent

Communicator certificate. After the evaluation comments from my last speech, I decided to ease off a bit. Rather than another spiritual speech and since God is always linked to gratitude, I decided to approach gratitude from a more scientific angle. I called it "The Quick Fix" to relate to the American cultural preference for instant gratification. It was not preachy and proposed gratitude for non-spiritual reasons. It was a fun one to write and it is always a good reminder of the mindset that should accompany the truly blessed, of which we all are, regardless of any possible perception to the contrary.

"Madame Toastmaster, and fellow Toastmasters, when it comes to our health and well-being, we Americans have come to expect the quick fix, and this quick fix often involves the taking of some kind of pill." I get smiles.

"But what if a quick fix pill really existed, that was completely safe, *free*, with no side effects, and able to deliver the following results:

- ✓ A higher sense of personal well being
- ✓ An improved quality of life
- ✓ More happiness
- ✓ Less depression
- ✓ Less stress
- ✓ More life satisfaction
- ✓ More satisfaction in our relationships
- ✓ Enhanced personal growth
- ✓ A greater life purpose
- ✓ Increased self-acceptance
- ✓ More positivity when coping with difficulties
- ✓ More emotional support from others
- ✓ Improved problem solving
- ✓ Decreased negative coping strategies such as avoidance, denial, blame or substance abuse

✓ Improved altruistic tendencies
✓ Increased economic generosity and monetary giving
✓ Increased likelihood of sacrificing individual gains for communal profit
✓ Increased empathy
✓ Increased helpfulness
✓ Improved sleep
✓ Improved mental health

"Wouldn't it be *amazing* if we could benefit from all of that just by taking one safe, free, quick fix pill? Well . . . surprisingly enough, empirical findings have linked gratitude to all of these benefits, and more!

"We hear a lot about gratitude, especially during the month of November, but *why is gratitude so vitally important? And exactly how does its cultivation and application in our lives positively affect us in so many different ways?*

"Renowned neuropsychologist and author Dr. Rick Hanson, in his New York Times bestselling book *Hardwiring Happiness* says gratitude is at the crux of joy and healing in our lives and is absolutely vital to our character.

"His book is grounded in neuroscience and explains in detail why gratitude is so important to our human brains. And it is because our brains have a negativity bias, which means it is like Velcro for negative experiences but like Teflon for positive ones." More smiles and knowing nods.

"This negativity bias evolved to help us survive in the ancient world, but today it just makes us feel needlessly frazzled, worried, irritated, lonely, inadequate, and depressed.

"So, gratitude serves as a buffer to this depression and unhappiness by enhancing the coding and retrievability of positive experiences within our brain. It acts as a bridge to the greener grass we all want in our lives. Another author states that gratitude unlocks the fullness of life, which is basically saying the same thing but without all the neuroscience.

"Dr. Hanson says the more we practice gratitude through the mindful absorption of positive experiences, the lusher our life becomes, and the sooner we begin to enjoy all of those rich rewards and benefits that come to us through gratitude. He also says we can use gratitude to tap into a hidden power that actually changes our brains, as well as our entire lives, for the better.

"How does this actually work? We have all heard of the Law of Attraction, that we attract what we think about. But along those same lines is the Law of Vibration, which states that *everything*, from the tiniest electron to the entire universe, is in a constant state of vibratory motion. And energy, which cannot be created nor destroyed, is constantly being manifested in millions of varying degrees of vibration according to its specific frequency on an electric wave spectrum called a "Scale of Vibration", which has no definite lines of demarcation.

"In other words, we all have the creative ability as humans, through our thoughts, feelings, and actions, to cause vibratory changes in ourselves by merely changing the frequencies of our own electromagnetic thought waves.

"Two recent studies were performed in which over thirty of the most commonly studied personality traits were analyzed to see which ones affected our happiness and well-being the most. Can you guess what they found correlated with happiness and well-being more than any other personality trait? *Gratitude.* Nothing else can change your current state of vibration more quickly or powerfully, and you can change frequencies easily, just by holding a single grateful thought in your head.

"When you do this and show gratitude, nothing else in the world may have changed, and yet suddenly everything feels totally different. So, what has changed? Gratitude changed your frequency, or your rate of vibratory energy, and bridged the negativity bias in your brain. The way you interact with life, your attitude, perspective, and viewpoint are all now changed and different, with just one grateful thought. It's the same world, but with much different results.

"Cicero stated, 'Gratitude is not only the greatest of virtues, but the parent of all others.' Since gratitude is the greatest virtue, and since it positively affects your happiness and well-being more than anything else ever can or will, then we should not underestimate the importance and sheer power that gratitude can have in our lives.

"An attitude of gratitude is the one common denominator of every single truly happy person in this world. Gratitude changes your brain, acts as a bridge to happiness and well-being, elevates you to the highest vibratory state in the universe and is the quickest, easiest and best fix you'll ever find. Living our lives with gratitude is not only the best way to live; it is the *only* way to live if we care about living well and obtaining the best results we possibly can. Madame Toastmaster . . . . "

That spring Kaya had a piano recital at Keawala'i Congregational Church, a historic church in Makena that was founded in 1832 and first built of pili grass, before later being rebuilt as a stone and wood building. Kaya liked Margie and knew she liked music, so she suggested we invite Margie to her piano and singing recital. We did, and Margie came. She enjoyed seeing the kids perform their music as we sat in the pew together near the front of the church. Before Kaya's performance Margie mentioned that she had taken piano lessons for about thirty years, from elementary school well into adulthood, which I didn't know. As Kaya was delivering her performance, I proudly looked over at Margie to see if she was enjoying it and she was crying. Tears were literally free falling down her face.

The privilege of witnessing tears of joy elicits a very specific emotional empathy, and Margie blesses me with this privilege often. Whenever her heart is filled with love and gratitude, which is frequently, the waterworks cue and remind me of the immense joy she constantly feels just by being exactly as she was created, full of love, joy and peace, without ego obstructing her true nature. I leaned over to check in with her and make sure she was okay, already knowing she was. She tried to regain her composure, and when she did, all she could say was: "I'm just so grateful." I put my arm around her and leaned in and told her, "So am I. Thanks for pointing me in the right direction." Before I was even able to finish expressing my gratitude to this remarkable woman, my eyes were moist also.

ACIM marries love and gratitude, stating "Love can walk no road except the way of gratitude." It also says, "When your forgiveness is complete you will have total gratitude." It makes perfect sense that gratitude is inseparable from love and linked with forgiveness. I remembered Margie's admonition that everything hinges on forgiveness, since it is the means of ending separation and leading us back to oneness with God. If forgiveness is the messenger of Love, then gratitude is the compass Love provides to find our way home once forgiveness has delivered us the message in the field, ensuring the smoothest roads and the shortest journey. Gratitude is a natural byproduct of the Love which emanates from the Source of all creation, which we are all connected to. Welcome home. "The connection is complete."

Chapter 13

The Science of Spirituality

"Spirituality is unseen science,
and science is seen spirituality."
Kaba Hiawatha Kamene

The research I performed to write my final speech on gratitude was interesting and fun for me. I enjoyed the challenge of secularizing spiritual concepts. It seemed like it could be an easier way to bridge acceptance of a spiritual message for those who may prefer to segue more slowly from the seen science of our apparent reality into the unfamiliar territory of our unseen spiritual reality. Because, I'll be honest, if my own personal pain and suffering had not caused me to cannonball into a pool of paralytic surrender in a desperate attempt to find truth then my skeptical nature would have simply tuned Margie out, labeled her as crazy and left her alone to fly her freak flag.

Now I was the freak holding the flag and wondering if there was a better way to relay this message than passing notes saying I have a message from the Holy Spirit. I didn't know much about science, but I always enjoyed my high school and college classes that tried to understand and define the laws this world is governed by. But I also believed in God, a belief which wasn't always reinforced by the rigid rules of science. My impression of science was that it looks at and studies objects objectively. While spirituality looks at and studies the objects together with the subject, subjectively. Science looks at the outer world, and spirituality looks at the inner world. Science is about studying the root, while spirituality is about enjoying the fruit. It doesn't hurt to understand the root, but not at the expense of missing enjoyment of the fruit. Especially when the fruit is low-hanging and accessible, requiring us only to "look up" instead of down.

When my family traveled to Costa Rica, one of the things, we were most excited about was seeing wild monkeys. We had read about them, seen videos of them, and couldn't wait to see them in person. The shuttle driver at the airport confirmed they are everywhere and admonished us to look in the trees and we should see plenty of them. But despite Kim and Kaya looking in every tree as I drove across the tiny country to our condo that day, they saw nothing. After checking into our condo, we took a long walk around our heavily wooded area that afternoon and another walk the morning of the following day. We looked in a lot of trees but still had not seen any monkeys. Then we talked to somebody who told us a whole troop of monkeys were hanging out near the corner of the property. Kim was exercising so Kaya and I quickly went there but couldn't see any monkeys. I'm scanning the horizon, looking far and wide for apparently invisible monkeys. Standing with my hands shading my eyes and squinting into the sun as I scanned a forest of trees, I thought I saw something far off in the distance. I tried to point out to Kaya the ant-sized monkey in a faraway tree when I hear her sarcastically say, "Daddy, look up." I looked up higher in my distant tree, to which she excitedly tapped my shoulder, causing me to look down at her smug smile and her index finger pointing right above my head. I looked up to see a monkey's hairless ass sitting on a branch about three feet above my head. The monkey's proximity startled me, so I jumped, which delighted Kaya into giggles as I moved away into a safer and less distasteful view position.

My point in telling this story is not to compare monkeys to low-hanging fruit, it is to say sometimes we look down when we should be looking up, or we look out when we should be looking in. We need to balance our perspective, look up and down, in and out, study science but also practice spirituality. I know for many it isn't easy to remain open to the likelihood that there is more to this world than science can explain, but I had the advantage of direct mystical experience so I already knew there was more to this world than our primitive science can explain. I personally knew that just because something is beyond the reach and understanding of science, or sensory experience, that does not necessarily mean we must presumptuously doubt its reality.

It is good to know how the physical universe works, but a balanced perspective would also ask and wonder who or what causes it to work that way. Could it just be a crazy coincidence that our universe is inexplicably fine-tuned for intelligent life with such beautiful, harmonic, perfectly organized and structured mathematics? In a 1944 speech on the nature of matter, the architect of quantum theory, Max Planck, made a statement that reverberated throughout the scientific community like the shockwave of a huge earthquake and revolutionized our understanding of atomic and subatomic processes. While speaking at a conference in Florence, Italy, Planck stated, "There is no matter as such! All matter originates and exists only by virtue of a force which brings the particles of the atom to vibration. We must assume behind this force the existence of a conscious and intelligent Mind. This Mind is the matrix of all matter." To further clarify that he was referring to a singular consciousness here is another of his quotes: "I regard consciousness as fundamental. I regard matter as derivative from consciousness. We cannot get behind consciousness. Everything that we talk about, everything that we regard as existing, postulates consciousness."

This may have been a shocking statement in 1944, but it is not an uncommon scientific position for quantum physicists today. Physicist Klee Irwin, founder of Quantum Gravity Research, speaks of a universal collective consciousness and the idea that our whole universe may be a code-based simulation, just like the movie Matrix.

Of course, we should learn what we can about the world we appear to live in, but let's not neglect to learn about the consciousness of the Mind that created this universe, or the matrix of all matter derived from this consciousness. Another of the world's most famous scientists understood this need for a balanced perspective. Albert Einstein once said,

> "A human being is a part of the whole called by us 'Universe,' a part limited in time and space. He experiences himself, his thoughts and feeling as something separated from the rest—a kind of optical delusion of his consciousness. This delusion is a kind of prison for us, restricting us to our personal desires and to affection for a few persons nearest to us. Our task must be to free ourselves from this prison by widening our circle of compassion to embrace all living creatures and the whole of nature in its beauty."

Einstein knew the conscious limitations of this human experience, as well as our need to liberate ourselves from them. He was also convinced of a higher power beyond the boundaries of our primitive science, as evidenced by this quote:

> "Everyone who is seriously interested in the pursuit of science becomes convinced that a spirit is manifest in the laws of the universe—a spirit vastly superior to

man, and one in the face of which our modest powers must seem humble."

Those who knew science best also knew its study was only the tip of the iceberg and either implied or blatantly referenced something much greater and way more intelligent behind it.

For this reason, I shake my head and smile whenever some simpleton tells me the extent of my consciousness is limited to my brain and will cease when my brain does. That is one way to believe. Another is that what I really am formed an errant thought that unintentionally created a universe, and as spacious as that universe appears from my tiny human perspective, it is still only an inadvertent and barely noticeable blemish within the reality of what I truly am. There are lots of ways to believe. Some people will rightly say my belief doesn't necessarily make it true. Ditto. But what if it did?

What if life really is a controlled mental hallucination that serves a very specific learning purpose, and our only limitations within this matrix are the limiting beliefs we form and adhere to? What if transcendence of those limiting beliefs was the only thing keeping us from moving mountains, walking on water, or conquering death? What if the only thing humanity lacked was our discovery and acknowledgment of the pure intelligence projected all around us, providing a mirror for consciousness to learn to connect with the Divine Mind and recognize our intimate connection with the infinite and unlimited Source of all that exists? Even better, what if this discovery was not a choice, but being the Will of God, was our only option? "God will not fail, nor ever has in anything." If that is true, then our free will only applies to *when* we decide to choose this exclusive option. *ACIM* says our Creator has "set the limits on our ability to miscreate." Then why does our choice even matter? It doesn't, unless you want to end misery and suffering. Until we desire that end, we can take all the time we like pretending this world is real or relevant. But who really wants to prolong unnecessary misery and suffering?

I could already see a union between the usually discordant belief systems of science and spirituality, and it excited me to continue researching to find a stable, secular bridge upon which I could dovetail these different disciplines. The more I researched the more I was pleasantly surprised to find an abundant confluence of science and spirituality. Professor Kaba Hiawatha Kamene sees science and spirituality as inseparable. In his book *Spirituality Before Religions* he says, "Spirituality invoked and inspired the visible principles of science; and science explained and revealed the eternally invisible presence of spirituality."

Then I heard Dr. Bruce Lipton, author of *The Biology of Belief*, say "The most valid, truthful science on planet earth is quantum physics. There is no science that has been tested or affirmed more. Quantum physics recognizes that consciousness is creating our life experiences. Through our minds we are manifesting our reality." Naturally, that statement made me want to dive deeper into quantum physics, where it appears reality only becomes real when somebody begins to observe it.

Quantum mechanics is the physics that governs the behavior of the universe at the very smallest scales, and it is . . . incredibly weird. According to the laws of quantum mechanics, nature's building blocks are quantum particles which can either behave like particles, located in a single place, or they can act like waves, distributed all over space or even in several places simultaneously with no definite location in space. How they appear to us seems to depend on and require an outside observer to measure them in order to push them to "choose" a definitive state, since before we measure them, they seem to have no definite properties at all. They discovered the "observer effect" which states that the process of observing a particle changes the way the particle behaves.

Leonard Susskind from the Stanford Institute for Theatrical Physics says with quantum mechanics when you try to show something doesn't happen by doing an experiment, the experiment makes it happen. It's as if the particles are waiting to respond to our intention and perception of them. When physicists performed the same experiments without any variation at all, where nobody watches the experiment and then again with the experiment being observed, they found that the actual scientific results changed, based upon whether the experiment was observed or not. Matter exhibited intelligence and feedback at a sub-atomic level, depending upon our observation. This proves Planck was right, and that the force binding matter is conscious and intelligent. This also reminded me of Wayne Dyer's quote: "If you change the way you look at things, the things you look at change." Apparently, this is not just a spiritual law; it is also a law of quantum physics.

This phenomenon really bamboozled physicists, and they could not figure out why the same experiment, performed in exactly the same way, somehow defied scientific explanation by behaving differently and producing different results depending on whether or not the experiment was observed. It was as if the matter itself was waiting to manifest a reality according to the consciousness of the observer. Its cue for both a behavioral response and identification as either a wave or a particle was coming from an external observational consciousness that the matter was somehow required to respond to. Obviously, the idea of a universe where things don't exist until they are observed opens itself up for comparison to a simulated reality, since a need-based simulation would do the same in order to preserve computing resources.

ACIM often repeats the message that what we are seeing is not true. "What perception sees and hears appears to be real because it permits into awareness only what conforms to the wishes of the perceiver. This leads to a world of illusions, a world which needs constant defense precisely *because* it is not real." This Course quote is consistent with the quantum physics concept of a universe where things don't exist until they are observed, since it is our perception that creates our seeming reality. Without an observing awareness or consciousness to perceive, and thereby create our physical reality, then it does not exist. Once perception creates it, we see an illusory world that fits our perception but still isn't real. Because if perfect oneness of spirit is our only reality, then physical matter would indicate resistance to that reality (illusion). Therefore, it is our perception that causes the creation of our simulated reality and its illusion of separation. In other words, we are doing this unto ourselves, and if so then we can undo it simply by changing our perception of it. Interesting, but the intrigue was only beginning.

Another fun phenomenon about science and the building blocks of the universe being simultaneously waves and particles is the ability of these particles, once previously entangled, to affect one another's "choices" instantaneously, no matter how far apart they are. This is called quantum entanglement, and this phenomenon connects quantum systems in ways that are impossible in our world. When two particles are entangled, it is not possible to measure one without learning something about the other. Their properties are inextricably linked, regardless of location. They not only appear to send information faster than the speed of light, which is impossible according to all known physics, but they do so instantaneously. Physicist Dr. Gary Sjolander suggests this is because there is no separation between the particles, in space or time, classifying them as non-local and non-temporal. This insinuates a connective reality that exists outside our perception of the physical world. There is no information being sent between them because they are already connected and sharing this information on the quantum level, although our present level of perception would disagree.

Andrew Friedman, an astrophysicist at UCSD, said "Entanglement itself has been verified over many, many decades. The real challenge is that even though we know it's an experimental reality, we don't have a compelling story of how it actually works." Although this experiment has been verified over and over for decades, some still say it is impossible, just because they can't accept the impossible results. Even Einstein doubted the validity of these results, calling it "spooky action at a distance." Although physicists have learned to control and study quantum entanglement, they've yet to be able to explain it, which leads to a conundrum about the nature of our basic reality.

I felt I was successful in identifying how spirituality is consistent with quantum mechanics, but what about a possible correlation with cosmological physics, which are often discordant with quantum physics due to the massive changes in scale of measurement? So, let's now discuss the larger, cosmological nature of our apparent reality and see if spirituality can somehow help science explain the mysterious and unknown nature of our origin and how it correlates with the verified scientific impossibility of quantum entanglement.

The universally accepted cosmological creation of the universe occurred about 13.8 billion years ago, but physicists have estimated that a full resolution of our existing universe would have most likely required about 1.4 trillion years to achieve randomly, another confirmation of Planck's theory of a conscious and intelligent Mind behind the force that causes the existence of matter. Extrapolating backwards using the known laws of physics suggests that prior to the precise moment that speeding particles of light abruptly and forcibly departed from an extremely luminous celestial object, there was singularity, which simply means the nature of the celestial object was infinite and not subject to space, time or entropy. Shortly after the initial rapid expansion of the Big Bang, when the universe swelled from a size smaller than an electron to nearly its current size within a tiny fraction of a second, it cooled dramatically to allow the formation of subatomic particles and then atoms. Once this cold soup of particles reached near absolute zero, it formed what is called a Bose-Einstein condensate where giant clouds of primordial elements form new matter, such as stars, galaxies, and planets.

An interesting side note of particles in a Bose-Einstein condensate forming new matter is that even when particles are separated this way to form new matter, they always remain quantum entangled. It is not significant if the matter is many light years away from each other, their response to each other is not only faster than the speed of light, it is instantaneous, suggesting a zero-time neural network. In other words, even though matter may appear separated, it is all connected as one at the quantum level. *ACIM* would say it this way, "There is no way in which a gap could be conceived of in the Wholeness that is His. The compromise the least and littlest gap would represent in His eternal love is quite impossible."

In fact, astrophysicist Anirban Bandyopadhyay says the whole universe is a single, timeless photon, a massless subatomic particle that is the quantum of the electromagnetic field that our universe is contained within. This statement correlates quite well with the Big Bang's nearly instantaneous rapid and continual expansion to its current size from an initial subatomic particle, such as a photon. He says a single photon has no distance of separation, so any distance or space between us doesn't really exist. That would surely explain the mystery of quantum entanglement. And if you ask Anirban about the separate self, he will say there isn't one; there is only a part of the whole. That sounds familiar. "The recognition of the part as whole, and of the whole in every part is perfectly natural, for it is the way God thinks."

Author Michael Talbot often attempted to assimilate religion, spirituality, and science and in 1991 he published *The Holographic Universe*, advocating a theoretical model of reality that suggested the physical universe is comparable to a hologram. Then I read about a study done a few years ago that is believed to offer the first observational evidence that our universe could be a vast and complex hologram. This fascinated me, because I had recently listened to an online lecture by physicist and author Leonard Susskind, a professor of theoretical physics at Stanford University titled "The World as a Hologram," in which he said very sharp mathematics can confirm that the world is a hologram within an accelerated expanding universe. That didn't sound like any mathematics I wanted to dive into anytime soon. But now I'd heard the word holographic used to describe time, the Mind of God, *ACIM* , and now the universe. I decided to do more research on this term.

Anything holographic refers in some way to a hologram, which is a three-dimensional projected image reproduced from a pattern of interference produced by a split coherent beam of light. The image is not real, but it's an accurate three-dimensional projected image that is created by a source splitting light beams and then later putting them back together without the original light source being present. Some of the unique properties of holograms is that they split or divide light in order to have the appearance of creating more than the original. Also, all parts of the hologram carry the image of the entire object, or "the whole in every part." Each part or piece is identical to the whole and all formed images are illuminated by a coherent light source. The only thing is holograms aren't real. The only reality is the light source projecting the hologram. Physicist Dr. Gary Sjolander asks,

"If the universe is projected, what is the source of illumination? The mind of God? If so, this entangles physics and spirit."

In this study, theoretical physicists and astrophysicists investigated irregularities in the cosmic microwave background, or the "afterglow" of the Big Bang, and found substantial evidence to support a holographic explanation of the universe. The idea is similar to that of ordinary holograms where a three-dimensional image is encoded in a two-dimensional surface. Except it is the entire universe that is encoded, according to this study. An example of a holographic universe is like watching a high-definition 3-D film in a movie theater. Our eyes somehow witness moving pictures having height, width and crucially, depth – when in fact eyes can only see low resolution 2-D images. Susskind also said this, calling it a conflict of principle and a trick of the eye called stereoscopic vision, since our eyes cannot see in 3-D and must extrapolate depth from 2-D images. These images must therefore originate elsewhere, within perceptual space or mind space, created by electrochemistry within the brain that converts otherwise colorless photons into a colorful 3-D high-definition matrix that we call reality and that appears to occur within space and time.

The study says the difference, in our 3-D universe, is that we can touch objects and the "projection" is "real" from our perspective. What an interesting choice of words, "the projection is real from our perspective." But wait, if this is true and Susskind is right about cosmology proving with very precise mathematics that the universe is a hologram, then that would mean . . . it isn't real. We're not really here. We originated from a singular Source of light outside of space and time and we don't belong here in this illusory holographic projected image. Although we may appear as tiny, fragmented holographic projections of light that are an exact and identical replica of our Source, we don't really exist at all within this unreal holographic projection. It is, as a matter of scientific fact, an illusion. Who says science and spirituality can't correlate? Maybe we have always been talking about the same thing but calling it something different. Here is what *ACIM* says: "You dwell not here, but in eternity. You travel but in dreams, while safe at home."

In an attempt to define our reality by defining what is living, some will say if it perpetuates a pattern by self-organization then it is alive. But a virus, a tornado, a crystal, and the universe all do that. Physicist Klee Irwin makes the claim that everything observable, including humanity, is consciousness responding to information. He also contends that this consciousness is indivisible and exists within one mind, like so many others such as New York Time's best-selling author Larry Dossey, M.D. In his book, One Mind, he asserts there is only One Mind that is a collective, unitary domain of intelligence, of which all individual minds are a part. He claims minds are nonlocal with respect to space and time, and this means the separateness of our minds is an illusion in that all individual minds only form a single mind.

Even Nobel physicist Erwin Schrodinger proclaimed, "There is only one mind." Distinguished physicist David Bohm said, "Mind and matter are not separate substances. Rather, they are different aspects of one whole and unbroken movement. Deep down the consciousness of mankind is one." Bohm further states this intimate connection with one another could recalibrate the self-oriented Golden Rule, from "Do unto others as you would have them do unto you" to "Be kind to others, because in some sense they are you." He concludes that this unity of the one mind carries us beyond the isolation and frustration of a struggling individual to a renewed sense of meaning, purpose, and possibility. Transforming yourself also transforms the universe.

Irwin says our reality is information or meaning conveyed by symbolism. Further, this information that creates our reality can only come from mind. It requires an entity to choose to measure it and then interpret that measurement and ascribe meaning to it according to a subjective interpretation, or perception. This is how things change and why things appear different when viewed by the same people, because our subjective perception creates our reality. How is this possible? Because we are the perceiver that creates the feedback mechanism that ascribes meaning to this information that in turn creates our reality, at least as we see it and according to our own perception. In other words, what you believe is real for you, but this reality is nothing more than a reflection of your own perception about whatever information you are observing. So, then I guess we could say, "The world you see is what you gave it . . . . It is the witness to your state of mind, the outside picture of an inward condition." Which means we can change our reality simply by changing our perception, and perhaps we should "seek not to change the world but choose to change our mind about the world."

The evolution of quantum mechanics and its attempt to observe matter in its smallest form reveals that the smallest units of measurement do not break matter down into a measurable mass, but into energy, and matter is simply a "slowed down" version of energy.

This definition of matter reminded me of stand-up comedian Bill Hicks who said in one of his comedy routines, "Always that same LSD story, you've all seen it. 'Young man on acid, thought he could fly, jumped out of a building. What a tragedy.' What an idiot! If he thought he could fly, why didn't he take off on the ground first? Check it out. You don't see ducks lined up to catch elevators to fly south—they fly from the ground. How about a positive LSD story for once? Wouldn't that be newsworthy, just one time? To base your decision on information rather than scare tactics and superstition and lies? I think it would be newsworthy. 'Today, a young man on acid realized that all matter is merely energy condensed to a slow vibration. That we are all one consciousness experiencing itself subjectively. There is no such thing as death, life is only a dream, and we're the imagination of ourselves . . . . Here's Tom with the weather.'"

Planck correctly identified a field of electromagnetic energy that is everywhere, all of the time, and influences everything that happens in the world around us and within us. But Swiss physicist Nassim Haramein, the founder of the Hawaii Institute for Unified Physics, developed a unified field theory in collaboration with physicist Elizabeth Rauscher that he calls the Haramein-Rauscher Metric. In it he combines the gravitational, electromagnetic, and weak and strong nuclear forces into a single unifying framework. Leonardo Da Vinci said, "everything connects to everything else," and Haramein proposed the same by attempting to unite usually discordant quantum and cosmo-logical physics. His unification theory brings out some interesting ideas that demonstrate connection everywhere in the universe and iterates how entangled particles don't respond according to the known laws of physics, how all of the information in the universe is present holographically in each individual atom, and that consciousness and memory are not in the brain but exist as energetic feedback on the space-time continuum, with conscious-ness being omnipresent, omniscient and organizing everything. He even produced a film narrated by Sir Patrick Stewart called "The Connected Universe" that details his scientific search for a unified field theory to measure and understand this conscious-ness connection mechanism for everything in our universe.

Haramein says our universe is not as solid as it appears at the quantum level and is actually 99.9999 percent open space. He always thought matter defined space but realized from his measurements that space defines matter because space is not empty. It contains an astounding amount of connective energy which binds everything within Planck's electromagnetic field to everything else. A single cubed centimeter of space contains enough energy to power the entire world for millions of years if it could somehow be extracted. He also demonstrates how this conscious and intelligent space energy serves as a feedback mechanism that constantly receives, organizes, and responds to perceptual information in order to create our external reality from our inner perception. This reminded me of the Wayne Dyer quote that I used in my "Love or Fear" speech, "Loving people live in a loving world. Hostile people live in a hostile world. Same world."

Cosmological measurements indicate that only 4.9 percent of our universe is visible matter that we see as planets, stars and galaxies, with the other ninety-five percent being dark matter (twenty-seven percent) and dark energy (sixty-eight percent) that does not absorb, reflect or emit light and therefore cannot be detected by observing electromagnetic radiation. We know very little about dark matter and dark energy since we cannot see it. We only know what we do because of the effect it has on objects we can observe directly that are influenced by it. However, Haramein specifies that all matter, energy, and consciousness within our universe are interrelated and connected from quantum physics to consciousness and tracked through a constant feedback mechanism based in fractal mathematics. This dark energy permeates all of space and is the intelligent source of our self-organizing system, using the universe as an extension of space-time to look back and learn of itself as it makes constant adjustments during our cosmic dance with the universe, responding according to the conscious vibration of our individual and collective perceptions. On a universal level we are swimming in a Planck quantized soup of consciousness and our individual movement only occurs by forming, undoing and redoing our matter in Planck time intervals according to this constant conscious feedback mechanism, just like the frames of a movie.

In other words, we are not really here and are projecting our perception from a non-local mind, and everything we see is being created for us in real time like a movie experience. This reminds me of two additional quotes from *ACIM*, "Behold the great projection but look on it with the decision that it must be healed, and not with fear." Also, "There is nothing outside you." This is hardly new or controversial information since Deepak Chopra has talked for years about how when we are in touch with infinite awareness a single thought can trigger a non-local experience, and that seeing ourselves through this infinite non-local awareness that he calls God, we realize our consciousness is also infinite and cannot be contained within our bodies. He says the body, the mind and the world are all activities that emanate from a field of pure awareness within this infinite spirit. This is the same answer science provides, but it was sure interesting taking the scientific circuit to it.

Overall, this was a fun chapter to research. Who knew science could be so fascinating, or so strongly correlated with spirituality? I learned about famous scientists, quantum and cosmological physics, and our completely connected and holographic universal mind matrix created by the Big Bang. I marveled at how, in a fraction of a second, our universe of over two trillion galaxies, with a hundred billion stars per galaxy, was created from a luminous singularity and is now bound by an astoundingly strong, conscious energy that is still entangled with our incredibly luminous celestial source beyond all spiritual or scientific perception. I uncovered scientific evidence that although what we now appear to see as separate and divided, is in reality unified and connected. I was even able to answer some questions that science cannot explain, but *ACIM* has no difficulty explaining within a spiritual context. I don't know if all of this will help anyone understand our connection to God through entanglement with the Divine Mind, but it helped me understand Ocean and Margie a lot better.

Now as I read certain passages in the Course, I have an alternative scientific definition I can insert to secularize the message, just as I intended when I started this research. For example, "Into eternity [outside space-time] where all is one, [singularity] there crept a tiny, mad idea [of separation from singularity] at which the Son of God remembered not to laugh. In his forgetting did the thought become a serious idea, and possible of both accomplishment and real effects [the Big Bang]. Together, we can laugh them both away, [the holographic universe and its illusory effects] and understand that time cannot intrude upon eternity [singularity is the only reality]. It is a joke to think that time can come to circumvent eternity, which means there is no time [or space, or matter]." With the problem clearly identified, it is time to solve it. We simply need to remember, as Albert Einstein warned us, that, "we can't solve problems using the same kind of thinking we used when we created them." We need to approach the problem with a different perspective, which I have tried to provide here.

A Course in Miracles says that an idea never leaves its source, implying that we are the idea that our Source (God) created. We share the same likeness and since we were once joined, through entanglement we always will be. We have no definite location in space and information can be exchanged instantaneously between our Source and our projection of separated light in ways that science would say is impossible, even though they have tested and verified it. But it doesn't matter that science can't explain it, we are still entangled with our Source and can exchange information instantaneously through our Divine Mind connection. Everything wants to be whole. If once connected particles can somehow violate the laws of science and move faster than the speed of light to reconnect and communicate then it would seem this holographic universe was created with an escape hatch for consciousness, an emergency exit, a way to expedite the ending of this seeming event and return to reality.

The Divine Mind is slowly corralling us all towards that exit, and once there is not "a single 'slave' left to walk the earth," He will shut off the lights on the way out, voiding the illusory holographic universe. Gary Renard, in his remarkable book *The Disappearance of the Universe* states, "When everyone reaches the same state of enlightenment, the universe will disappear— Leaving only God's Universe of Heaven." An errant thought will have been corrected, and the singularity and perfect oneness of Heaven will have been restored. No longer will scary dreams incite fear in the Son of God. No longer will illusions appear real, and no longer will the arrogance of separation be thought possible. The entire projection will end because we'll have solved the riddle we originally proposed, and that created the appearance of separation in the first place, when an aspect of the singularity of I AM shortsightedly asked itself, "What can I become?" Answering this question not only required the creation of the universe to project an alternate reality, it also required a state of amnesia so we would think our illusory reality was real. But choosing again and changing our mind is the miracle that helps us perceive and remember our constant connection to Source and return to the grandeur of God, ending our projection into diminution that limits our otherwise limitless Reality. Rumi said, "Stop being so small, you are the universe in ecstatic motion." *ACIM* added, "God is not willing that His Son be content with less than everything."

I am excited about this Atonement. The Course is very descriptive of the state of singularity and perfect oneness that we enjoyed with our Source prior to our "detour into fear." In one place it says, "What [God] creates is not apart from Him, and nowhere does the Father end, the Son begin as something separate from Him." It also says, "Oneness is simply the idea God is. And in His Being, He encompasses all things. No mind holds anything but Him. We say, 'God is,' and then we cease to speak, for in that knowledge words are meaningless. There are no lips to speak them, and no part of mind sufficiently distinct to feel that it is now aware of something not itself."

Chapter 14

The End of Separation

"This course offers a very direct and a very simple
learning situation and provides the
Guide Who tells you what to do.
If you do it, you will see that it works.
Its results are more convincing than its words.
They will convince you that the words are true.
By following the right Guide, you will learn the
simplest of all lessons:
*By their fruits ye shall know them,
and they shall know themselves."*
A Course in Miracles

When I was ten years old, a stray dog that had been shot through
his hind leg followed me home. His leg had healed by the time he
came home with me and I only found out about this pre-existing
injury when I noticed his awkward running gait a few days later
and somebody else mentioned he was the dog who had been shot.
I don't know how he knew that, but when the dog ran his hind
leg kicked awkwardly sideways during his stride and became
more pronounced as he picked up speed, although it didn't seem
to slow him down at all. He weighed about fifteen pounds and
was tan with a white belly and had fur that was fairly short
everywhere on his body except around his face and mouth. Just
below where his floppy brown ears hung, each side of his face had
frizzled white hair that looked like it had been electrocuted. It

stuck straight out sideways instead of lying down flat like the rest of his body hair. He had a Duck Dynasty beard before it was fashionable. I used to grab his ears with my thumbs and fore-fingers and use the other three fingers on each hand to scratch the scruffy hair sticking out sideways on each side of his snout. He loved it and would half close his eyes but leave them open enough for me to see his love and gratitude shining through them as I did this. Due to his scruffy facial features, which indicated some mix of terrier, I named him Scruffy.

We bonded quickly and I loved that little dog about as much as a boy can love a dog, and yet somehow the flow of love always seemed lopsided to my benefit. There were not really any rules at my house, so nobody cared when he followed me home. We always had one or two dogs so what was one more? But Scruffy was different than any dog we ever had before because he was all mine. I knew it, he knew it, and my brothers soon learned it. As I mentioned in my Ice Breaker speech, I was the youngest of seven children and had four older brothers, so I got beat up a lot. Well, Scruffy laid down a new law regarding that. One time when my brother Danny was hitting me, as he often did, Scruffy ran between us barking at him and jumping up and down while trying to bite at his hands and arms as he struck me. Danny was 13 at the time and this was a fifteen-pound dog that he could have easily kicked across the room, but Scruffy didn't care. We were both kind of shocked because Scruffy liked my brother, just not when he was hitting *me*. Danny stopped hitting me and looked at the dog as if he couldn't believe it, and then he started laughing. As a test, he looked at the dog while pretending to strike me some more, and Scruffy did the same thing.

This canine behavior gave me great pleasure for two reasons. First, because he just saved me from a lot of future ass whooping, and second, because Danny was now jealous of *my* dog. He didn't have a dog that cool, that would risk its own life to protect him when he was in danger, but I did. If possible, it made me love Scruffy even more. From then on, Scruffy and I were inseparable for just about every minute of every day. I felt important with his Secret Service level of protection. At night when I went to bed I would get under the covers and then pull back one side and let Scruffy jump into my bed. He would lay down with me spooning him against my heart and I'd pull the covers over him and keep my arm around him until I fell asleep. This happened every night, and he stayed in bed with me until I woke up in the morning. Or if he did leave during the night, he always found his way back under my covers by the time I awoke in the morning. I was never completely sure about that.

Whenever I was eating, he always got some of my food, sometimes right from my plate as I was eating it. I could communicate with him simply by the tone of my voice. I could send him into a jumping and frolicking frenzy by bending down and chanting his name in a high-pitched voice along with some other stream of consciousness gibberish. He always came running, not walking, whenever I called him, and if he did something I didn't like he seemed to know it before I even had to speak. It was as if he was reading my emotions and understanding me completely before I even said anything. But if I ever did speak to him in a stern tone, he hung his head, tucked his tail between his legs and gave me a sad eye face that made it impossible to stay mad at him. If I ever shouted at him for any reason he retreated under the bed or somewhere else out of my sight until I calmed down.

And then there was school. I walked to elementary school every morning, and home every afternoon. I tried to get Scruffy to stay at the house while I was gone but he wouldn't have it. He walked with me, for protection of course, and when we arrived at school, I would scratch his ears and scruffy face, say goodbye, and go into the school building. He would curl up on the front steps of the school entrance and wait. I could hardly wait for recess because I knew Scruffy was outside waiting to play with me, and he always was. Everybody knew whose dog he was, because as hard as I tried to be the first one out the door for recess, I was often several kids back when we enthusiastically burst through the school doors to commence recess. Scruffy would always jump up with anticipation and anxiously look at all of the kids coming outside and show no reaction. But as soon I exited those doors the party started. He wagged his tail so hard when he saw me that he contorted his whole body and looked like a worm squirming on the ground, and when I got close enough for a greeting he would jump up and down by my side just to show me how happy he was to see me again. Everybody saw this and knew how loyal he was to me and how much he cared for me. They also saw how much I loved him, and I'm pretty sure they were all just as jealous as Danny was, since none of them had dogs waiting outside to play with them during recess.

I even showed them how he would bark and jump up and down between us if we pretended to fight. But I didn't do that too much because I didn't want to cheapen Scruffy's genuinely concerned reaction or have him figure out that I wasn't really at risk and stop doing it. Whenever the teacher left the classroom for a few minutes to go to the main office, I would position a friend near the door to watch the hall for the teacher's return while I ran to the window, opened it, and called to Scruffy sitting on the school steps. He would come running around the building, of course, and then I would lean my entire upper body out of the window, and he would stand on his hind legs and put his front paws on the wall just below the window to get within my reach, and I would scratch his ears and scruffy face until my stationed friend warned me of the returning teacher's approach. I knew in those moments every kid in that class wished they had a dog like

Scruffy, even the girls, because everybody wants to be that loved, even if it is just by a stray dog.

When I joined my foster family, they tried to accommodate Scruffy initially, but it just wasn't the same. They wouldn't let Scruffy sleep in the house, much less in the bed with me. Scruffy didn't understand this because he had always been a house dog as well as a bed companion. I tried to spend as much time as I could outside with him, but it always made me sad when I had to leave him outside in the cold and go back into the house again. He never seemed to understand this sudden exclusion and kept darting into the house whenever a door opened, and he knew I was inside. This became problematic so a year later I sent him to live with my dad and I never saw him again. My dad says he ran away, but he probably just went looking for me. I missed him to be sure, but I no longer needed his untiring emotional support. I was now in a loving family that provided that. Scruffy's designated role had been completed. He had bridged my early childhood emotional inadequacies admirably, for which I was profusely grateful.

It is only now in middle age that I can see the obvious parallel of my dog and the Divine Mind. In both cases they found me and made it clear that we were meant to be united. The flow of love from both seemed lopsided to my benefit. Both were inseparable from me and forgave anything I ever did. Both protected me and made me feel valued and loved. Both could empathetically understand my emotions and know exactly what to do to fix my state of mind. Both were completely honest, loyal, devoted and could be consistently trusted for unwavering friendship. Others quickly noticed the positive impact these companionships had on me. Both were always there, teaching me, when I needed their instruction the most. If I was angry, they soothed me. If I was sad, they cheered me up. If I was fearful, they gave me courage. When I was hurting, they healed me. Scruffy

although
widely accepted

was a good precursor of the Divine Mind, and the best part is, it is impossible to ever be separated or apart from the Divine and knowing that makes my dream a happy one.

Because Margie had undone her ego and identified so strongly with the Divine Mind, she enjoyed a daily connection to Its constant voice and guidance. She carried that connection everywhere she went, all the time. God's unobstructed love flowed through her effortlessly because she honestly believed she was One with God. This awareness of perfect oneness with God was expressed in everything she did, and it was a pleasure to witness, even though it was frequently misunderstood by those who had not yet awakened.

I remembered my initial response to her when we first met. My ego quickly judged and labeled her even though my soul was telling me to learn as much as I could from her. While you cannot be enlightened by the thinking or presence of others, they can sure point you in the right direction, and that is what Margie did for me. She pointed to something immanently desirable that she had found, and then showed me how to find it within myself. Ironically, my own discovery of it also strengthened it within herself.

After gathering hundreds of pages of written material from my communications with the Divine Mind, and upon being told numerous times I would be instructed what to do with such in "His time," I finally received the message I had been waiting for. I was instructed to tell the story of my awakening and my acquaintance with Margie during this process. I met with Margie on June 5, 2019, informing her of the Holy Spirit's instruction to write a book about my awakening and her involvement with it. Margie smiled knowingly and then shared her own dictation from the Holy Spirit that very same morning, received and written prior to our meeting. Here is what it said.

"Now the world will hear about your time with Don. He is My emissary. I gave you a message to deliver to him the night of your first conversation with him at Toastmasters. He has been commissioned by Me to write a book highlighting your acquaintance during his path to awakening. It will be a 'labor' of love for both of you and is My means of extending the *One With God* books beyond what either of you imagine. Enjoy this union of purpose. It takes place under My auspices and will bring you both great joy."

Of course, she received this dictation before I told her anything. Sometimes I forget that Margie, like Ocean, doesn't need me to communicate a message for it to be received with perfect clarity. You'd think that as many times as I'd seen this happen that it wouldn't surprise me any longer, and it doesn't, but it is a confirmation that we are simply being done and acting out our prearranged soul contracts as part of the same Mind. The confirmation from the hypnotherapist about my spiritual purpose involving Margie and my premonition that we had made an agreement together before commencing our current incarceration, I mean incarnation, now made perfect sense. Margie was to be an important voice of the Divine Mind's message, as told through my awakening.

The Divine Mind communicated the message and I recorded it as quickly as I could, but I was constantly interrupted by the distractions of life and being self-employed in an under-staffed business. I found a passion in writing what I was told to write and felt completely disconnected from how I used to identify myself. The frustration of not having adequate time to record this communication as quickly as it was downloading from my Higher Self caused me to imitate a distracted student pretending to study, or in this case typing a lengthy email to a client at the office that required quiet, when I was really typing and recording inner dictation from the Divine Mind instead. The bottled-up communication rattled around in my brain until I eventually made the comment to Kim that I wished I could just leave Maui by myself for a little while and sequester myself in a quiet place to finish recording the expression effusing from me and dripping wastefully into the insignificance of my illusory reality. Kim made a selfless decision and told me to do it. I had never done anything like this before, but I booked a three week stay in a condo by myself. I chose Bear Lake, a recreational area which extends from Southern Idaho to Northern Utah, which would be quiet during October. Before I even arrived, the Voice was speaking, providing valuable input on a process that I was completely ignorant about.

I flew into Salt Lake City in early October, and without telling any of my friends and family that I was visiting, I picked up my rental car and made the three-hour drive North to Bear Lake, knowing it would be quiet and allow peaceful solitude with my Teacher and the Communicator of the message. I passed through Logan on the way, where I was born fifty-three years ago. I had symbolically ended up at the place where I began, just as we all will. I drove along the Logan River and through the gorgeous Logan Canyon, pulling over to safely take in the allure of the fall colors causing a ripple of variant color coursing through the picturesque beauty of the Utah mountains in autumn. I exited the canyon and began the descent towards Bear Lake and saw its immense size spanning two states and covering my entire horizon ahead. I turned left when I reached the lake, knowing that if I turned right I would end up where I attended Boy Scout camp as a youngster and learned how to waterski while also earning merit badges on my path to becoming an Eagle Scout. I also recalled bringing my two sons here one summer and going to the marina up ahead on the right, and renting a boat and a giant banana that

I pulled them on behind the boat, until I turned too sharply and they bounced off the banana and launched into the air like little NASA rockets during lift-off, until gravity eventually reversed their direction and brought them back down to earth with an invigorating splash into the cold lake, which thrilled my oldest son but caused the younger one to cry. These reminiscent memories are happy ones.

I've traveled all day since Maui is a long way away, with an inadvertent overnight layover in Oakland that allowed for only three hours of sleep. I was delayed further in Seattle before making the final flight and then drove nearly three hours to this remote pastoral location. I checked into my condo, and unpacked my luggage, and did a little work since I had been unavailable to my office all day. Then I wrote for a while and did a little more work that found its way to me through the wonders of modern technology. It was late and I was exhausted so I decided I should not do any more tonight and went to bed so I could start early and refreshed in recording this remarkable story of transformation. The Divine Mind spoke to me as I lay in bed. I listened but kept trying to sleep. It was one in the morning and He was still speaking. At one-fifteen I replied that I've been traveling all day and I'm tired so the rule is I should go to sleep now and start fresh in the morning. He said, "Rule? There are no rules in this regard. You came here to write a book. How fresh do you feel now?" I noticed I was oddly no longer tired. Having been delivered an alertness that I couldn't wait to take advantage of, I got up, got dressed, grabbed a snack and started writing.

I had been overwhelmed by this entire process before and had no idea where to start and how to pull it all together and organize the story onto the written page. Now I wrote until 7:15 as six solid hours of book outline, stories and their suggested sequences were revealed to me and I wrote it all down as fast as I could until I noticed the sun had risen. I finally went to sleep, knowing exactly where to go from here and how to fill in the rest. It made sense that He would provide this information only after I made the effort to get myself here, my faith-based action being a prerequisite to providing the clarity of a concrete "how" only after the initial leap had already been made. This renewed and strengthened my trust in Him. This entire book was written within these three weeks, living without rules. I wrote whenever I could, I ate when I was hungry and slept when I was tired. Sleep was never regular, coming in three to five-hour bursts whenever writing was beginning to be obstructed by fatigue. Sometimes I'd wake up at ten pm and once I even made a meal at three am. I think I probably showered and brushed my teeth every day but who's to say, after all there were "no rules." I know I didn't shave the entire time, reserving that activity as a reward for completion when I finished. Having no gray hair on top of my head, I was surprised by the abundance of gray now revealing itself within my facial hair.

Mostly I just enjoyed my time alone with the Divine Mind. No distractions, no interruptions, just me and my Friend, and I was happy. The clock was irrelevant. I operated purely according to my Guide; my only mantra was "no rules." I did not acknowledge any fear, scarcity, or lack, only love and abundance, as the Holy Spirit guided me through the maze of a fully written book for a first-time writer in three short weeks. We partnered our efforts to communicate clearly and record that communication directly, as quickly as possible. When it was finished, I stood up, stretched my legs and back, got dressed in clothing not customary to my life on Maui, and took a walk while sharing my gratitude for the assistance He provided.

As I left my condo and stepped into the brisk outside air, I noticed the hills and small mountains appeared as powdered sugar pastries with a white layer sifted onto the top third of them, covering the ground but leaving trees and larger bushes exposed.

This is not the first time it had snowed in the past three weeks, but this early in the year it would be gone by the following day, if not sooner. Seeing my own breath is a novelty I have never experienced on Maui, but one that I remember well from many winters in the Utah cold. As I stepped onto the bike path that ran along the lake near my condo, I could faintly hear a rhythmic clanging of wire rigging against masts in the breeze, from sailboats stored for the winter. The sound waned and was intensified by intermittent gusts of wind, some of which caused me to adjust my clothing to keep the cool air off my bare skin. Magpies and blackbirds supplied song to accompany mother nature's ebb and flow of musical creation.

Further down, a large flock of migratory Canada geese emitted a cacophony of honks, barks, and cackles as they fed, mated, or performed whatever celebratory measure justified such an exuberant vocal display. The mix of sounds was unique, and a perfect complement to my view of the glassy blue lake and the occasional red, orange or yellow leaf that blew across my feet before being pulled into the folds of tall grass growing along the edge of the paved path. The overgrown grass often protruded onto the bike path to display a colorful intrusion and decorative accumulation of wind-swept deciduous leaves in an artistic display that could not be made any more beautiful by intentional placement. The wind rustled through the leaves that yet remained on the trees, causing them to dance and quiver in their own unique expression of joy that brushed my soul with peace. I tried to take a picture of this natural splendor but was unable to adequately capture it, compared to how it felt and moved me in person when not filtering it through a camera lens. So, I gave up trying and just appreciated what I was experiencing.

Again, gratitude infused me with a peace that has often been elusive on this mortal journey. I decided to exercise vigilance in holding onto this peace in an abiding way and ceasing to obstruct it with any further belief in illusion and misperception. The Divine Mind was pleased with this choice, and suddenly I was consumed by His peace and my entire being was united with all that is, and no separation existed anywhere. I experienced a mind healed of belief in separation. My Self being the creator of this world, I sensed my own singular presence throughout its creation. I recognized what had delayed my arrival to this place of peace and enlightenment, in that my creation had not extended from perfect oneness but had been projected according to a distorted perception of belief in separation. Creation from this perceptual disconnection with Source could only have imperman-ence, so I needed to transcend it. Although I could still appreciate it, I was shown the benefit of extending my awareness beyond it, and I was now clear that Heaven was not a place nor a condition. It is a state of mind, an awareness of perfect Oneness, and the knowledge that there is nothing else; nothing outside this Oneness, and nothing else within. God lives in everything, and everything lives in God. It was so simple. I was done, having no need of further questions because now I only heard one Voice. It was always true and usually saying that nothing within the illusion matters. I had brought my illusions to the truth and by so doing, became disillusioned by them.

Suddenly I heard Margie's voice, although she was currently three thousand miles away from me, but not really because we are one joined mind. Her crackling voice, which distracted and unnerved me the first time I heard it in a Toast-masters meeting years ago, was strong and confident, "Enlighten-ment is an awakening that changes the mind about the meaning of the world and denies dreams of misery to recognize God. It reverses all of the thinking of the world entirely. Now that you have completely awakened from the dream, you will see the face of Christ in every living thing and nothing is held in darkness, but rather the light of forgiveness shines on everything. Having seen the face of Christ the curriculum ends. From here on no directions are needed, vision is wholly corrected, and all mistakes have been undone. Peace has finally come, and the goal of the curriculum has been achieved. Thoughts turn constantly to Heaven and always away from hell. All longings are satisfied, for what remains unanswered or incomplete when Love looks on Itself?"

I walked home slowly, pondering my experience of perfect oneness and Margie's mystical communication. I didn't do anything for this enlightenment. I was chosen. Just as we all are. The Bible records Jesus as saying, "for many are called, but few are chosen." But *ACIM* says, "all are called but few choose to listen." Everybody is called because God Himself would not be complete unless each seemingly separated mind reached this state of awakening from the dream, when all of Christ will be restored and everyone who ever came to earth to die shall be equally released from what we made. In this equality Christ shall be restored as one Identity, in Which the Sons of God will acknowledge that they are all one. And God will smile upon His Son, His one creation and only joy.

After returning from my walk, I warmed myself in front of the fireplace before making a sandwich for lunch. After eating, as I reclined on the couch, the effect of my late-night writing combined with the fullness of the food and the warmth of the fire soon had me snoring. During my nap, the recurring dream that started eleven months ago returned. I knew the wasteland well by now and arrived at the bridge quickly. The kindly gentleman was there and looked at me with anticipation and asked, "Are you still seeking your own completion and what makes you whole in truth?"

We both smiled knowingly, and he extended his hand as he said, "You cannot ever be separate from anything bound by Love, and everything is bound by Love. Across the bridge is your completion. Fear not to cross to the abode of peace and perfect holiness. Only on this side is the completion of God and His Son established forever." His extended hand was irresistible, and I began to cross the bridge to him but hesitated. He offered this encouragement, "Seek not for wholeness and completion in the bleak world of illusion. This bridge leads to union in yourself and to knowledge, while fantasies deprive you of knowledge and are the veil behind which truth is hidden. To lift the veil that seems so dark and heavy, you only need to value truth beyond all fantasy and be entirely unwilling to settle for illusion in place of truth."

"I only want truth!" I blurted out.

He smiled again. "Your completion lies in truth, and nowhere else. Turn with me firmly away from all illusions now and let nothing stand in the way of truth. Crossing the bridge lifts you from time into eternity. When you cross it, you are directed straight to the Heart of God. There is no veil the Love of God in us together cannot lift. The way to truth is open. Follow it with me."

I began to cross, but when I did, thoughts of doubt shot frantically into my mind and lofted a desperate last-ditch volley of arrows, fired somewhere from the shadowy recesses of an ego mind that had fled to hide from the intensity of his light. However, my commitment to cross united with my will and created a momentum that caused my own light to surge forward and sear the arrows mid-flight before even nearing me on the bridge. They were powerless against this light and Love within that had decided to make the crossing. The arrows of dubious thought dissolved harmlessly against my surging light as it expanded to fill the width of the bridge and extended in front of me and behind me as I charged across the bridge with a sheer power that astonished me. This invulnerable unified power was within me and connected to me all along. I just hadn't been aligned with it. I surged forward, willingly allowing the protection of this steamroller of expanding light and Love to fill the length and width of the bridge. It was an unstoppable force, displaying the release of tremendous, imprisoned power in an astonishing surge for Truth and completion.

As I neared the other side my speed increased, and there was an opening in the expanded light that looked like a portal, tunnel, or a passageway. I went into it and was sheared of everything unreal. It pulled away from me and was either consumed by the light or left somewhere on the bridge behind. The moment everything unreal was behind me I stepped into a lightness and freedom that I had never imagined possible. Shedding whatever it was that had been twisting my perception into delusional distortions felt like removing burdensome body armor, and the combination of peace and joy wasn't just a result of freedom from the confines of the body, but from thought itself. It was a complete release that left me free of it all, and I heard the gentleman say authoritatively, "You are hereby released from the world you made and assured the Kingdom of God is within you and can never be lost."

Freedom, that is the best word to describe it. The mind's freedom had transcended the ego's incessantly disruptive and distracting thought system, and that sensation was even better than the freedom from the physical limitations of the body. I had finally escaped the ego's entrapment and freed myself from everything untrue. I was beyond all doubt and perception. All that existed here was the knowledge of God by experiencing Him as myself. I had lifted the veil that separated truth from illusion and stepped into perfect union with the heart of God, and the immeasurable love, joy and peace within this freedom was unimaginable. I was embracing the peace that passes all under-standing, and the all-encompassing Love I felt was beyond any conditions or restrictions. I *never* wanted to leave! As I bathed in this pure Love, rapturous with joy beyond description, the man's voice gently and happily stated the obvious, "This is Love without illusion. This is Truth and completion." Just like my previous dreams of the bridge, when I awoke, I remembered everything in vivid detail so clearly that it was hard to believe it was only a dream. The illusion of love deprivation kept me from crossing the bridge for almost a year, but after all of the debate and discussion, the end result of my decision never required the sacrifice of anything because Kim and Kaya were already on that side, and so was I. It was only my perception of them that wasn't. I really had been at home in God the entire time and was only dreaming of exile.

For the rest of the day I reflected often on the bridge crossing. I tried to call Margie but was unable to reach her. My continued reflection distanced me even further from the world, and that distance pulled my perspective back, away from fear. I realized that when you remove judgment, all that's left is Love, which filled my awareness where ego and fear had been. My crossing revealed the unseen reality with true perception, aligning my will with the Will of Him Who created me, and it caused me to look upon the world with apathy. How could I ever take it seriously again? No sooner had I thought this question then I heard Margie's voice again, "How can you *not* be apathetic towards an inconsequential dream?"

I smiled and picked up *A Course in Miracles* and turned to Jesus' ending prayer for all of the seemingly separated as he concludes his message:

> "I thank You, Father, for these holy ones who are my brothers as they are Your Sons. My faith in them is Yours. I am as sure they will come to me as You are sure of what they are and will forever be. They will accept the gift I offer them because You gave it me on their behalf. And as I would but do Your holy Will, so will they choose. And I give thanks for them.

Salvation's song will echo through the world with every choice they make. For we are one in purpose, and the end of hell is near.

In joyous welcome is my hand outstretched to every brother who would join with me in reaching past temptation and who looks with fixed determination toward the light that shines beyond in perfect constancy. Give me my own, for they belong to You. And can You fail in what is but Your Will? I give You thanks for what my brothers are. And as each one elects to join with me, the song of thanks from earth to Heaven grows from tiny scattered threads of melody to one inclusive chorus from a world redeemed from hell and giving thanks to You.

And now we say 'Amen.' For Christ has come to dwell in the abode You set for Him before time was, in calm eternity. The journey closes, ending at the place where it began. No trace of it remains. Not one illusion is accorded faith, and not one spot of darkness still remains to hide the face of Christ from anyone. Thy Will is done, complete and perfectly, and all creation recognizes You and knows You as the only Source it has. Clear in Your Likeness does the Light shine forth from everything that lives and moves in You. For we have reached where all of us are One, and we are home, where You would have us be."

Towards the end I had to blink tears from my eyes to keep my vision clear enough to read. With a full and grateful heart, I closed *A Course in Miracles* and placed it on the coffee table that was already piled high with my notes, research materials, and

Margie's *One with God* books. I contemplated the phrase, "The journey closes, ending at the place where it began." Perhaps that was why it felt more like a beginning than a completion, reminding me of T.S. Eliot's observation, "We shall not cease from exploration, and the end of all our exploring will be to arrive where we started and know the place for the first time."

The joy of knowing Self overwhelmed me and caused my throat to constrict, as more tears of gratitude welled up in my eyes. Once again, I felt my soul elevate and get pulled up into Love and enveloped in an eternal embrace that swelled my heart, upon which I heard, "You are My holy Son, forever innocent, forever loving and forever loved, as limitless as your Creator, and completely changeless and forever pure. You have awakened and returned to Me, and what was lost has been found. Welcome home. Let's celebrate, for I am your Father, and you are My Son, and we are One."

Bibliography

ACIM Annotation System

The numbering of A Course in Miracles provides a method to reference a specific passage within the Course and its Supplements. Here an example:

"You will first dream of peace, and then awaken to it." (T-13.VII.9:1)

T = Text
13 = Chapter 13
VII = Section VII (of Chapter 13)
9 = Paragraph 9 (in Section VII)
1 = Line 1 (of Paragraph 9)

Another example:

"We say 'God is,' and then we cease to speak, for in that knowledge words are meaningless." (W-pI.169.5:4)

W = Workbook
pI = part I (of the Workbook)
169 = Lesson 169
5 = Paragraph 5 (of Lesson 169)
4 = Line 4 (of Paragraph 5)

Another example:

"Forgiveness is the final goal of the curriculum." (M-4.X.2:9)

M = Manual for Teachers

4 = Section 4
X = Part X (of Section 4)
9 = Line 9 (of Paragraph 2)

Additional abbreviations:

In = Introduction
C = Clarification of Terms (in the Manual for Teachers)

Chapter 1: Meeting Margie

https://www.toastmasters.org/about/all-about-toastmasters
Holy Bible, Romans 12:19

Chapter 2: The Light Enters

Chapter 3: A Memorable Tea Party

ACIM T-8.I.4:1-4
ACIM T-29.I.1:1
ACIM T-31.VIII.1:1-2; T-31.VIII.2:3-4; T-31.VIII.6:5
ACIM C-4.1-3
ACIM W-pI.80.1:1-5; T-1.VI.2:1-2
ACIM W-pI.56.5:4-5
ACIM T-27.VIII.6:2; Holy Bible, Luke 15:11-24
Holy Bible, Luke 15:11-24, Genesis 3:23, Revelations 12:9; ACIM
      T-2.I.2:1
ACIM T-27.VIII.6:2-3; T-18.I.5:2-3,6; T-29.VIII.6:4-5
ACIM T-12.VII.5:6; T-26.VI.1:1-2; T-2.III.3:4,6

Chapter 4: Gathering Mentors

ACIM W-67.2:3-8

Holy Bible, Matthew 25:40, Matthew 7:20
ACIM W-pI.94.1:2; W-pII.240.1:1; T-1.VI.5:4; T-2.VII.3:13-15
ACIM T-1.II.3:10-12
ACIM T-9.V.6:3
ACIM Preface
ACIM Introduction
Wapnick, Kenneth. *Absence From Felicity* (pg. 156), Foundation for
    A Course in Miracles; 1991
ACIM T-4.I.4:7; T-4 I.9:11

Chapter 5: A Different World Emerges

ACIM T-31.VIII.9:1-2
ACIM W-pI.In.8:1-6, 9:1-4
ACIM T-15.X.9:3
ACIM T-3.VII.3:3; T-25.II.3:3

Chapter 6: Glitches in the Matrix

ACIM T-6.III.2:3-4
Newton, Michael. *Journey of Souls*, Woodbury, Minnesota:
    Llewellyn Publications; 1994
Byrne, Lorna. *Angels in My Hair* (pg. 315), New York: Harmony
    Books; 2008
ACIM T-15.IX.1:1
Gospel of Thomas (113)
ACIM T-4.III.1:1-4; T-10.V.1:2-3
ACIM C-5.1:1, 3:5
ACIM T-18.IV.7:7; T-13.XI.5:2-4; CL-5.2:1-5; T-1.VII.5:6
ACIM Introduction; T-29.I.1:1; T-4.II.10:3; T-29.IX.2:1-5
ACIM T-10.V.11:3-7
Renard, Gary R. *The Disappearance of the Universe* (pg. 17), Hay
    House, Inc; 2002

Chapter 7: Humorous Speech Competitions

ACIM T-3.IV.2:3; T-24.I.6:7; T-4.II.7:1-2, 10:3; T-4.IV.3:2-3; T-4.I.10:1,3, 11:1-2, 4

Chapter 8: Struggling with Ego

ACIM T-11.V.4:1-2; T-7.VII.11:1; T-8.I.6:2

ACIM Preface; T-31.V.2:1-3

Pollan, Michael. *How to Change Your Mind* (pgs. 366-67), Penguin Books, 2018; ACIM W-93.5:1-5; T-31.V.7:5; T-11.II.7:1

ACIM T-3.VII.1:7; Pressfield, Steven. *The War of Art* (pgs. 7-17), New York, Black Irish Entertainment LLC, 2002

Pressfield, Steven. *Do the Work* (pgs. 94-95), Do You Zoom, Inc. 2011

McKenna, Jed. Theory of Everything (pg. 104), Wise Fool Press, 2013; Holy Bible, Matthew 12:25

ACIM T-4.II.3:2,4

ACIM T-2.I.1:1-3, 5-12; T-2.I.2:1

ACIM T-29.VIII.6:2,4-5

ACIM T-5.V.3:8-11; T-5.V.4:1-4; T-4.III.3:2; T-21.III.3:3-4

ACIM T-9.VIII.1:1-3, T-9.VIII.4:1-2

ACIM T-3.VII.2:4-6; T-3.VII.5:1-3

ACIM T-2.III.3:3-6

Chapter 9: An Unexpected Tragedy

Remnick, David. https://www.newyorker.com/news/news-desk/an-american-tragedy-2, November 9, 2016

Tyler, Marjorie. *One With God* (pgs. 225-227), Sacred Life Publishers, 2020

Tyler, Marjorie. *One With God* (pg. 231), Sacred Life Publishers, 2020

ACIM M-13.1:6-7; M-13.2:1; M-13.4:2-10
ACIM M-13.8:2-3
ACIM T-12.I.8:7

Chapter 10: Applying Forgiveness

ACIM T-27.VIII.1:1-3; 2:1; 3:1-5; 4:4-5; 5:1,3; T-7.VII.4:1-2,5
ACIM T-27.VIII.5:4-7; 6:2-5
ACIM T-27.VIII.5:10; Shakespeare, William. *King Lear* (pg. 4) Act
    1, Scene 1
ACIM T-27.VIII.7:2-4; T-21. I.1:1,5; Preface
ACIM T-26.V.5:4; Bhagavad Gita 8:16
ACIM T-26.X.4:2-4,7-8; T-27.VIII.9:1-5
ACIM T-27.VIII.10:1-6
ACIM T-27.VIII.11:1,6; 12:4; 13:1-2,6-7
ACIM W-pI.122.1:1-6
McKenna, Jed. Spiritually Incorrect Enlightenment (pg. 333),
    Wisefool Press, 2010
ACIM T-13.IV.8:1; T-27.VIII.6:5; T-6.I.5:3-5; 6:1-2,6-7; 9:1-3
ACIM T-6.In.1:2; T-27.VIII.7:4; 8:1-3
ACIM T-18.IX.13:1-4; 14:1,3-5

Chapter 11: The Pursuit of Peace

ACIM T-23.II.22:6-9
ACIM T-9.IV.8:3
ACIM T-7.VII.11:1; W-pI.16.1:2-7; W-pI.16 2:1-3; T-23.I.12:6-7
ACIM T-15.III.5:4-5

Chapter 12: Transformation

ACIM W-pI.92.9:1; T-8.III.4:2-5
ACIM T-21.In.1:1-2,5-7; T-26.IX.1:2-6; 2:1

ACIM T-13.In.2:1; T-14.IV.1:1-2,4; T-14.V.2:1

ACIM T-14.III.4:2; T-31.VII.15:5; T-15.XI.10:7; T-14.IV.7:4

ACIM T-25.II.2:1-2; T-14.III.4:2,6

ACIM W-pI.93.6:1-4

ACIM T-5.V.5:1; T-13.X.10:4

ACIM T-13.VIII.10:6-7

ACIM T-31.I.4:5-6

Barks, Coleman. *The Illuminated Rumi* (pg. 98), New York, Broadway Books, 1997; ACIM T-26.III.1:1-5,8,12; T-26.III.2:3,5-6; T-26.III.3:1; W-pII.195.6:1-2

W-pII.195.2:2

Hanson, Rick. *Hardwiring Happiness*, New York, Harmony Books, 2016

Chapter 13: The Science of Spirituality

ACIM T-14.IV.4:4; T-2.III.3:3; Kamene, Kaba Hiawatha. *Spirituality Before Religions*, independently published, 2019

ACIM Preface

Dattaro, Laura. https://www.symmetrymagazine.org/article/the-quest-to-test-quantum-entanglement, November 6, 2018

ACIM T-29.I.1:3-4; T-16.II.3:3; Talbot, Michael. The Holographic Universe, HarperCollins Publishers, 1991; Susskind, Leonard. https://arxiv.org/abs/hep-th/9409089 September 15, 1994

ACIM T-13.VII.17:6-7; Dossey, Larry. *One Mind*, Hay House, Inc., 2013

ACIM T-21.In.1:2,5

ACIM T-21.In.1:7

Haramein, Nassim. *The Connected Universe*, A film by Malcolm Carter, 2016

ACIM T-22.II.10:1; T-18.VI.1:1

ACIM T-27.VIII.6:2-5

ACIM T-1.VII.3:13; Renard, Gary R. *The Disappearance of the Universe* (pg. 263), Hay House, Inc; 2002
ACIM T-15.III.4:10; T-2.I.2:1; W-pI.132.12:4; W-PI.169.5:1-5

Chapter 14: The End of Separation

ACIM T-9.V.9:1-6
ACIM T-18.VI.1:5-6; M-28.1:2; 2:1-2,6; 3:1-7; 5:2
Holy Bible, Matthew 22:14; ACIM T-3.IV.7:12; T-16.IV.9:1-3
ACIM T-16.IV.9:4; 10:1,3-4; 11:5; 12:5; 13:4-7, 9-11
ACIM W-pI.77.3:2-3; T-10.I.2:1
ACIM T-31.VIII.10:1-8; 11:1
ACIM T-31.VIII.11:2-5; 12:1-8; W-pII.10.5:1-3

Acknowledgments

Gary Renard – Your books have inspired me. It is an honor to have an author I respect so much endorse my own book. I enjoy having you as my ACIM teacher and I can't wait to read your next book. If Hawaii continues calling to you, call me. Mahalo Nui Loa!

Marjorie Tyler – This story was foreordained and fun to experience and write with you. Thanks for being such a good sport and allowing me to exaggerate your eccentricities. I look forward to our continued tea parties and additional writing projects.

Ed Tate – What a great speech mentor and example you have been. Thank you for all your coaching help and excellent advice. I still have a lot to learn, so I look forward to continuing to improve my speaking skills with you.

Ocean Love - Wherever you are, I know you're making this world a better place with your light and love. I will never forget you and I sincerely hope our paths will someday cross again. If so, the fish tacos are on me. Peace, love, and trust.

Ron Hirsch – From the moment you hired me to first manage, and then sell, your rental condo on Maui, I have enjoyed our spiritual conversations. But I never thought you would someday endorse a book I wrote. It has been quite a journey and I'm grateful.

Gary Sjolander – Thank you so much for your corrections, contributions, and improvements to Chapter 13. When writing about science, it always helps to know a rocket scientist and a super smart guy. You input has been invaluable and I enjoyed our discussions.

Jordan and Marcus McEntire – From my initial rough draft to the final manuscript, you both have always been eager to read and discuss my writing. Your lifelong love of books and reading has been admirable and fun to watch, and your feedback on this one has been invaluable.

Deelia Nelson Photography – I hope people *will* judge this book by its cover. Thank you for taking such great book cover pictures! You visually encapsulated my holy relationship with Margie so effortlessly and are a lot of fun at a photo shoot.

Sacred Life Publishers – Much thanks to Sharon Lund for her tireless late-night efforts to assist with all aspects of this book publication, and also to Kaitie Palm for her multiple readings and great editing suggestions. You guys are the best and I couldn't have done this without your help.

Meet the Author

Don McEntire

Don McEntire is the founder and Principal Broker of McEntire Realty, a real estate sales and property management firm in Maui, Hawaii. In 2009 Don was named one of the state's Top 100 Realtors. He is a member of Toastmasters International, where he met Marjorie Tyler, scribe of six published volumes of *One With God: Awakening Through the Voice of the Holy Spirit.* In 2017 he placed 3rd in the District 49 Humorous Speech Contest for Toastmasters.

Don is the youngest of seven children and was only four years old when his mother and grandmother were killed by a drunk driver. He moved around a lot until eventually finding stability as a teenager at a Mormon foster home in Utah. This resulted in his volunteering to serve as a full-time church missionary for two years as a young adult and remain a lifelong Christian. In 2016, the psychological suffering induced by a separation from his wife and daughter effected a strong spiritual awakening.

After his awakening, Don credits *A Course in Miracles* with helping him transition to the Divine Mind. He is no longer affiliated with any organized religion. Don never imagined writing a book until Margie appeared and demonstrated a better way that magnified his personal peace and happiness while eliminating fear. This inspired him to share her message of divine love and hope that illuminates our true reality and spiritual identity.

Don has three children and one grandchild. After growing up in Utah's cold climate he now enjoys living and working in one of the most beautiful places on earth. His interests include traveling, reading, playing golf or basketball, beach time, boogie boarding, snorkeling, and diving. His favorite days are daddy/ daughter or granddaughter days.

CPSIA information can be obtained
at www.ICGtesting.com
Printed in the USA
LVHW050255221220
674834LV00016B/175